DANIEL PULE KUNENE

1923 - 2016

DANIEL PULE KUNENE

Surviving South African and American Racism Through Education

Edited By
Fritz Pointer
and
Liziwe Kunene Pointer

©2022

AFRICA WORLD PRESS
TRENTON | LONDON | CAPE TOWN | NAIROBI | ADDIS ABABA | ASMARA | IBADAN | NEW DELHI

AFRICA WORLD PRESS
541 West Ingham Avenue | Suite B
Trenton, New Jersey 08638

Copyright © 2024

All rights reserved. No part of this publication may be reproduced, stored in a retrieval system or transmitted in any form or by any means electronic, mechanical, photocopying, recording or otherwise without the prior written permission of the publisher.

Book design: Dawid Kahts
Cover design: Ashraful Haque

Cataloging-in-Publication Data may be obtained from the Library of Congress.

ISBNs: 9781569028506 HB
        9781569028513 Pb

*This book is dedicated, with
Eternal Love and Memory to:*

*Liziwe Boitumelo Kunene Pointer
(October 8, 1956–October 22, 2021)*

CONTENTS

Acknowledgements	ix
Foreword by Fritz Pointer	1
When I Was a Child	13
Lady and Charlie	33
Secondary Education	39
Back To Edenville	53
Leseliyana la Lesotho ("*Little Light of Lesotho*")	67
Johannesburg	73
Apartheid	95
Getting Married	109
Exile to America—UCLA	131
UW-Madison	151
About the SOWETO Poem	177
The SOWETO Poem – Prologue	193
The SOWETO Poem	195
Holland—The Performance	199
The Struggle Continues	207
Return to the Roots: South Africa, Thirty Years Later (Part 1)	213
Did We Not Say?	235
Return to the Roots: South Africa, Thirty Years Later (Part II)	237
Return to the Roots: South Africa, Thirty Years Later (Conclusion)	263
Epilogue—for Selina	287

Edenville (1996)	289
Nkosi Sikelel' iAfrika (Dr. Phyllis Jordan–1998)	297
Honor at University of South Africa (1999)	299
Nkosi Sikelel' iAfrika (Dr. Daniel Kunene–2002)	303
A Second Marriage (2003)	307
Honor at Cape Town University (2013)	309
Sixteen Days	315
Afterword by Raj Shukla	319
Bibliography	323
Inde	333

ACKNOWLEDGEMENTS

This book could not have been written without the knowledge, assistance, and love of: Selina Claurina Kunene, Liziwe (Liz, Lizzie) Boitumelo Kunene-Pointer, Sipho Thamsanqa Kunene, Luyanda (Lu) Themba Kunene, Linda Fowells, Wandile (Wandi) Pule Kunene, E.T. and Henrietta Sekhuthe, Sarah Sekhuthe, Mary Sekhuthe, Miriam Sekhuthe, Marci Starks Kunene, Sophia 'Manyefolo "Mama" Kunene, Elias Tsoebera George Kunene, Magdeline Kunene, MaMorake Kunene, Mamosa Kunene, Peter Sello Abrahm Kunene, Phillip Kunene (and their children and grandchildren), Sarah and Elton Pointer, Inez East and Ray Dones, Bill Fowells, Sue Falk Fowells, Somori Kunene Pointer, Thiyane Kunene Pointer, Tracy Pointer, Jackie Pointer, Anita Pointer, June Pointer, Shegun Toure Pointer, Nandi Toure Pointer, Jadah Toure Pointer, Aaron and Leona Pointer, A.C. and Phyliss Ntantala Jordan, Bernard Makhosezwe Magubane, Gerard Sekoto, Roger and Pauline Mayer, Margaret Njobe, Muriel Island, Bob and Odile Robinson, Jack and Pat Vogt, Harold Sr. and Anna Robinson, Evelyn Reid, Freida High Tesfagiorgis, Vernon February, Ralph and Nancy Knudson, Neil and Meg Skinner, Michele Goodwin, Greg Shaffer, Sage Cammers-Goodwin, Ed Garvey, Laurence Giles, Don and Karen Hester, Chris Antonuzzo and Wade DallaGrana, Judy and Tom Brady, Raj Shukla, Dustin Carrell Cowell, Hugh Masekela, Caiphus Semenya, Letta Mbulu, Sister Mary Paynter, Bernard van Beurden, Chris Swanepoel, Jimmy and Jeannie Cheatham, Roddy and Hermine Wengrowe, and our publisher Kassahun Checole, and editor Frank Bilsard.

Special Recognition: "To those," Papa was wont to say, "who made me *Great*. My Great-Grandchildren": Selina "Len," Phoenix, Daniel, Amaru and Kendrick. And Somori Kunene Pointer for researching, finding, editing the Photo Gallery.

Daniel Kunene & Fritz Pointer

FOREWORD

INTELLECTUAL BRAINDRAIN:

THE CASE OF DANIEL PULE KUNENE

BY
FRITZ POINTER

"We were exiles from our country, South Africa, which had rejected us and our talents, including a kaleidoscope of paintings, poetry, stories, novels and music that we would have contributed."
(Daniel P. Kunene)

Gandhi said his life was his message. Daniel Kunene's life was likewise his message—civil rights activist and committed fighter against apartheid; paragon of love, dignity, knowledge, peace, passion, and the pursuit of justice; wellspring of song, poetry, fiction, and music; epic linguist, acclaimed scholar, and translator of African oral and written literatures. His legacy, its breadth and its depth, lives with us. Pinnacle of family—Husband, Father, Grandfather, Great-grandfather, Teacher, Community Leader. May we carry his generosity of spirit forever forward.

Daniel Pule Kunene (April 13, 1923–May 27, 2016), born in Edenville, South Africa, is an icon in African Studies. Forced to flee his homeland in 1963, with his beloved first wife Selina, daughter Liziwe, and son Sipho, during the Rivonia Trial (in which Nelson Mandela was given a life sentence), Dr. Kunene first made his way to London, then to Los Angeles, where two more sons, Luyanda and Wandile, were born.

He lived in exile from his home country for 30 years and found, upon his arrival in the United States in early 1964, that the injustices of racism had followed him from South Africa to North America. A year earlier, Vivian Malone had taken the first steps past George Wallace to register alongside white students at the University of Alabama. A young President Kennedy committed the nation to desegregation that very evening. Just one day later, in Mississippi, Medgar Evers was murdered in front of his wife and children for the crime of working toward a country free of discrimination. Two months later, Dr. King brought his dream of a just America before hundreds of thousands at the March on Washington, just weeks after white radical Christian terrorists murdered four black girls in the process of bombing the 16th Street Baptist Church in Birmingham, Alabama. Two more months later, President Kennedy was dead.

So, Kunene joined a list of South African intellectuals, writers, and artists in exile, including A.C. Jordan (*Tales of Southern Africa*) and his wife Phyllis Ntantala, author of *A Life's Mosaic* and one of Kunene's secondary school teachers; authors Dennis Brutus (*Sirens, Knuckles and Boots*), Bernard Magubane (*The Making of a Racist State*), Zakes Mda (*Ways of Dying*), and Keorapetse "Bra Willie" Kgositsile (*Spirits Unchained*); painter Gerard Sekoto; musicians Hugh (*Grazing in the Grass*) and Miriam (*The Click Song*) Masekela; composers Caiphus Semenya, Letta Mbulu, and Jonas Gwangwa; and so many others whose talents were rejected by their home country.

"They made the decision to stay in America and to leave everyone behind," recalled Sipho Kunene of his parents. "That must have been incredibly difficult." Perhaps their choice was made easier because they believed a stay in the United States would be temporary. Liz noted that, much like so many immigrants, "They left South Africa believing they would return." To their surprise, the Kunenes were not to return to South Africa for three decades.

At the beginning of his sojourn and exile in the US, Kunene would say by way of explanation or confession:

Foreword

This was 1964. The Civil Rights Movement was on the ascendancy. For one thing, we soon realized, my wife and I, that once they met you, and once they knew you were from outside the United States – we were from South Africa – then you were more embraced by White liberal society, than if you were a Black American. Quite clearly, they didn't feel you were someone in contention with them. African Americans, who were then called Afro-Americans, were automatically considered the people, who were in contention with them about jobs and rights who might look at them with some hatred.

> Whereas you come from some place outside of the United States from Africa, South Africa, Nigeria, wherever, you are no threat. All that I could think of is that I am not a threat. I am not going to fight for Civil Rights here because I don't belong in this country. Not being in a position of someone who might be a Black Panther, who might belong to SNCC, I was not considered a threat.

His son, Luyanda (Lu), said his activism was as personal as it was political. Lu remembers an image of his parents reading poetry to children in a local elementary school.

> Part of their activism was to educate the community about Africa and South Africa and apartheid. Some of my dad's poetry – he came to a parent show-and-tell and read some of his poetry and asked the kids about it. And the kids got it. They understood. That's how he used art to undermine an unjust system.

Then, in 1970, he was recruited to the University of Wisconsin–Madison to replace his mentor, A.C. Jordan. Upon their arrival in Madison, both Dan and Selina became active members of the Madison Area Committee on Southern Africa (MACSA). Their mission was to support the liberation struggle in the Portuguese colonies of Mozambique, Angola, and Guinea Bissau as well as in Zimbabwe, Namibia, and South Africa, and to educate Americans about the role the US was playing in propping up these regimes. MACSA issued several publications on Wisconsin Corporations in South Africa and on South African ties with Israel, edited a monthly newsletter, hosted a national conference of anti-apartheid organizations, and made numerous presentations to school, church, and community groups. On such occasions, Dan and Selina were "superstars," speaking from the heart about their experiences growing up under apartheid.

A trained nurse, Selina spoke about the deplorable health care available to black South Africans. Daniel spoke of the violence of uprooting families from their homes and banishing them to arid "homelands" where they had never lived. He related how the odious passbooks controlled one's every move and how a peaceful protest to symbolically burn the passbooks had led to the massacre of 69 men, women, and children in the town of Sharpeville.

The Kunenes and MACSA became increasingly involved in boycott and sanctions work, setting up high-level meetings with Wisconsin companies like Johnson Wax that were doing business in South Africa. They persuaded the Madison Chapter of the Postal Workers Union to spearhead, at the national level, the boycott of Polaroid, which produced not only the badges that workers in the US were forced to wear but also the photos for the odious passbooks in South Africa. They put pressure on first the university, then the city and county, and finally the State of Wisconsin to divest their portfolios of stocks in companies doing business in South Africa. Dan and Selina were the face of South Africa at these demonstrations and delegations. All of these actions required intellectual muscle, fortitude, and courage.

Daniel taught for 33 years at UW–Madison in the Department of African Languages and Literature in addition to the University of Cape Town, University of London, University of California Los Angeles, and the Johannes Gutenberg University in Germany. During that time, with his incredibly gifted and honed intellect, he managed to author and publish 16 books, in incredibly diverse genres addressing incredibly diverse themes,of which the following is but a small sample:

- *The Heroic Poetry of the Basotho* (scholarship);
- *Chaka* (translation of classic novel);
- *Pirates Have Become Our Kings* (poetry);
- *From the Pit of Hell to the Spring of Life* (short stories);
- *Dawn to Twilight* (novel).

Foreword

I first met Prof. Kunene in the spring of 1976, my first year as graduate student in the Department of African Languages and Literature. I had been in his company back in 1971 at the University of California, Los Angeles (UCLA) when he was on the faculty and I was a graduate student there in African History, and, our mutual friends, Hugh Masekela, Caiphus Semenya, Letta Mbulu, and Jonas Gwangwa and I were hanging out in recording studios and clubs around Los Angeles. They would sometimes go by to visit, Dr. Kunene (I tagged along, and listened) to discuss anti-apartheid activities, fund-raising for the freedom struggle, and such.

I never took a course with him, though throughout the years I attended many a lecture and poetry reading at which he held forth with his melodious tenor. I joined the African Poetry group he had started some years earlier to read poetry and do improv drama. It was during one of those improvisational dance productions that Liziwe, his daughter (dancing) and I (reading poetry) noticed each other. To music and dance, I read my poem:

Upon Meeting Liziwe

I come into your orbit
Asking questions,
About the capacity of poems
To stop bullets.

You come into my orbit
Smiling and dancing
To Soyinka's poetic cadence
Clasping the flesh
Between a dead man's thumb.

We ascend
Spiraling
Arabesque on a pinpoint
Together

I embrace your world
Clapping my wings against the wind
Perched like an eagle

On a high, rocky nest
Hugging the planet.

You watch rivers
Red with blood
Rushing over the skin of your earth,
Damning, flooding the heart
Of the west
Of the west
Oh! Daughter of Noah.
We sit
Lacing feet and fingers
Around this globe
Like rocking a cradle, or a coffin. (1976)

Liziwe and I created, edited, and published the first issue of *BaShiru*, the Journal of the Department of African Languages and Literature, with invaluable help from the good Doctor himself and our dear friends Steven Moyo (poet/professor and father of Dambisa Moyo, *Dead Aid*: *Why Aid is Not Working and How There is a Better Way for Africa* and *Winner Take All*: *China's Race For Resources and What it Means for the World*) and artist/professor Freida High W. Tesfagiorgis. And this gave me pause, as I remember being one of the editors of the first issue of *Ufahamu*, a Journal of the Department of African History at UCLA. After our wedding in the Kunene family home in Madison, officiated by my mother, Sarah Pointer, Liz and I have enjoyed forty years of companionship and love.

    Professor Kunene traveled extensively with his family, conducting research and performing poetry across Africa, Europe, and South and Central America. It was, for example, when he was a guest professor at the Johannes Gutenberg University in Germany in 1986-1987 and attended an anti-apartheid rally in Paris that he first met fellow South African artist in exile, Gerard Sekoto, where, according to Kunene's poetic reflection,

> ...we were caught on camera as if dancing a tango. . . . It was a super-joyous occasion. It was emotional. We seemed to be seeking answers in each other's eyes about our experiences of

exile. We both knew the loneliness of exile. ("Song for Sekoto: 1913–2013," p. 82)

Daniel Kunene and Gerard Sekoto, Paris 1987

In Kunene's book of short stories, *From the Pit of Hell to the Spring of Life*, published in 1986, he describes "Sekoto's vivid painting of African prisoners marched in a public place by a white armed guard; indirectly reminding us that white prisoners were never displayed in public in that manner, that only blacks committed crimes. White power!" ("Song for Sekoto," p. 83).

Kunene's awareness of and familiarity with Sekoto's work was protracted and deep. He says:

> I first heard of Gerard Sekoto, a black artist living in Sophia-town, from my older brother Elias (alias "George"/"Geo"), who was then himself living in Johannesburg. I was a student at Kroonstad Bantu High School in the Orange Free State at the time.
>
> Geo's enthusiasm and vivid descriptions of Sekoto and his exciting paintings stimulated my own imagination and I would visualize them in my head. This was around the late 1930s, to the early to mid 1940s. By the time I too had ended up in Johannesburg , Sekoto had left. And, it was to take several decades, and the crossing of oceans and continents, for me to eventually meet him.

This was mostly-almost entirely – because we were both exiles from our country, South Africa, which had rejected us and our talents, including a kaleidoscope of paintings, poetry, stories, novels and music that we would have contributed.

One of the contributions we would have made to our country was, ironically, to help turn it from a path of destruction to a new, vigorous, thriving country rich in its diverse colors, languages and cultures. Instead, our energies were spent away from home, on transforming our host countries into our allies in fighting the demon of apartheid and its barbaric, genocidal acts that killed our children, our cultures and our dreams, threatening our very existence with extinction. Countries like France, Germany, the Netherlands, England and others followed the humanitarian path and used our presence to promote them.

They took our message to anti-apartheid groups, to their children in schools, to churches, and to other similar places. Secondly, my translation of C.L.S. Nyembezi's *Mntanami! Mntanami! (My Child! My Child!)* also carries a Gerard Sekoto painting, *Yellow Houses in Sophiatown*.

It is magnificently edifying to appreciate and accept Daniel Kunene's erudition and passion in translating Nyembezi's Zulu novel, *Mntanami! Mntanami! (My Child! My Child!)* into English, for which he received the FIT Karel Capek Medal in 2011.

The intellectual rigor, courage, and discipline required to provide the world this gift is further testament to his genius. The FIT international translation award is designed to promote the translation of literary works written in languages of limited diffusion. The objectives of the award are to improve the quality of such literary translations and to draw attention to the role of translators in bringing the peoples of the world closer together in terms of culture. Professor Kunene's noble endeavor is to unite mankind across cultures through the astounding might of this intellect and the pen. We should also remember that Kunene had already given us an English translation of Thomas Mofolo's marvelous Zulu novel, *Chaka*.

So, from one talented artist to another: "Thank you for your gifts, my brother, Gerard Sekoto" Kunene concludes: "I hope this helps to complete the story of a man we all adore, whom we all miss, but who left us gifts that we cherish, by which we will always remember him, and through which, in a way, he remains with us" ("Song for Sekoto," p. 83). Ironically or fortuitously, this poignantly and accurately describes Dr. Daniel Pule Kunene himself.

In the summer of 1993, months before her death, he returned with his beloved wife, Selina, to South Africa after thirty years in exile for a profoundly emotional reunion with their families.

Meg Skinner, a neighbor and friend of forty years and founding member of MACSA, in a tribute letter to the family, observes that Selina, later that year, hospitalized in a semi-conscious state, before losing consciousness, exhibited a smile and rapid eye movement as we sang *Nkosi Sikelel' iAfrika* and she expressed a strong wish to see her sister, Miriam, one last time. Professor Kunene did everything in his power to honor his wife's last wish, but it was not easy, as Miriam had never been out of South Africa and so had neither a passport nor a US visa. He appealed to an Afrikaner colleague at Witwatersrand University, an institution he once boycotted, who was able to expedite the issuance of a passport.

According to Meg, by the time Miriam was on her way, Selina was in a coma, with all of us around her hospital bedside. Dad excused himself to collect Miriam from the airport, and upon his return, announced that he had kept his promise, and brought her beloved Miriam. Sadly, no response. Miriam then leaned down to Selina, mom's ear and said, in Sotho, their shared language: "This is your big sister, Miriam. I have come a long way to see you." And, to our amazement, with her last ounce of strength, Selina attempted to sit up, managing about a 45-degree angle, and moaned, acknowledging that she was aware that the family was complete. She breathed her last shortly thereafter.

A man of deep passion and feeling, I include here one of the chapbooks of poems he dedicated to Selina:

Were It Not For This Thing

Were it not for this thing
This closing of the eyes
This stopping of the breath

This stiffening of the limbs
This cessation of speech
This departure of the body heat

We would have been playing our favorite game
Chasing the butterflies of our dreams
Lolling in the enveloping warmth' of the world we molded with our own hands
Which is the real world
Which is always around us
Which is invulnerable and strong in its frailty

But this thing
This closing of the eyes
This stopping of the breath
This stiffening of the limbs
This cessation of speech
This departure of the body heat

It came upon us
It came between us
It came to spite us
Yet we shall dream on
Beyond failed speech and breath
And eyes that don't see
Eyes that, for their blindness, see more
Take in new landscapes beyond the limiting horizons
As we leap with nimbler limbs
Unfettered by tendons and ligaments and veins and vessels
That defy our orders
And our heat shall rise
And we shall talk and we shall laugh
Beyond
The prison
Of mortality

In November of 2015, at the age of 92, Dad, Professor Kunene came to give a lecture to my Humanities class at Contra Costa College in San Pablo, California on "Leitmotif in *Dawn to Twilight*," a novel he had completed and published at age 90. It was for all of us gathered there—family, faculty, students, and friends—an unforgettable, incomparable experience.

A master teacher, Professor Kunene began by requesting two volunteers from the packed classroom to assist in acting out a passage `his still powerful voice led the students through the reading. Then he asked the students to explain their own interpretations of scenes and character motivations. And the overarching question: "How does water function as a metaphor and *leitmotif* in *Dawn To Twilight*?"

"When he got up before the class the years melted away," recalled Lu. He found the same solace and inspiration in the poetry he composed to enlighten others. Said youngest son, Wandile, of Daniel's motivation: "He got so much out of the creative process and what he did. He would acknowledge and appreciate how it affected others. But like a lot of artists who are doing what they love, he was so focused in that moment of creation—that was important." Sipho described what so many experienced in Daniel's poetry: "My dad always had a way of seeing things through a different set of eyes."

At one point during his presentation, he stopped suddenly and gave a thunderous clap with his hands, like a grandfather would, to stop three young men in the back of the classroom from speaking over students attempting to ask questions. In all it was a wonderful experience, with students getting copies of their books signed and posing for a picture with the author—Daniel Pule Kunene. He was a scholar, an artist, a dissident, and an activist to his last days.

Daniel P. Kunene's books, monographs and documents, research materials and private library collection are now a part of the Melville J. Herskovits Library of African Studies Archive at Northwestern University in Evanston, Illinois. This will preserve the life's work of Dr. Kunene for historical and research purposes. His recent donation (2016) is to be added to his materials donated some years ago. His legacy will be secure for generations of researchers and students.

Daniel Pule Kunene

WHEN I WAS A CHILD

This opening story is going to be largely about me . Naturally therefore, it will carry much of the "when I was a child" theme. I will share with my audience the various environments that conspired to make me be me.

I'm glad, in fact extremely happy that I am who I am, that I have the wonderful family I have. Which means to say, what I am today, where I am today—all of these are not what I was hoping for, what I was striving for. Mostly, that is to say.

I was born in a little town called Edenville, in a state called Orange Free State in South Africa, on the 13th of April 1923. At that time there was strict segregation. People seemed to only want to think about apartheid when they talked about South Africa, the segregation that was merely strengthened in 1948; but there was historically strict segregation, typified by residence—where you had White people living in a white area that was called "Town" and Black people living in a black area ... that was call "Location." The term "Location"... I don't know its origin, but the Black people certainly did not originate it. The whites, way back, to designate the place where only Black people lived, originated it.

I grew up under the keen observation, tutelage, and guidance of my father and my mother. Also some of my siblings, since I was the third, and more were yet to come. The tutelage and guidance referred to above was both by example and by direct intervention.

We, the community of Edenville *Location*, and indeed all black adults, had the right to intervene when we, children, did something contrary to the values of the community, and ultimately to the society. So we were aware of being under constant surveillance, even when we might not be. Even though we might not have a cause to be so. Thus it came back to us censoring our own behavior, to the benefit of the entire society.

So, as we grew up, actually, in our ordinary conversations, the terminology of "Town" and "Location" became understood to mean "Town" for whites and "Location" for Blacks. In terms of your postal address, you gave the same name, Edenville, and then if you're living in the Black area you said "Edenville Location." The Whites just said "Edenville"—White and privileged.

There were only two Zulu families in Edenville Location—the Kunene family and the Sithole family. *Baba* (Father) Sithole was clearly as much Zulu as my father. Maybe as nostalgic at times too. My mental picture that made me to believe this, was how *Baba* Sithole visited our house, and he and my father would sit outside, against the wall, side by side, and hold a slow conversation, in *isi-Zulu*—staring into space as if far away. Laughing! Using language mechanics that emphasized the cultural link they shared. These eyes that seemed to open far away distances were eloquent. It seemed to me they were connecting not only their language, their longing for a time that had passed, but also the longing for it to come back…the missing of it. Nostalgia.

The occasional silence between their speaking was not silence; it was deeper communication, deeper speech than the speech of sound. I felt it too in sympathy with their longing. *Baba* Sithole's house was some distance from ours. Edenville Location, being its size, the phrase "some distance" should be qualified—about ten minutes slow walk! It was near the then-only black cemetery. My father's (our) house, in the direction of the stream you crossed to get into the "no man's land" where cattle and horses grazed. Some sheep too!! So my father visiting *Baba* Sithole, or *Baba* Sithole visiting my father, had to be something they wanted to do—memories of home for the two gentlemen—nostalgia, for example. Also, Edenville Location being as friendly as it was, *Baba* Sithole might run into another friend and stop to chat for a while.

When I was a child, that is, prior to the formation and inauguration of the church choir, discussed a bit later, I was a child of a different kind. I reveled in moonlight singing and dancing and simply getting lost in the moment. I got lost in the singing and dancing of my compatriots. People always remarked about my head, which they said was big—meaning too big. So also about my nose—too big too! To top all, they said I was short, meaning too short!

That too did not mean anything to me. I nearly forgot my nose. That too they judged Too big! Ha! Height too short! Nose too big! My height! Too short? They love it! They love it! They loved the whole of me! They said they wished they could simply cuddle me in their arms—the girls, that is! Well! I did not know why they wished so!! Much later I knew.

They loved to form a circle on the lower street side from our house and sing and clap their hands. This took place near the *tshinabelo* tree that grew there. They formed a circle and sang the play song:

Tiki-tiki semankorojane
Tiki-tike semankorojane

Saka-saka semankorojane
Saka-sake semankorojane

I was in the center of the circle dancing lively gyrations with my little body. They accompanied it with vigorous clapping and laughing, and dancing in place. The more they laughed the more lively and varied my dancing would be, and the more joyous and friendly dust they raised.

We children were embracing the setting of the sun as the darkness slowly drew an enormous dome—at first slowly, then quicker—around the earth. It would be like an instinctive reaction to this heavenly mystery, like the birds that were beginning to twitter at the time. We too, children, came out of our homes to embrace this phenomenon with our songs and dances. These are the children's welcome of the daily phenomenon. These are the moonlight games, singing and dancing and clapping, all harbingers of the night. We were mixed groups—boys and girls. And there were sometimes songs whose words and movements suggested our beginning awareness of our sexual maturing that was slowly creeping upon us too.

The whole of Edenville Location would be filled with young voices floating into the darkening vault.

As "the sons of Ham," we were to be constantly pursued with labels that warn whites who saw you that you might be dangerous. The word *Location* in those days did what *Township* does today. Whites do not live in *townships*, anymore than they lived in *locations* when those were available. Blacks do. And they did. Very often, the warning "Beware of wild animals and Natives" was posted on gates or fences, especially of white farms.

The street that passed in front of our house—you know, the one with the "Rock at the Corner"—that street, at that time, if getting out of our yard to the street you turned left, then you would be going toward the "evangelist" Morake's house; but also on the right, shortly after you passed his house, you would be getting to Uncle Jerry's house. And then, if you took a turn to the right, and then you took another right, you'd pass one house and the next one would be my grandpa's house. Right next door to my grandpa's house—no fence, no nothing—was one of my aunts, one of my mother's sisters.

That thing of families not being too far from each other, which was a traditional thing, I think I'm right that *clans* started on the basis that we all have to always be not too far from each other. In terms of mutual support, it's within calling distance, it's within crying distance. If you hear, for example, "Oh, my child is burning!"—which is one of the things that actually happened—and people come to help, not just relatives but those within hearing distance.

A cousin of mine, a little girl, who was living in the house next to my grandpa's house. She was sitting outside next to a fire, the *Mbawla*—the brazier —and her dress caught fire. And being a child, the first thing she thought of was running. As she was running, of course, the flames were being fanned, and she was running cutting through fences, yelling and screaming. And, just coincidentally, a young teenage girl in a house she was passing was just at that time getting ready to throw out the dishwater; she had just finished washing dishes; and she saw her and threw the water on her and the flames went out.

When such things, like a fire, happened, the whole community would get involved. It was not a matter of "This is not my business";

rather, the thinking was, to survive as a group we had to survive as individuals. When there was a death, someone was dispatched to knock on doors or windows to announce the passing. The same was true of a birth or wedding for that matter. It was not a private matter. It was a community matter.

Town was where the Whites lived and where the jobs were. Location was basically a dormitory place, where our fathers came, tired from their manual labor, ready to eat and maybe sit around the fire for a little bit, and have some stories and then go to bed. So, we did have some little time to interact as families. We would have time, often after our evening meal, for us to do some storytelling. My mother was the expert as far as that went. She was an expert storyteller. And we sat around and got absolutely thrilled by the stories. My mother used to put a lot of passion into her storytelling. She actually lived the parts that she was narrating about. My father did tell stories from time to time, and they were a bit ponderous. He had one favorite story he told almost every time he took over the storytelling.

To be clear, the Blacks in the Locations were cheap labor for the Whites in the Towns. So there was this daily migration of people from the Locations to the Towns, of people going to work as domestic servants, petrol station attendants, workers loading trucks that went to the railroad station—all that sort of thing. That was the order of the day.

In fact, this reminds me that, for quite some time, actually for a few years, when I was still small, our parents working in a place like a store, a general dealer store, were not given time off for lunch. They worked straight through from the morning when they got there until they came back home, and they had to sneak time in. One might go and make a fire, quickly, out in the back room over there and cook some "mush"—you know, corn meal mush. Then, before he is missed, he would have to rush back and another one takes over until they are done. And they'd have to sneak and go out and eat standing.

Eventually, after several years, a law was enacted that required workers be given an hour, in the middle of the day, to have their lunch, without having to be harassed while trying to eat.

My father worked for a white general dealer where you bought everything. He carried heavy bags of merchandise to load on the waiting lorries, or bales of sheep's wool to be driven to the little railway station called a "siding." Likewise, he carried other heavy items off the lorry on its return from the siding. There were blacks being similarly exploited by their white employers.

At that time, at my age, that was how life was. No one complained. No one asked why. For me, looking back, I wonder why my father did not think that God was unfair in creating white people rich and black people poor. Whites always had more than they needed, and they threw away some, and blacks scrambled to scrape with their fingers for any refuse that the white people did not want, let alone need. White men always jingled some coins in their pockets.

On top of all that, it seemed that, my father did not only accept this utter discrimination, but he actually actively preached the goodness of God on Sundays, as well as two evenings a week, and sometimes one additional evening on Sunday. That's a lot of preaching!

My father also seemed to know the entire *Bible* by heart: he knew the hymns, the psalms, the catechism—not in English or Afrikaans or any European language, but in *isiZulu, isiXhosa, seSotho*. He could preach in two of those languages as well, namely *isiZulu* and *seSotho*. To praise the word of God! He also sang well, with his voice ranging from tenor to bass. My God! What child wouldn't imitate an example like that! He could also sing the leading voice if necessary, a sort of male soprano that was an octave lower than the female soprano. If you can imagine a male choir, he and many other men would provide the male "first part." So would other male voices provide the alto, tenor, and bass.

Our Location and the Town were separated by well over a mile maybe a mile and a half, of what you might call "No man's land." It was pasture ground, for people who had some animals like goats and cows. They herded their cows or horses during the day and brought them home in the evening. So we had this sort of spatial "No-man's-land" kind of separation so there could be no mistake as to where the Blacks lived and where the Whites lived.

If you stood outside in the morning, you saw black men walking towards *town* to go and work for white men. You might also later see some women domestic workers treading the same path, to pick up the white people's dirty laundry to go launder it, or carrying the clean washing back to the white people's part of Edenville!

Whites did sometimes come into the Location, but it was always a scary thing when we saw White people, and we would think: "What's wrong. What have we done?" Say, for example, a farmer might come on his horse-cart, selling some produce. Sometimes a Superintendent would come to find people who hadn't paid their rent. Whites never came to visit, just as Blacks never went to them, in their White Town, to visit. It was a strictly *Master-Servant* relationship.

When the *Master* came to your humble dwelling, it wasn't usually for something good. To say nothing about the police: The police raided to find out if people were having drinking parties, because drinking was illegal in the Locations, even our home brew. Our parents had to get permission to brew beer at home with corn and sorghum, and without that you would be arrested.

This was, of course, a form of both economic and cultural control. The police would raid at night, from time to time. There was a curfew as well. After 9 p.m., no Black person should be seen in the White Town, or they should expect to be arrested and go straight to jail. In terms of the severity of the segregation in South Africa under apartheid, it is comparable to that experienced by Black Americans throughout the South.

It was almost as if you were natural enemies. I remember a house, a little bit away from Town, standing by itself. It was owned by a White and he had some function in the municipality. His young boys would sometimes make a point of waylaying young Black children, boys and girls passing there, attack them, and beat them up. There was this revulsion or hatred or at least dislike of one another. Even as children, there was the feeling that White People are not our friends. You never expected that they would be your friends. So these animosities, even those expressed by older White boys to beat up Black children, were a way of exerting their feelings of *superiority,* that they could do whatever they liked.

Obviously, Blacks and Whites were not going to the same schools. I attended school in the Location. In Edenville, there was no school building—notice I didn't say *buildings* plural because there was not even one—where classes were held. Classes were held in churches, in church buildings. I do remember my first two years of classes, called Substandard A and Substandard B, were held in the Wesleyan Methodist Church; Standards 1 and 2 were held at the African Methodist Episcopal (AME) Church; and Standards 3, 4, 5, and 6 were at the Dutch Reform Church.

I started school at the age of seven at the Sub-standard A; the following year, at age eight, was in Substandard B. The raw and uncovered earthen floor of the Wesleyan Church soon rubbed off on to your clothes and/or your skin, which was mostly exposed, partly because the boys wore short pants which sometimes also had tears in several places. The girls wore short gym dresses. More often, though, they wore any dress of any cloth since many parents could not afford the price of tailored, pleated, gym dresses. It was, of course, the second year of the same physical earth "punishment."

One day I was squatting on the floor, since there were not enough benches for the number of pupils in the classes held there. My left knee was bent, supporting the slate I was writing on. The right hand held a slate pen which squeaked its way through the hard surface of the slate. Mistress, as a female teacher was called, was in front of the class reading short sentences, phrases, and letters for spelling. She was motherly, with her bundles of covers that reached down to her ankles. Sort of like the Victoria's secret! I looked alternately up at her face, read her lips in addition to hearing her voice, and squeaked it all on to my slate.

Suddenly, a sound came floating from the direction of the AME Church. It was harmonious and soothing. Briefly I stopped writing and my eyes turned in the direction of the sound. It happened several times—just one chord, held for a few seconds, lingering and then stopping. I listened intently to these beautiful chords, floating and then stopping. Mesmerizing! The Mistress's voice kept its demand for my attention. I was seduced! I loved both! Fortunately, I was able to do the seemingly impossible: I brought into a kind of "harmony" the Mistress's unrelenting voice, the squeaking slate as I pressed on with my writing, and the musical chord that came like fluttering, singing butterflies.

I reached home. I went straight for one of the four hard dark wood chairs with legs secured at the bottom with thick steel rods strung very taut with bolts at each of the four corners. I sat down on the step leading outside, turned the chair up-side-down and picked and twanged the rods with my fingers, as one would a guitar. I listened intently to the "music" that came out. It was good. I even tried to produce chords and any other harmonic sounds by picking several of the strings at the same time. I relished whatever sounds I could produce from this "instrument."

Sometimes a comparable experience came to me when I was sitting outside against the wall, basking in the sun. This was something everybody did in the autumn and early winter months. If I fell asleep, which often happened, my waking up was slow and gentle, and I saw, through my as yet unopened eyelids, unbelievably beautiful streaks of countless shimmering colors. Red dominated, and then a miscellany of what I can only describe as a harmony of colors.

At that same time, a chorus of extraordinarily tall women, draped in multi-colored shoulder-to-ground gowns, were singing a song without words, humming, as if sailing backwards, drifting away from me. The wearers were emitting, through their mouths, a single, harmonious, powerful chord, that sailed backwards with them dying, dying, and then, finally dying completely when my eyes opened.

From singing in church—and, for us children, at school as well—it was clear that my entire family (my father and mother and siblings)were endowed with the gift of singing and harmonizing. We sang at church, naturally. We sang at home, naturally. We sang in our games, naturally. At school and at church we sang or were taught to sing from a notation system called *tonic solfa,* which was based on certain letters of the alphabet. A straight octave without sharps and flats consisted of the letters *d-r-m-f-s-l-t* going up, and the descending *d'-t-l-s-f-m-r* going down. In a conversation such as this, we do not need to go into details of accidentals and so on.

To complete the picture, I will add the sharps and flats to the above "rise" and "fall" of the scales: The Rise: d-*de-r-re-m-f-fe-s-se-l-le-t.* The Fall: d'*-t-ta-l-la-s-fe-f-m-ma-r-de.* The fall is rather rough: *ta* sounds like *TORE, la* sounds like *LORE* or *LAW, ma* sounds like *MAW* or *MORE*. Time values were sometimes helped along with punctuation marks like a *coma*, a *colon*, a *semi-colon*.

I've gone farther than I intended. This is not a music lesson, which I'm not qualified to teach anyway. There are things like transition from one key to another, etc., etc., but I should add that these notations are so detailed, so meticulous, that, at high school, parts of Handel's *Messiah*, including the "Hallelujah Chorus," were transposed from staff notation to *tonic solfa* and sung to the finest detail without a flaw. I'm sure that there are people who know this a lot better than I do.

From here, the singers need only four notes to make a basic chord. Just like the one I heard floating from the school at the African Methodist Episcopal (AME) church, to the Wesleyan Church, where the slate and the pen were in contradiction to the luring harmony.

The Dutch Reformed Church also had a pulpit. It was quite a bit larger than that of the Wesleyan Church. That too had a message on a heavy cloth draped on the preacher's semi-seclusion in the mysterious pulpit. It was written in Afrikaans to the reader that God loved him or her.

I leave it to the reader of this book to come to grips with the fact that these messages of the word of God, of the kindness of God, of the magnanimity of God, were facing an audience which knew nothing of the languages that were addressing them. It brings to mind the Tower of Babel, and God's intention in declaring a plethora of languages where presumably there had originally been only one, once upon a time. Now there were so many, sowing the seeds of racism. Look at the results!

We children, in our innocence, played and sang and clapped hands and danced when we should have been crying. But not knowing we should have been crying was our salvation. That's true. We were saved by our ignorance, our innocence. Innocence became our salvation.

Among the adult conversations I heard, unintentionally, that my father, before he became my mother's husband, and therefore before he became my father, lived somewhere in rural Natal. He went to the gold mines as a voluntary contract laborer. Like many other laborers from remote villages with no money for the train, my father walked. Again, like other such laborers, he depended on kind people in the villages and small towns for overnight accommodations and food, to open their doors and their hearts to him.

Edenville, a semi-rural place at that time, was near such a route. My father, on one such excursion, stopped there on his way to the gold mines, or from there as he walked through the Orange Free State, asked and was received at Edenville. He met my mother and never went any further, despite his Zulu culture and Zulu origins. He became bilingual, bicultural, learned the Sesotho Bible, as indicated above.

Then, among other things, he met my mother and later became the father of my two older siblings and then me. Which means the world became different. For one thing, I would not be here writing this story if that had not happened.

One day my father surprised me. He and I were looking at a music book. In our talking about some songs written, of course, in *tonic solfa*, he started calling some of the embellishments and modifying signs by name, such as *da carpo, diminuwendo,* etc. My open-mouthed amazement left him laughing and patting me on my shoulders.

In some of his nostalgic moments, he taught us some Zulu traditional songs. One of them was as follows:

Inhliziyo yam ayikho lapha, ipheshiya koTukela
(My heart is not here, it is beyond the Tukela) (twice)
Hambani sihambe lusapho lwakowethu
(Come! Let's go, my kinsmen!) (twice)
Siye ezweni lawokhokho bethu
(Let's go to the land of our ancestors)
Phesheya koTukela (twice)
(Beyond the Tukela River)

As we sang it, I felt in my father's voice that he was full of nostalgia, which got into the hearts of all of us also.

In this totally *seSotho* linguistic and cultural environment, my father still deeply wanted two things: One, that at least one of us boys should marry a Zulu girl; and Two, that we should all learn to speak *isiZulu*. Well, we tried. I know I did. That, I thank my father for.

All the churches in the Location, just like the houses, had mud floors. People in the Location, from time to time, used mud mixed with dung to plaster the floor. At the church buildings, every Friday, we school children had to be engaged in the process of *renewing* the floors by plastering them with mud. The ritual was this. The boys dug the soil, then went to fetch water—there were no water taps in the Locations; you had to go to a little stream or creek to carry water from there to come and mix this mud.

Then it was the girls' turn, at this point. They tucked their little jean-dresses into their bloomers and knelt down and plastered the floor, moving backward, plastering and plastering, until they had covered it. That's what it meant, at least partly, to be in a church building that didn't have wooden floors.

And then there was the syllabus. The syllabus was very, very Bible-oriented. Any subject—let's take Humanities—stories you may have read were Bible-related and pepped up with Biblical references. Only exception: courses like Arithmetic, where nothing could be done to make it "Biblical" Arithmetic—one plus one is two and two plus two are four, no matter what religion one subscribes to.

But, generally, Bible Studies was one of the most important things, to the extent that, every morning, school began with an assembly where we sang hymns and prayed before going to our classes. Then, every Monday morning, our teacher would line us up and one-by-one would ask us: "Did you go to church yesterday?" If you said "No," then, "Why?" If you said you were sick: "Can someone verify that?" "Can I ask your mother?" If you said "Yes," then, "Who was the Preacher?" "Oh, it was Father So-and-So." Then, "What part of the Bible did he read from?" "Well, he read from Genesis." "Can you tell me what he said?"

So, you were quizzed to make sure you had gone to church the day before, or that you hadn't gone for a valid reason, such as sickness. The consequence for not having gone to church without a valid reason was punishment: you were going to get some lashes and be warned, "Never stay away from church."

Apart from this, you were surrounded by images that reminded you that God's eye was on you. Always! You can't escape Him. I remember the pulpit in the Wesleyan Methodist Church, which the preacher entered by climbing two or three steps that elevated him from the congregation he had come to teach about God. It endowed the preacher with a new "godliness" that made you want to kneel before him. It had a wooden book support that made it lean, to be more easily accessible to the preacher's eyes. Draped down that book supporter was a small heavy cloth with a crocheted holy message about God, something like "God loves you," in *seTswana*, facing the congregation.

Even at home, our mothers bought pictures of God and hung them on the wall. He, God, was white. He wore a large bush of white hair that reached down to his shoulders and a bushy beard, even lower, almost like the mane of a wild beast! He had blue eyes. Our parents looked at the picture with veneration. Or pictures of Jesus either on the cross or being dragged there. Or Mary! White and sad. Why?

All these were reproductions by white European artists of their mental pictures of the supposed suffering of Mary when she was about to give birth to her son. Or when Jesus was a baby, white, chubby, and ugly. I don't remember whether or not we ever saw his naughty little front dangling innocently. They say the highly pregnant Mary resorted to having her labor in a manger because the rooms in the inn where she should have been given dignified accommodation for her holy birth were full. Sounds like they were sold out to rich merchants, and to hell with Mary.

All these stories were later shown to be untrue. Where Mary gave birth to Jesus was the normal place for that event to happen in that society in that era. Furthermore, these fraudulent images were sold by itinerant, indigent-looking, starving-looking, dirty-looking homeless white men for a shilling, a florin, up to a half-crown from hard-working, under-paid blacks like my father and my mother.

The Standards I and II classes met in the African Methodist Episcopal Church (which, for short, was called the AME Church). There was no pulpit, thus no hanging message. A very low earth platform was all that separated the preacher from the congregation. On that platform stood a table, often rather rickety, where the preacher placed his Bible, his hymnal, and any other printed material he might need.

Unlike in the Wesleyan and Dutch Reformed churches, therefore, the preacher was free to move back and forth to the extent that the table and the platform would allow him. Most of the time he took advantage of that space to walk back and forth as he preached, to pound the table with his fist for emphasis, thus carrying his message not only with his words, but also with the dance, with his strutting back and forth. Mostly he spoke his message loudly. The success of his sermon was judged partly by how many women cried aloud, which, of course, also made the preacher raise his voice even louder.

The emotional level of the sermon sometimes rose so high that the preacher had to stop in order to recapture his composure. If that happened, anybody in the congregation might sometimes intervene by starting a hymn, which was eagerly received by the now spiritually charged congregation. We children would be kneeling on the floor. Some of us cried too, out of some deep fear that this kind of preaching instilled in us.

I too cried. But, for me, it was mostly when I heard my mother crying. I knew her crying voice, and I immediately cried too. A choking feeling suddenly crept up to my throat. To support her, maybe? Maybe to say the world was indeed at last coming to an end? All the terrible things! Where do we go if there is no world anymore? And to think I didn't even have a pair of shoes to walk there.

Having recovered, the preacher would pick up his sermon to the end, whereafter he stood calm. And when we got outside, the earth was still there. To this day, I cannot say what I felt the crying did for me. I felt cleansed. Cleansed of all evil things. I think I can say that's exactly what it did to me and for me: It cleansed me. Purgatory once more.

You see, there would have been no "Daniel" anywhere had not Christianity imposed itself. My African name is Qhoboshiyane (Fortress) Pule (Rain). As far as Daniel is concerned, I was told it comes from an uncle who looked down on me in the crib and said, "Something tells me to call him 'Daniel'." Now, 'Phanuel' is another of my names: my uncle, my father's younger brother, who lived in Natal, and he had Phanuel as his name. And I was also named after him.

Why European names, Biblical names? For one, children would not be accepted into school unless they had a "Christian" name. One of the things Europeans who came to South Africa did, one of their intended missions, was to make Africans totally forget their origins. The real owners of the land became owned by the conquerors. How much more upside down can a situation be than that?

And, one of those things was to destroy our names from our culture. Remember how, in Alex Haley's *Roots,* Kunta Kinte was beaten until he accepted the white man's name, "Toby"? Christianity came along with colonization…robbing people of their lands, their stock, and, by some twisted turn of logic, the culture of the people, demeaning and denigrating it. Calling every belief the people had "heathen." So, some people were "converted" and began to call the unconverted "heathen."

School for Africans was not compulsory, but Black parents wanted their children to go to school and would raise heaven and earth to have their children go to school. We as Blacks had hurdles that the Whites did not have. We had to pay quarterly school fees; and if our parents could not afford to pay, you stayed away from school. No questions asked. You just don't show up when the *books* say your parents owe school fees.

Whites did not have to pay school fees. We, that is, our parents, bought our own schoolbooks. Whites did not have to buy schoolbooks, they were provided. So, the poorest people were being burdened with all these extra expenses to have their children educated, that the richer, quite a bit richer I must say, White people did not have these additional financial obligations imposed upon them.

So, here we are now, we're dealing with poverty, we're dealing with every possible hurdle put in the way of children and their parents who want their children to go to school. I remember that, in fact, sometimes there were White golfers who played on Wednesdays, early afternoon and Saturdays. We went there to offer to caddy for them. I don't think you could guess how much we were paid, but we still appreciated it. We were paid three pennies for caddying a nine-hole course—three pennies!

On Saturdays they played two rounds, then you got six pennies. We still did it because we needed the money, to the extent that we could, to be of some help to our parents. I remember one time my older brother and I, at our mother's suggestion or our own, but whenever we went to caddy, we would give our money to our mother to keep for us. We ended up very excited because we had collected six shillings, that would be less than a dollar.

Also, in order to caddy on Wednesday, we had to skip the second half of school. When there was a break in the school day for a brief interval, we would run home to get something to eat, and then we might just sneak away, go and caddy, and bring those few pennies home.

As anybody can guess by now, the drop-out rate for my peers was very high, because of the hurdles—the school fees, books, clothes, etc.—and hard for parents who, even without paying your school fees, were finding it difficult to give you decent food, decent meals. We slept on the floor without a mattress.

Of course, one of the reasons for dropping out was that, whatever you can earn, doing whatever job you could get in the White town, would help the family income. So, dropping out was such a common thing, because they were being discouraged at every turn—left, right, front, center, there were hurdles. You had to have some kind of will and determination to go on. Sometime parents actually encouraged their children to drop out because of these hurdles.

Still, I can't emphasize enough how much our parents appreciated education, how much they wanted us to have education. They took education as something that gave you power. It gave you power, for example, you get to a certain level you could get a job, maybe a teacher, and that gave you status in the community, but also earning a reasonable amount of money. For all these reasons, our parents were very keen that we get education.

The fact that people were so proud, as a community, as a whole; of course, there were exceptions—people were jealous, envious, and so on—but the community was proud our young people were getting educated. Hence the value that was placed on education, even by those who were not able to keep their children in school for financial reasons...mostly for financial reasons.

Let me give you an example of *community* I'm talking about. If there were a funeral, of someone who was not related to us, just to be there it was a matter of pride, by the people who were next of kin—the bereaved—that we be there ... for the services, at the church, at the house, at the final service at the gravesite. At the end of it all, we would be asked to go quickly to the "Exit" gate and we'd stand on each side and count the people, just as a matter of record. Again, to show that *education* was most prized, for the individual and the community.

There were four boys and two girls in our family. And the eldest was a girl. We were all, at one time, together, in primary school. This love to have children educated manifested itself also in the appreciation of an educated child. Now, at Edenville-Location, you were educated, basically, when you learned to read and write your own language; and a little bit of English, which was also regarded as a mark of distinction—the more English you knew, the better.

But, when you were able to read and write, even if you were a little boy in the community, everybody in the community prided themselves on your skills. And they had also the privilege, almost the right, to call you: "Hey, young fellow come here. I got this letter from my son in Johannesburg, could you please read it for me?" And, after reading: "Now, you must come again tomorrow, son, to write the letter back to my son?" They give you a pad and dictate to you what you're to write. Sometimes you have to ask the narrator to "please go slower, I'm writing"—his words are just popping out.

I guess the point I'm trying to make is that this community got a communal profit from any child who had got some education. Our parents didn't mind and were actually proud when people would call us to say, "Come and write a letter for me." We were like secretaries for the whole Location. What we could do did not just belong to us, but to the whole community. We didn't feel exploited. We'd be feeling built-up! Actually, it built us up.

I look back at that with some nostalgia, because I don't know if I appreciated it at that time as much as I do now, that the whole community was benefitting from the writing and reading skills we were learning from school. I was doing this from about the time I was nine or ten years old.

You know, there were many lay preachers, who could identify songs by number and sight in a hymnal, and books of the Bible like *Exodus*, but when it came to *reading*—standing there in front of the congregation, struggling, trying to read when they really couldn't—he would call us from the audience, during the service: "Hey sonny, come here. Come and read these verses for me." And, I would go to the front of the church and read the verses from the Bible. "Thank you, my son. Go sit down." And, then he starts his sermon.

You see, we were very important. We were very highly appreciated by our community. I cannot emphasize that enough, the extent to which people appreciated what we had got by being in school. And every parent would have liked their child to be in that position of having learned the skills of reading and writing. Any parent who would have called you from the street and said: "Hey, hey, young man, come here and read this letter for me," or "Come and write this letter for me"—by that act alone, you know that they would have been very happy to have their children to also have those skills.

At this time, both my parents were working. My mother was a Mosotho of the Bataung group. She spoke Setaung. Her names were Martha Mahloli Kutoane. Her totem animal was "Tau," the "lion." She belonged to the Wesleyan Methodist Church, her father's church, as was the custom. When she got married, she joined her husband's church, namely the African Methodist Episcopal (AME) Church, as was the custom.

My mother, mostly, took in washing, laundry from Town, from the Whites. My mother would go to the White Town and pick up washing, or send us children to go and pick it up; and then she washed it. And, not any source of water anywhere except that stream; and, that's where they did the washing. They had skills to not only wash laundry, but to bleach it—by soaking it, then spreading on the grass and letting the sun do some bleaching, bring it back, rinse it, take it home to iron it. Then, either my mother would take it herself, or she would send us to deliver it.

This was kind of a once-a-week thing if she did washing for just one family, one White family. But some people did it for several families, so they were occupied more days in the week than just two (washing day and ironing day). So I think about myself being exploited by working at caddying, being paid three pennies for a nine-hole course.

Everybody was exploited. Every Black person was exploited. It was cheap labor because they had no choice.

My father, was Zulu—last name (surname) Kunene; first names Ephraim, Edmund. Remember, descriptions like "surname" and "last name" suggest European, especially missionary interference with the then traditional naming practice of naming by descent (e.g., "Son of…").

He was born and raised in Oliver's Hoek near Ladysmith, which was the nearest railway station. Oliver's Hoek was a rural area in Natal with scattered villages. His brother, Phanuel, lived a day's walk from my father's village, with rivers to cross and gentle hills to climb. I think my "little father's" (younger "paternal uncle's") abode was also in the Oliver's Hoek area. Some of my father's praise names, which are poetic, and refer to *warrior* qualities, are as follows:

uMashishiwane
uNdlovu-zidl'ekhaya-ngokuswel'-abelusi
uMthakathi
uThiyane-ngokuthiy'-amadoda'-emazibukweni
uNdimande
uZikhode-ka-Langa

His totem animal was "*Ndlovu*," the "elephant." Since the praises above were often spread among clan praise poems, there are probably others that I don't know, since I don't have the poems themselves.

Before he left Natal to live in Edenville, Orange Free State, after marrying my mother, my father belonged to the Lutheran Church. Arriving at the tiny town of Edenville, where there was no Lutheran Church, he joined the AME (African Methodist Episcopal) Church, where he soon became a lay preacher. He earned his living through manual work for a Jewish general dealer shop owner.

Unfortunately, I know nothing about Mama's (Selina's) side and, with Uncle Ezekiel and Aunt Henrietta gone, there's no one I can turn to. As regards my father's side, I just remembered one item which might help the search for family roots and origins. It is the fact that the Great world-wide Depression, which led to great suffering, was, in South Africa, accompanied by a severe and prolonged drought. The scarcity of jobs was exacerbated by crop failures. In addition, great dust storms, always reddish in color, increased starvation and a general sense of inertia.

LADY AND CHARLIE

My father lost his job at the general dealer's store mentioned earlier. This was in the early 1930s, with 1933 being the worst. He left on his horse to look for work in a little, privately owned mine about 12 to 14 miles away, called "Lime Works." The laborers dug the lime stones in a quarry, loaded them on cocopans and pushed them on rickety rails, up to the kiln where the stones were burned and ground into lime powder and shipped away. Back-breaking work for a pittance.

I was in, maybe, Standard 2 or 3, which would be the early 1930s, when the great drought that seemed to have gripped the earth was on top of us as well. By "us" I mean the South Africa I knew at my age, somewhere between nine and ten years of age, which would have been around 1932 or -1933. Every day was greeted by a morning that seemed to promise rain, but the supposed rain clouds would soon begin to change into a gripping red that slowly wrapped itself around the earth and blurred our vision. As I grew up, I came to know that that time coincided with the world-wide drought that led to or coincided with the Great Depression in America. Whatever the connection was or was not, we were attacked by the same drought that was not only frightening, but physically diminished even the meager amount of food we had. We, the Location dwellers, raided the white people's dumps, which, we believed might have some left-over food from their tables. We scratched them, and whatever seemed edible we ate.

Churches preached sermons beseeching God for rain. No rain came. Small pools and lakes and streams dried up or got dangerously close to doing so. Everybody appealed to whatever powers might know what we meant when we said: *We are thirsty.* Cows died because no green grass grew. Cattle bellowed, first in anger (*Where's our grass?*), then in despair (*Where's our water? Save us from the thirst!*).

The water had begun to retreat from the shore, luring whatever, or whoever, with the little gleaming pools far into the strips of water: *Yes, you may come and drink me, but beware of the treacherous way hither.* The bellowing grew louder. Some risked it. Dipped their legs close to their knees, drank from the pool, and stuggled, one leg at a time to return to the shore. But at least for now they had quenched their searing thirst. The choice was between death from thirst, and a more cruel and slow death by sinking slowly in what had become a quicksand of mud.

Generally, the black people in South Africa did not eat horse meat, except if they had been born and raised in Lesotho. Necessity and hunger taught them otherwise. They began to eat horse meat. Horses they saw die in the grazing camps for lack of grass to eat. We had two horses which were very fond of my father. A white mare, the older of the two, called "Lady." The younger one, of a brown color, named "Charlie." These horses loved my father and always pranced towards him as they saw him walking home through the grazing camp footpath. They would walk behind him homewards. They would get into their pen and my father would give them generous amounts of the forage he had brought.

The black churches prayed for rain. No rain came. The water continued to recede farther and yet farther from the shore.

The schools—oh yes. Black schools. The Whites chided themselves. God would yield to the prayers of children. Straight out of the children's innocent mouths. *Why have we waited so long?* Was it the self-deprecation of the white power. The Edenville black primary schools came out in force to the higher of the two rocky hills in the grazing fields. They were led by their teachers and spiritually by the Wesleyan evangelist who started the proceedings with a regular prayer.

In the middle of it he switched to the voices of children speaking in the first person: "God we appeal to You. The cattle are dying.

There is no water to drink. The crops cannot grow because the land is so dry! Our feet burn as we walk on this hot, hot ground."

The prayer was much longer, naming the cruelties of the drought and the heat and so on and so on. Well, surely God will feel sorry for the children. No one believed in that more than we, the children. As we walked slowly down the hill, back to the Location, one little boy of about my age, apparently seized by a religious moment, said: "I saw a cloud the size of a man's hand!" We opened our mouths hearing this prophetic statement. We were amazed by this miracle about to happen. Especially from the mouth of an innocent child!

The adults too, including the whites, were also hopeful. Surely God could not ignore this innocent plea from suffering children.

He did. No rain came.

Now what?

The owner of the general dealer where my father worked kept reducing their pay. His explanation was: "You can see that times are bad. I am not making as much money as I used to."

"Yes. But it's the same with me—my children and their mother and myself," said Father in reply. "How can I support them with this little bit you give me? It's been very difficult even without the drought and famine. But now? No, Baas. Is too much little money! We're hungry! Maybe a little more. Just a little more!"

"Well, Ephraim, I am doing my best. If you can find another place to work, you may leave. What can I do?" he added, shrugging his shoulders. This was a dilemma that took some days, maybe ten days, before my father had the courage to tell my mother and my mother in turn told us. We had known the dark, bitter secret. But now when it hit us bluntly like a heartless bullet, we stood dumb. It was as if someone had died.

There was silence. Merciless tears dribbled down our cheeks when our parents were no longer able to protect us by forcing their own sadness in their own chests, when they could no longer press down their tears as my father said, more than once, "I don't know what to do. Edenville is dead. I have thought of going to find work at that cursed place called *Limeworks*. If they hire me there, it will be a difficult job, digging lime stones, pushing it in cocopans on little rails and loading them on the machine that grinds them into powder called *lime*. "I don't know what else I can do."

He kept quiet for a little while, sniffing gently from time to time. My mother continued crying gently. Then she abruptly stood up and said to us: "You have heard for yourselves, my children. Your father is going to leave and work in that place where they dig lime. He will stay there. He will not come home every day." Then she said in a harsh, desperate voice: "That's what the white people do to you. You work for them, then when a difficult time comes, they do not stand by you. They throw you away like an old dirty rag!" She walked suddenly to the bedroom, where we could hear her sobbing.

We were all choking with emotion—anger, despair, sympathy with our parents whom we never wanted to see crying. Two days later, my father saddled Lady and rode to Limeworks. We would miss Lady, we would miss our father, and we would continue to starve, as things looked. The sun had continued to come out of the earth red, sucking the last remaining moisture in the air, if there was any at all. We saw my father's back and Lady's full tail as they turned the last corner before disappearing from our house.

The house was very lonely for many days. Crying came easily. Sniffling sounds came too often. The house felt empty, especially in the evenings. That chair where my father sat, where he could see all of us, whether with a frown or with a smile, was empty. A ritual at most. The throne of authority was empty.

I missed the ritual that happened most evenings when my father was home: walking to our parents' bedroom to hear our father's prayer for out safety for the night. My mother's determination for these goals was so palpable, you could touch it.

In my father's absence, my mother was the only adult who carried the responsibility to feed us, to clothe us, to keep us alive, make us continue to want to live. In other words to keep on believing that our striving to overcome difficulties, to go to bed at night and get up in the morning, to tell ourselves all this is going to reward us one day. For me, the main reward from all the sacrifice and hard work was that one day I would qualify for a job—a respectable and well-paying one, to thank my parents for the sacrifices they were making to ensure that I would achieve my educational goals.

Meanwhile, we had to get used to living in Edenville with what was there to live on, which clearly was below what we needed to survive. Yet, we stayed and did what we could to help our mother to keep us and her alive. The more the sacrifices like these faced us, and the more little victories we achieved, the more I was determined that one day I would reach that level of working, earning enough to support my parents. I did not know then, I do not know now, the power of this motivation.

The drought persisted. More animals died. Charlie died. Signs of his getting to this point had been obvious. They had got more obvious as more moisture was sucked out of the earth. Thus, Charlie's death was not quite a surprise. Sorrow, the fact that another living member of our household was gone—all these made the burden on our bodies and souls increase. My Mother decided that since Charlie was her horse, she was going to make an exception, and have him prepared for his resting place, namely the sustainer of our lives. She was sure these considerations exonerated her from her previous determination never to eat horse meat. Our starving bodies were the most holy place for Charlie's final resting place.

There was a man who had come to South Africa from Lesotho, and my mother asked him to undertake the job of skinning Charlie, preparing him as any animal prepared for eating, like cow or sheep meat, would be. The man from Lesotho would get a generous amount of the meat. My mother and my brothers and sisters made the appropriate sounds of disgust, but soon saw our mother's reasoning: Eat Charlie! We all agreed that it was rather different, the texture was somewhat slippery, a few uttered this or that not to eat Charlie. But we did eat Charlie.

My father used to ride Lady to visit home from time to time. But there came a time when he did not, and we heard no more about Lady. We guessed what had probably happened to Lady. Limeworks had several Basotho men working at the mine. Most of them had their families with them. Whether my father ever shared any secret about Lady's fate I never knew. We assumed that Lady had come to the same end as Charlie. We feared to ask our father.

Martha, mother of Daniel

Ephraim, father of Daniel

SECONDARY EDUCATION

I mentioned earlier that the first two years of school were called Substandard: Substandard A and Substandard B. And then, from there it was Standard One, Standard Two, so on and so forth. Standard Six was the highest level that we could reach in the Location. There was no school offering anything beyond Standard Six in Edenville Location.

It was different in the White schools. They could go to the Secondary Level, and still be at home beyond Standard Six by two or three years, before they would have to separate from their parents. Now, for us, Standard Six was the highest.

Now, the Final Exams, and this was considered so important, were set in the capitol of the state. They were printed there and put in sealed envelopes there. We didn't write our names on our exam books but were given numbers. So there was this anonymity that they wouldn't know who you are; and, the sealed envelopes were torn open while we were sitting there ready with our pens, in our presence—often in front of another witness—just to say, "These are being opened right this minute, everybody is going to see them now…never before." Then they were distributed and you were told, "Keep it upside down, until they are all distributed." Then, at a given signal, you were told to turn it right side up and begin to write your answers.

It was almost a great, solemn occasion for the Location, for the community. These highest educated young people, these children of ours, having to write this high examination; that the questions come from Bloemfontein and are sealed. It was a ritual, but not just a ritual; it was to insure that nobody knew what the questions were going to be until they were right there in front of you.

When I did Standard Six, by that time, my older sister, Sophia, and my older brother, Elias—we all got bunched up in Standard Six, because I had got automatic promotions because I was going through courses so easily the teachers didn't see any reason to take me through the formality of "spending a year here, spending a year there" when, in fact, I could just go and join those who were already in Standard Six and do as well if not better than them.

So, when the final results came, I was top. My brother was second and my sister third. The extent to which this was an achievement that was felt throughout the Black community was heightened by the fact that Reverend Madlomo, who was then the Minister of the Dutch Reform Church in the Location, was also the appointed *Invigilator*, watching over us as we were writing the exams, distributing the papers, collecting the papers.

But what he did do, which made it even more significant, was, every day of the exams, to indicate the beginning of the first exam, he would have the church-bell ringing. It would tell the whole Location that it was the beginning of the Standard Six exams. Everyone knew. And we felt very proud. At that time, I was thirteen.

I should also mention how strict the requirements were, for passing a certain Standard; to go to the next one depended on how you did. If you got marks below a certain point, you stayed back there for another year. That's why when we first got to this country (America) and I heard about *automatic promotion* in the elementary schools, in order to keep the peer group together and all that, I was amazed. What's the purpose if they're not going to earn promotion to the next grade, by showing mastery of the work that they have learned in the previous grade? So, what's the point?

We had mixtures of heights and ages in the same class because people had to *earn* their passing on to the next grade, by passing their exams. Either you passed or you failed; and if you failed, you stayed back for another year.

The exams might go over three days. Reverend Madlomo, every time we finished writing the first papers in the morning, would invite us all to his house for tea and cakes; cakes baked by no less a person than the Reverend's wife, Mrs. Madlomo. Of course, this was such a special treat for us; it wasn't often we had cake. Marie Antoinette comes to mind.

My mother was the one, the staunchest one making sure that we continued to get our education. She was not educated herself. She could barely write. My father could read and write some and had had more schooling than my mother. But they, like others in the community, consider education as something that gives you power, in all kinds of ways.

For example, the more educated Black people were less afraid of confronting Whites. They had that sense of "Don't try to bully me…I have some power."

To begin what you might call Middle School or Secondary School here (in America), we had to leave home. It was not available for Blacks in Edenville. There were no school buildings for blacks. All eight years: Substandards A and B, and Standards 1–6, were held in church buildings. This served Christianity well, for it meant that the children were surrounded by God's symbolic presence six more days of the week. Basically, the entire week.

The nearest bigger town where they had secondary and high school, up to what we called Metric, where you're matriculating, being prepared to go to a university.

Before this there would be Form One, otherwise Standard Seven; Form Two, Standard Eight; Form Three, where once again there was another milestone. This is where you would sit for exams that would give you a Junior Certificate. The Certificate comes from the State Capitol, your name on it.

Now, when my parents saw that we had all three passed Standard Six, they had to decide: they couldn't possibly afford to send us all to Kroonstad, financially. They could not afford to send us to start our Secondary Education. After a family gathering, it was decided, "Oldest son first." So, it was my older brother who was chosen to go to Kroonstad.

What do I do? The first year that I could have gone to Secondary School, but did not, my parents, with the advice of the teacher, let me go back and study Standard Six again. I already had a first class pass for this class. So, I repeated. It was now 1936. I got another first-class pass.

The following year, my brother went back to Kroonstad for a second year. I still could not go. This time I did three little jobs. The first one, there was this old Dutch woman for whom my mother did washing and who lived alone, Mrs. Coetzee. She looked forward to my mother coming because she was lonely. In cases like this, my mother would just do the washing there in the woman's house, rather than bring it home, to give her a little company.

We all had to learn the *master's* language. Our parents, in the Location, spoke a kind of Afrikaans, derivative from the Dutch language, by communicating with their employers. This was getting to be my third year repeating Standard Six. I had to do something. This was getting too monotonous.

My mother talked to this old Dutch woman and asked if she could give me some little job. She agreed and gave me work as a sort of handyman around the house, fixing what I could, running errands. She also owned a cow, and I had to get there early enough in the morning to drive the cow to pasture. Then bring it back in the evening, for milking.

I did that for one month, for which I was paid a penny a day. At the end of the month, thirty pennies would equal two shillings and six pence or half a pound. And I quit. I just couldn't stand it. And then, somehow, my teachers got me a teaching job at a farm school.

I had no experience as a teacher, just the knowledge I'd got from Standard A to Standard Six. I sort of knew how my teachers taught me, and I was going to try to mimic their way of teaching, and I did that.

One thing that I didn't do, which people said, "Hey, you're lucky you didn't get into trouble with the farmer" (the white farmer). Remember, this was a White farmer's farm, with the Black workers separated living in their little houses and their children having to come to school; sometimes it would not only be children of this farm, but other adjacent farms.

I held that job for about three months. It was temporary to begin with. Then I got another teaching job, this time in Edenville itself. I was teaching in the lowest grades. I was a teacher wearing shorts.

You see, there was this significance of long pants versus short pants. A child wore short pants. The father and the older men wore long pants. No child wore long pants. Sort of ritualizing the length of pants. So, teacher or no teacher I had to wear short pants.

As far as controlling the students is concerned, there is again this difference with American schools as I know them, and I think it's getting more and more so. Discipline in our school, when I use to go to school, was understood to be part of the building of your character. Discipline would take any form, including physical punishment, getting lashes. I know I had my share of that.

As a young rebellious youth, I was skipping school. It must have been around Standard Three. I got it in my head that I was just not going to school. I can't even remember why. I just went to town and just wandered about, aimlessly. On the second day, I went to the golf course. The school sent two older boys after me. They chased me through a farm until I came to an old woman doing washing. She asked, "What are you running from?" I told her "Because I don't want to go to school…because I have a sore foot." She laughed. And as we stood there, the two boys caught up to me. They forced me back to school where I got a thrashing like I'd never had before.

Of course, my mother was concerned but the teacher was *in loco parentis* in your relationship to them, and as long as you were away from your parents they had all the rights of parents, to discipline you.

I was one grade below my older brother and my older sister, who were, respectively, about three and five years older than me. The Primary School levels were arranged so that I was something like two or three grades behind them. By level of achievement, I was at least their level if not above. The principal decided to promote me so that the three of us ended being in the same level of Primary School.

This began at, I believe, about the fourth level. We ended doing the last level of Primary in the same year, with me earning a first class pass to their second and/or third. After being held back for two years by my parents for lack of money to send all three of us to the black secondary school at Kroonstad at the same time, now at last was my turn. The school was lovingly called K.B.H.S., that is

Kroonstad Bantu High School. Now at last was my turn, the third Kunene student to tread its waters.

So, in 1938, when I was 15, I got my chance to go to Kroonstad for Secondary Education. Here I am having this additional expense on my parents' part, that Whites did not have to have, and having the trauma of separation; and, in addition, going to Kroonstad where there were no dorms. No dormitories, no facilities for students who came from out of town to live.

My mother took me to Kroonstad on a lorry. Blacks in Edenville Location from time to time rented a lorry belonging to a white man in town, who set his total price that included his regular black transport driver. The would-be travelers sat on the black deck towed by the engine. In turn, the male travelers were responsible for carrying off whatever loads or merchandise were on the lorry and loading them back on when they got back. He set his total price, which the negotiator divided among the potential travelers.

The lorry stopped at a central spot in B. Location, and all the travelers walked to whatever their ultimate destination was. My mother and I had none. She had heard we had some relatives in Kroonstad. She looked this way and that, like a radar: Where were they now when she most needed them? "Let's go, my child. God will be with us." I did not ask go whereto . I simply trusted in my mother as she trusted in God.

In fact, right then, she mumbled a little prayer: as we walked: "*Oh God, please guide our steps.*" I felt a little choking in my throat. She had heard vaguely of some distant relative, and she would see if she could remember any of the names and trace them. She started to walk, with me in tow. She would take the chance of stopping at any home she simply felt good about, even before she decided for us to enter or pass.

She stopped at one gate, where a woman was outside, apparently about to walk back into the house:

"*Dumela, mma!*" (Greetings, mother!) The woman looked briefly at us and quickly turned and disappeared in the house.

My mother could not believe it. Is this how people behave in the big towns? We walked on, with our earlier hope almost crushed.

Our feet had become more dusty, almost as if we were dragging them in the dust.

"Mother, let's rest a little so you can take that bundle off your head," I said. "I can carry one or two small ones."

"Just a few more steps, my child," my mother responded. The "few steps" over, we stopped and were looking for a place we could sit more or less comfortably.

Two or three houses a little forward from where we were, someone called: *"Mama! Mama!"* and as we looked around, we saw a woman who was signaling to us, "Don't sit there. My daughters will come and help you." No sooner had we located the source that we saw two young girls running towards us.

"Dumelang, mma."

"Yes, my children," said my mother as she took the load off her head. One of them took my suitcase and put it on her head. Our feet were dusty and tired. The woman who called out to us came and greeted us and helped the girls to carry our loads into the house. She came out with some food, which she offered us with a little bow. My mother welcomed it with equal grace and we started to eat. My mother and I ate, at first rather silently. Our kind savior broke the silence, briefly, first about the weather, how hot it was. "I hope you're not in a hurry. It's too hot to be walking around with luggage like this. Just rest a little. Can I help you?"

I could see it was hard on my mother, but she held back her tears. "We've just come from Edenville. My child is going to join the big school here, Kroonstad Batho…." My mother and the woman both laughed. My mother laughed long enough to disguise the crying tears. "Not *Batho*," said the woman, and I saw the same effort in her. *"Don't cry, don't cry.* They call it *Bantu*." "Yes," responded my mother, "Kroonstad Bantu *Hayi Sekolo*." We all cracked up laughing. Praised be my mother, I thought. "I'm looking for a place for him to stay."

So, what our parents did is if they knew somebody or even had any distant family and say: "I'm bringing my child to school here. I'm looking for a place. Can he stay with you? We'll support you the best we can." Nothing formal like, "It's going to be so much per month" and all that. And, they would either say "Yes" or "No."

Especially, if they were family members, they would find it difficult to say "No." But sometimes, total strangers would see you and your mother walking in the dusty streets with your luggage, knocking on doors, because that was the only way you're going to get a place to stay, in order to get this education.

Many of them exploited the situation: you scrubbed floors, polished furniture, went to town to buy groceries, and sometimes you had to write home and say, "I cannot stand to be in this family anymore."

I stayed with quite a few families while I was studying there. Sometimes a family might have a separate room in the backyard where you might do your own cooking. Otherwise, you stayed in the house as a kind of unpaid, free house help. But that's how my Secondary Education began at Kroonstad Bantu High School.

Kroonstad was about thirty miles of unpaved road form Edenville, and at that time thirty miles was a very long distance. Again, the issue of poverty: I didn't even own a bicycle, essential if I wanted to occasionally visit my parents without getting on a train. Sometimes I would borrow a bicycle from somebody and cycle those thirty miles, maybe two to three hours.

Sometimes almost tragic things can happen during a ride like that. I remember one where I was caught in the rain cycling back from Edenville to Kroonstad, having left around mid-afternoon. I hadn't gone very far when I saw the rain coming in my direction in no time, first a few drops, and then a downpour. The road just turned to mud. Then, I heard a sound, a hissing sound, and noticed the bike slowing down. I stopped to inspect it and found that the inner tube was bulging out and I rushed to release the valve and expel the air before, it seems, the tire would explode. Now, I had to push the bike the rest of the way, and I was still very far.

Now, late afternoon passing by a farm, a white farm, Blacks did not own farms anymore; and, I had to be careful to stay on the right side of the fences: if a dog barked, a white farmer could come out of his house with a shotgun, and shoot you, and that would be the end of that—Private property and all that.

You know, in *oral societies*, people talk, you never find a house full of people totally silent. I don't know if I ever told you, of course;

years later, about when Mama and I were in Germany. One time, it was beginning to be quite dark, the sun had set, and we walked to a shelter where we were going to get a tram to wherever we were going. It was dark and there was some slight rain. When we came around to the front, we were really surprised that the place was full of people: looking straight ahead, no one saying anything to anyone. And I just thought, "If this was South Africa or anywhere in Africa, an African community," we would have heard as soon as we turned the corner that there were people there, talking, because people are talkers. People here, in America, are afraid of the dark. Rather than coming out, joining one another, enjoying each other in the moonlight, we fear each other.

Eastern Transvaal, A laborer's house 1961, Photo by Ian Berry

I looked for a place where the Black farm laborers lived; I got there and they were absolutely kind. The men there repaired my inner tube, inflated it, gave me warm tea and generally treated me as they would any traveler who got caught in the rain, in the night, or needed a place to sleep or rest. They treated me like their child. They tried to persuade me not to continue.

But I was driven by one thing: I had an exam to write the next morning. I couldn't miss that exam. I knew if I could make it to a certain hill I could coast down a good distance. Soon it was getting dark and a bit scary. We were always warned and aware that that there were some mischievous whites who could hurt or even kill you. Only white people owned cars, at this time, so I knew that whenever I saw an approaching car it was white people. Often, I had to hide in gullies and behind trees. I tried a White farm and was chased away by a dog. I again found where the Black workers were and they took me in. They took my wet clothes and hung them up, fed me, and insisted that I spend the night. I did.

The next morning I was able to make it to Kroonstad in time and freshen up before going to write the exam. We were inspired. Those of us who had the good fortune to be in school were inspired. The whole saga is based on the need to write that exam. We drove ourselves. We didn't need to be beaten and scolded, we knew what we needed to do and we did it.

Several very significant things happened at Kroonstad Bantu High School. One of them was that was where I met one of my teachers who was to be my life-long mentor, Professor A.C. Jordan. He, himself, ended up here at the University of Wisconsin and was part of the establishment of the Department of African Languages and Literatures in 1964. I had met Professor Jordan when I was in high school in 1938.

Shortly after I got to Kroonstad, the choirmaster was auditioning new arrivals for their voices and selecting students to add to the choir. I was selected to be one of the ones going into the choir. I loved singing! I just loved singing!! Also, it was then that I first composed a song. I wrote a four-part song that, from time to time, during a break in school, a holiday or interval, I would collect some of my fellow students, a few of them, and we would stand around and sing this song I had composed.

This was for soprano, alto, tenor, and bass. I composed the words as well, and they were in Zulu. Zulu was my father's Mother

Tongue, not my mother's. Now, as we get into a little family lore here, the story that we were told as children of how my mother and my father met was that my father used to be, around the beginning of the 20th century, a *contract laborer.* He was born in Natal, Zululand, now called Kwazulu Natal, thoroughbred Zulu—language, culture, everything.

Many who went to sell their labor at the mines, gold mines in Johannesburg, had no means of getting there except walking. And they spent days on the road, nights on the road, getting shelter from strangers who took them in as travelers, in the same way I had been helped by workers when I was on my bicycle. Black people would never turn you away when you needed shelter, when you needed a place to stay for the night, when you needed food; and that's how many people went from their homes in the rural areas to the mines in Johannesburg… and so did my father.

To get from Zululand to Johannesburg, in the Transvaal meant going through the Orange Free State, where, by the way, Edenville is. One leaves back and forth, coming back, going back home to Natal after the contract is over, going to Johannesburg, and so on and so forth. My father met my mother who was in the Orange Free State where the culture, the language, everything is Sesotho, not Zulu. They are both African languages, Bantu languages; structurally, they compare very, very well, but they are different languages. Even culturally there are significant areas of difference. Met my mother, fell in love, and married her, and never took another step.

He did not go back to Natal. He stayed there. His church had been the Lutheran church in Natal, but when he came to Edenville there was no Lutheran church in Edenville, and he joined the AME (African Methodist Episcopal) church. He became a lay preacher—laborer during the day, visiting church members in the evening, preaching on Sunday, doing any repair work that needed doing, making sure the organization of the church, meetings, evening services and the like ran smoothly. People like my father had to be there to continue the congregation together to provide a ritual and, if you will, business structure.

My father, being a preacher, learned *seSotho*. And he would tell us that one way that he helped himself to know *seSotho* as well as he did was by having a Zulu Bible here and *seSotho* Bible here, and comparing: *How is this said in Sesotho? How is this said in Zulu?* He ended up being quite versatile and was able to preach in both languages.

He never forgot his roots in Natal. He very much wanted for us, at least one of us, one of us boys, to go and get a wife in Zululand, with pure Zulu blood. Well, we didn't. Not because we didn't want to; the opportunity just never arose.

My father was trying to cultivate our awareness of our Zulu origins, our Zulu roots, through him. He taught us several songs about his longing for home, for Zululand: *My heart is not here, my heart is over the Kukela river, come on, let's go, let's go back to our home.*

I think one of the motivating modes of thinking in people is the thought of *survival*. The first thing, it's survival. Our parents survived by not fighting their bosses, and being exploited, and being looked down upon, and every bad thing that could be done, a white could do it to a black…with impunity. And they survived, our parents. Because sometimes you have to use your judgement and say, "In this circumstance am I going to expose myself, just to say I'm casting a stone for liberation even if it means I die right now. Or am I going to just work, support my family with the bit that I get and *survive* and hope that tomorrow will be better?" That is a choice that is not made very easily, and so I applaud my parents for having just *survived* to bring us to where we are. They were seeing the future through us, their children—and we through our children, who will be stronger and better equipped to challenge the system than we are.

Like the Israelites of old, the Boers, the Dutch believed they were God's chosen people and had the right to kill African "heathens." What became known as "The Battle of Blood River" is a case in point. Due to a superiority in weaponry, the Boers killed an advance of Zulus until "the river ran red with blood." The Boers then built a church on that spot, which they called, "The House of Weeping" and thanked "God" for helping them kill so many Africans. This is the Christianity our parents and grandparents faced. So, as we grew in consciousness and awareness, we became—certainly I became— disillusioned with Christianity and organized religion per se. What so-called "God" would support this kind of treatment of our people?

The wars against the Boers were called "Kaffir Wars," the equivalent of "Nigger Wars." As they say, "It is the victor who writes history." Africans, today, would call those "Wars of Liberation" and the like.

BACK TO EDENVILLE

"*I'm going back to Edenville,*" I said when I was age seven and I was in Substandard B. One afternoon, and I don't know how long this had been going on before it struck my consciousness, I was in the church building where the Substandards were taught, the Wesleyan Methodist Church, and within voice distance was the AME church where Standards One and Two were taught.

One afternoon, sort of towards the end of the school day, we were having our class, with our very motherly teacher—and *Teacher* was not used for a woman; she had to be called *Mistress*. The word *Teacher* was for a man; a male teacher could be called a teacher but not a female. That's how we grew up: Woman *Mistress*... Man *Teacher*.

So, this Mistress was just so motherly it was unbelievable. There was a class going on, and then suddenly I heard a most glorious sound of harmonized voices. I pricked my ears. It would come from the direction of the AME Church floating in the air...hung sometime and then...quiet. Then it would start again. And, it was one chord, all the time, just one chord.

My mind was divided between being present in my class and hearing these Angelic sounds. I appreciated music a lot. I found out afterwards that in fact those sounds came from the teacher who was the choir director for Standards One and Two. He was tuning the choir for the pitch where the song they were about to sing would begin. If it were going to be the key of C, it was by estimation, mostly by ear; there were no tuning forks in Edenville Location, that I knew of anyway.

So, he would pitch a song for a major chord, then shout, "Chord!" and the four parts would sing that chord—not words, just sound. The notation system that I used for my pieces, and that was used in our schools to teach us to sing as well as in church hymnals, was *tonic-sol-fa*. In other words: *Do, Re, Me, Fa, So, La, Te, Do*. Not staff notations—which I use to see as golf clubs.

When he gave them the chord, four parts were expected to know their letter: *D* for *Do*, *R* for *Re*, *M* for *Me*…and so forth. It was beautiful. I was so very attracted to what I was hearing. The music was in my blood. I loved to sing and I loved to try to create music. In the poverty that we were, as you can imagine, there was no musical instrument of any kind at home.

I used to take these chairs made of very dark, very hard wood, very straight chairs. Underneath the seat, to reinforce it, there were these steel rods; in the corners, they were held tight by steel bolts.

I would turn the chair over, and "pluck" on these rods, put my ear there to listen, trying to make sounds, trying to make music.

Of course, I was not the only one who liked music or singing, but one more inclined to want to write it, to compose. We were a singing family. One of the pasttimes that we would have, after the evening meal, in addition to stories, would often be singing. My mother would sing soprano, which we called "first part" (*fesoata*); my older sister would sing alto "second part" (*sekene*). For some reason, tenor and bass were not called "third part" and "fourth part." They were *tinoro* (tenor) and *beso* (bass). Myself and my older brother would sing tenor, and my father would sing bass. It came rather naturally for us to sing in that kind of harmony. We were truly surprised to hear that in the white church the entire congregation, including the men, sang "first part!" Like women! A man singing *fespata* was unheard of! With some exceptions.

We used to be amused to hear that at the White church, everybody sang *first part*. Now, *first part* is the melody, the melody would be sung by women, so would the *second part*, the alto. We never could understand how men could sing *first part* like women. So, with a little sour grapes, people would say that's why they need an organ in their church: to make the music sound better.

We were the first and at that time only Edenville Location singing family. We sang for our own entertainment. This mostly took place in the evening after supper. This time was sometimes occupied by storytelling, with my mother the main, one might even say the only, storyteller. My mother went into the story with her whole body and soul. She reacted to the story, she went through the emotions, she sometimes had tears in her eyes.

My father sometimes took the storytelling role. He did his best. What I recall are stories about little girls lost in the forest where they became espied by the evil deformed being called Zim. My father impersonated Zim with a deep, harsh voice that would make us tremble by repeating a terrifying threat: *I am going to eat all of you, beginning with you, then you, then you* and so on, pointing at each of us in turn. My father laughed a lot, both at his imitation of the girls' shivering, and his own uncontrollable clumsiness in his efforts at Zim threats. But who could compete with my mother's re-enaction of life itself?

We children sometimes took over by teasing each other around the fireplace. There were riddles aplenty, and other ways of getting under each other's skin.

But singing brought us all together, whether from memory or out of our favorite source, *Congregational Anthems*. Hymns too. One evening as we were thus singing, suddenly my father's attention was somewhere else, looking up away from the book in the direction of the door. The rest of us followed his eyes with ours. At the now-half-open door we saw a white policeman in full uniform, his handcuffs strapped to his shiny belt by his side and now and again caught by the feeble candlelight.

Taken by surprise as we were, we laughed. He was accompanied by a black constable who stood a couple of paces behind the white official. He too laughed, though clearly deferentially. The brief laughter ended when the white official stopped laughing and, in a moment of humanity, explained why he was there. He was on duty, checking out the Location when he heard the sound from our house. He instantly rushed there, thinking it might be a group of men drinking beer, and it was not good. Then he decided to sneak up to the door. He was pleasantly surprised to find that it was "*Ou*

Ephraim singing with his wife and children." We all embraced that rare moment of respect, let alone civility, generated by music, *music by us*, and acknowledged by a white policeman. We were not rebel-rousing.

He left together with the black constable. We were quiet for some time, communicating solely with our eyes. Then, without further ado, we resumed our singing, my mother leading.

Many nights we observed another ritual. At a certain point in our self-entertaining activities—singing, storytelling, etc.—my father would say, "Let's all go to bed." Then we would all get up like an army and walk in a line towards our sleeping quarters; the leader of this line carried a candle. We walked from the kitchen, through the pantry, then the boys' sleeping room, through the living room which we called "the big house." Here, visitors relaxed and held conversations with our parents, eating together.

Our bed-time procession ended finally in our parents' bedroom. Father sat on the bed, or in a chair if there happened to be one on that occasion. My mother or father would start a short hymn, or one verse of a long hymn, followed by my father commanding, "Let us pray." We knelt on the floor, shut our eyes, and my father would say a prayer, the gist of which was his beseeching God to protect us from all dangers of the night till we reached the safety of the morning. When father reached "Amen," we said our "good nights" to our parents and went to our various sleeping areas.

No mattresses, just old empty sacks instead. Several empty sacks might similarly be stuffed with dry grass, for a mattress. But that, we seldom felt was worth the trouble. Why, instead of lumpy raw floor, you might end with unbearable pricks from the dry grass. Pillows? Rarely. Instead, smaller sacks stuffed with dry grass. We blew out our lamps or candles, lay down our heads, and fell asleep. I have to confess I didn't know the origin of this ritual, the procession to our parents' room, and how it came to an end.

"Hey, why not have a house concert?" said my mother one day. "We can do it! We can do it!" So, besides singing for amusement, and enchanting some prowling white policeman, my parents decided to stage a house concert from time to time. The first one was held right there in the rather confined dining/sitting room of our house. It was announced by word of mouth, and by nailing a handwritten notice on to the sturdy rough wooden pole that served as a corner anchor of one of the grazing camp fences. You could not avoid it, going to or coming from town. The big letters at the top read: **TSEBISO (NOTICE)**.

Members of the community were charged a *tickey* (roughly three American pennies). But if someone showed up clutching a penny or two, with eyes that said, "That's all I have," they would never be denied admission. Or if a child stood outside listening through the cracks in the door or peering through the window curtains because they did not have a penny, they would be let in without charge. Those were the instructions my parents gave the doorkeeper.

So, in addition to entertaining ourselves, occasionally there would be a *concert* held in the house. People were charged a minimal, maybe two pennies or three pennies to enter, notices nailed onto some corner posts. The *concert* was a very, very lively thing. There was a *Chairman* who announced the pieces that were going to be performed, but also who controlled a process that we in *seSotho* call *buying and blocking*.

Any member of the audience could get up, go to the Chair's Table, and say, for example: "*I want to buy the song that I heard this choir sing some time back.*" Or "*I'm buying so-and-so to come on the stage and sing.*" Somebody in the audience could also go up to the Chairman as the choir is busy singing and say, "*With this money I want that choir to stop! I don't like that song! I say stop it! I don't want to hear it again, it hurts my ears.*" And the choir had to stop. The Chairman announced and the choir had to stop.

The *blocking* would be someone coming to reverse what you just did, saying, "*With this money I want that choir to continue singing.*" But the *blocker* had to *block* with a slightly higher amount of money than the original *buyer*.

I should add to my story, particularly this house concert part of it, that we, the choir, aimed to amuse ourselves too. That would be one big reason for adding an item like the song *Bolomfanteni* in our program! No one in the choir, basically being the family, knew how it was created and by whom, and not its funny tune. All we did know was that there was a much larger town, called Bloemfontein, quite a way south of Edenville and Krooonstad. How it was ever made into a song, and especially the one we sang, remained a mystery. It was funny, amusing, sometimes sort of irritating and annoying to anyone who tried to solve those riddles. Well, that was one of the songs we usually sang during one of our house concerts. Here it is:

Nno-o...Nno-o!
Mma-Botha-Buthe!

Samariki!!
Nno-o...Nno-o!

Bolomfanteni
Taramteni

Diswibi Taramteni
Dikommoro-kommoro

Di ya Sawule!

The song *Bolomfanteni* was usually repeated twice from beginning to end. The choir would then begin to leave the "stage," which amounted to a clear space that the performers occupied as they performed their act.

At this point someone in the audience might walk to the table, already hollering at the chairman: "Mister Chairman! Mister Chairman! I never heard anything like this. What is this song saying? I really don't want to hear it again. It gives me a headache. With these two pennies, Mr. Chairman, I say let them sit down!"

Another voice might then shout: "That's why you must hear it again. You can't just learn it the first time you hear it. Mr. Chairman, I say, three pennies, let them sing it again!" The choir would begin to walk back to the "stage."

A "buying" or "blocking" action might be introduced with some colorful preface such as: "With these four pennies that I earned with my sweat loading and unloading trucks for Baas Piet, I say 'Block it!'" If the bidding became lively, the choir might stand at the edge of the singing square or circle waiting to know whether they were going to sit down or go back to the "stage." The chairman might whistle and shout, "Hurray! That's money! That's money!" meaning we're succeeding in raising money! "That's what we're here for." The concert was thus very often a noisy and lively affair, with occasionally one member of the audience calling encouragement to one of the performers they particularly liked, even as they were in the middle of a performance.

Granny Old Martha, revered by the whole Location, sometimes came to some of our concerts. I remember one occasion when she got up, took her time walking to the chairman as our choir began to walk away from the stage after performing *Bolomfanteni*, and waved her hand, shouting: "Not so fast! Not so fast! You *khwaere*! What were you saying there standing and shouting things some of us don't understand? I say go back to that *seteichi* (stage) and sing some sense. Sing it and then tell us what it was saying. Go!" The chairman laughed, the people laughed. The choir laughed! The whole room was choked with uncontrollable laughter more than ever before *Bolomfanteni* was repeated one more time.

On these occasions, my mother would sometimes, when there was a concert like that, cook what was called a *sechu*. S*echu* was a Sesotho-ized form of stew. But it had ceased to mean just a stew as we knew it, but to mean any delicacy of meat, including rice and potatoes, and this would be sold. It's brought to him or her, while the concert is going on and they're sitting there… very often on the floor, because there were not enough chairs, eating while listening.

When the concert was over, people would often hang around to continue part of the convivial interaction just ended. The conversations and comments would last for some time before dying slowly to yield to the night.

These are various ways of our family being involved in the community, especially in music. Combine church and singing family and it wasn't too long before my mother formed a church choir for the Edenville AME Church. We practiced for an *Investiture*, we were going to have the next time the Minister controlling the District came; we would be *Invested*.

The surplices were made by someone special who was sent from the town where the Minister resided. It was very strange because we were told that the surplices that we were to wear, there was one person, who made them, who tailored them, and who sold them. We would have to have him come for several days before the Investiture to take our measurements, buy pieces of cloth, and he would sew these surplices.

I remember one family, this man saying, "Ah, I can do that myself. I'll just make one for my son. I don't have to have this guy make it." And we were rather shocked, and we thought, "Well, come on, yours won't be as *'Holy'* as ours; because they will not be made by the *official* person."

The day came when the choir was to be *invested*, in their robes; also, a choir, from the town of the Minister who was coming to preside over this, came. So, when we marched from my parents' house up the street to the church, they were marching with us, accompanying us, almost like protecting us.

We were to march with the visiting choir, the more seasoned choir accompanying us. Our church, AME, did not have any attached rooms of any kind. It was just the four walls.

In bigger towns, the churches would have attached rooms. The choir would assemble there and put on their surplices, march out of there, through a back door around to the front and through the congregation to the platform. For us it was marching through the streets. We started from a private house where the minister was staying. It was a long march.

That occasion just absolutely took this little Black Township by storm. It was wonderful. Now, we were carrying our surplices over our arms—because we were not "official" yet—while they had theirs on.

We eventually got to the church and the Investiture Service took place. Two other Ministers, who had been invited from other bigger towns, were also on the dais for this occasion. Also, the church choir from the headquarters where this superintendent lived also came. And my older brother and I sang a duet. I sang first part and he sang alto. Something titled "Someone Will Enter the Pearly Gates Bye-and-Bye." The choir marched to and from the Investiture Service. We were congratulated. And the Minister, in recognizing my mother's effort that resulted in this event happening, forming the church choir, actually compared her to Queen Victoria—as a woman of leadership and vision. She was very proud of this honor. At one point, someone, some voice from the crowd, called out my mother's name, praising her achievement together with her children. This is what that voice said: "Well done Mahloli, together with your children."

These seeming digressions are integral to my story, to who I became, to who I am. And the music is always there. I, at that point, had already composed several pieces from when I had just started high school. But it has to do with my religious upbringing, this immersion into church—my father was a lay minister; my mother and other women of the AME church had their Thursday afternoon prayer meetings wearing their uniforms. We were expected to be in church Sundays twice a day (morning service and evening service) and Wednesday as well (there was a church service).

Not only were we expected to go to church by our parents, and by "we" I mean people who were really into religion, into church, but we were expected by our teachers to go to church. When I was Substandard A and Substandard B, our teacher, who was sort of bulky—in a kind dignifying sense—she wasn't obese, that's how women as they grew in their years would be. She was very much like a mother to us.

Not only were we under that kind of *pressure*—you're being watched all the time by your parents, by your neighbors, and by your teachers about going to church—but the Bible was a constant part of our schooling. Not only the *Bible*, but, the first thing when we assembled in the morning was: sing a hymn, prayer by the teacher, then we would go to our seats. Right up through high school: we assembled in the morning, the teacher said a little prayer, then we went to our classrooms.

The Bible every morning and prayer just before the end of school as well; and in religious families like mine, there was prayer just before eating for food; there was prayer at night where the whole family assembled in our parents' room and knelt down and my father prayed (or my mother) and we broke up to go to our individual rooms.

In those circumstances, you can understand there was a time when I composed *religious* songs. Titles like: "We're Going to March to Heaven One Day." Our church choir, I taught them the piece and we used to sing it: "We're going to march to heaven one day. We're going to cross the River of Jordan. We're going to march to heaven one day." I was writing the music and the words and the harmony. This was not the only one, another one I wrote that was religious was called, "My Prayer." Another one was "If I Pray," and another one was called "For My Work Is Done."

Looking back, I cannot believe some of the words I used. "For My Work Is Done," for example: "A flame is burning in my heart. I will spread the word of God. I shall go to my heathen brothers and will teach them how to pray. Praise the Lord praise the Lord for His time has come. Praise the Lord praise the Lord for my work is done." To think that I called Black people who had not accepted religion "heathens" is incredible. I could not believe that I had said that, once I became more politically conscious. That was a part of my life I cannot and will not deny.

At one time, I worked in a hospital kind of continuing education—this was a Black hospital, of course—for students whose studies were interrupted by illness. Those who were comfortable enough, we went around the wards, teaching whatever they needed to be taught to continue their education. Black hospitals were so crowded. Sometimes patients had to sleep on mattresses on the floor. Sometimes patients had beds in the corridor.

One girl that I taught, her name was Alice. One day I came looking for Alice to do our lesson and the bed wasn't made, there was nobody in it, and I asked, and Alice had died. That struck me very forcibly. Part of it must have been the fact that it took me so by surprise, it was a shock. I had been expecting to find Alice lying there and she had died, overnight I suppose. And I wrote a four-part song, quite a long piece, in Sesotho this time: "She Is Now An Angel of God."

In this same mode of religious compositions, I also created choirs just about everywhere I went. One such experience was, I created this choir of adults in Johannesburg (one has to understand that these things were for our personal enjoyment and entertainment). We were invited sometimes to go and perform on certain occasions, in a Black Township—maybe even pay our own fares on a train—at concerts, and sing for nothing, to just entertain ourselves, to enjoy doing it. Sometimes, we came together on a Sunday afternoon, maybe we had decided to go and sing at somebody else's house and being dressed up—suit and tie and women wearing very nice Sunday clothes—walking to this place, if the weather was good, nice and sunny, and just enjoying this, watching life pass by, we pass by the tennis courts, we get to the place, and we perform.

I also sang solos accompanied by piano in various places; especially I remember the *Odin Cinema*. It was very elegant. Its capacity was between one thousand five hundred and two thousand. It had a foyer with mirrors and walls with paintings; it was a kind of a Black middle-class place. People realized that was the place you showed your middle-classness: you dressed very nicely to go to a concert there: you wore your suit and tie, gloves; women wore furs, nice dresses. Occasionally, there was a small White liberal orchestra who would come to perform for us. This was Sophiatown.

Now, I sang solos: *O Solo Mio, Where'er You Walk*. In the final audition for the show, I was singing in the microphone and then I was told, "You don't need the microphone. Your voice is powerful enough, you project well enough you can fill this hall without a microphone."

The following day was the performance. When my turn came, I got on the stage and the previous performer had had the microphone at center stage. With a flourish I picked up the microphone and put it at the far end of the stage and came back to center. The accompanist begins to play and I'm preparing to enter, when a voice – and the whole hall has been darkened – right below me, from the stage, a woman's voice whispers, "Why don't you use the microphone?"

At that, I forgot the first line of the song. The first few words just went blank. I went blank. I went totally blank. I was in such despair. The introduction was finishing, just a few bars left before I was to come in and then suddenly the words came back.

Never did I sing a song with so much passion, with anger that I had to control. I didn't know what I would have done. It was such an incredible experience that I wrote a poem about it:

"A Moment of Terror At The Odin Cinema." (an essay/poem)

Johannesburg, Sophiatown, Black Township Odin Cinema,

Most modern Black cinema in the Southern Hemisphere

Large wall-size mirrors in foyer,

Where the aspiring Black middle class look at their furs and suits and smile at what they see as they file into the auditorium.

Odin's gently sloping floor, semi-circular rows of seats, filled-to-capacity on this Sunday afternoon.

And I, cloistered in the wings with my accompanist mentally rehearsing, "O Solo Mio," "Where'er You Walk," "La Paloma,"

Awaiting my turn to become one mo' tenor

Anticipating that moment of entry I'd cause a sensation,

I'd carry the microphone off the stage-center, then return to offer my naked voice. I did.

My pianist, a few feet to my left, plays the Introduction and I stand poised like an eagle ready to take off.

And near the stage, right below me, a woman's voice rises towards me in a whisper: "Why don't you use the microphone?"

With bated breath, the audience awaits the miracle of the voice that would fill the two thousand capacity auditorium without a microphone.

I could see myself bowing a deep bow lifting my head to look at the mystified audience.

I could see myself walking with unbowed pride to my equally mystified accompanist, holding his hand and whispering, "Let's bow and exit." Four or five more bars, maybe, toward the fateful moment.

Then seated one day at an organ, burst the memory bar.

Never had I ever sung the lost chord with such passion as I held my anger in leash.

I try to emphasize the loneliness of that moment: the audience doesn't know: my pianist doesn't know: I only know. I then put the line, "Nobody knows the trouble I'm in."

Leseliyana la Lesotho
("Little Light of Lesotho")

It should be remembered that the missionaries had established a newspaper, around 1856, *Leseliyana la Lesotho* or "*Little Light of Lesotho.*" One of the writers for *Leseliyana* got very excited—in fact, there was great excitement among the Basotho in general—about the introduction of writing and reading and the fact that anybody could write anything if they knew how to write. For instance—

> Last Sunday, I went to visit my brother across the river. And I found him and he was just fine. One of his cattle had just died.

—that sort of thing.

The serious aspect of this was that ordinary people became like "reporters." They reported their journeys, where they went, what was happening there. In this way, people continued to be intertwined with information. For a long time, you could write to the *Leseliyana* and have your story published, about whom you went to visit—your uncle, grandparents—and whom you met on the way.

Then, after some years, about 1869 or so, this excited Masotho wrote a letter and said:

> Well, now this paper should not be called *Leseliyana* anymore. It has grown big and should be called, *Leseli*, "Light"—Not "Little Light" but "Light."

There was such excitement that so many new things were happening.

Some Basotho, in fact, became afraid this excitement about what the missionaries had brought was beginning to make them forget about their own values. And it wasn't only among the Basotho. There are stories written about the Xhosa, by A. Soga, and he was disturbed. He said:

> Look, we have *always*, in our villages and homes, opened our doors to any traveler—who's caught by night, tired, hungry, who needs help; who needs a place to stay; who needs food; who needs a place to sleep, and we've given those abundantly, with pleasure.

> Now that the missionaries have separated us and calls the group who has not accepted their religion "heathens,"—and there are now villages that are villages of the "converted" the Christians. A traveler comes along, and night is upon him or whatever; he happens to be near a village of the "converted." She or he goes to knock on a door as she or he is used to, looking for shelter or food. She knocks there, and as soon as they recognize that the person is one who still uses, for example, the traditional red ochre, they slam the door in her or his face. "We are Christians; you are heathens. Get away from here."

These are true stories by people, the Sogas, who themselves were converted. The Sogas were a line of missionaries; one of them had actually gone to study in Scotland to become a minister, married a Scottish woman, came back, and you can still see the results of this union in the descendants. Now, he was not a "heathen" but one of the "converted" and yet he was saying:

> These are not our values. We are people who accept *anybody* who needs help, who needs shelter, who needs food. Now it seems our people are now thinking that "to be a good Christian, they have to chase people away because they're not Christian."

But the enthusiasm of many people who became "converted" caught the attention of missionaries and teachers, who would write about how excited some black people were about their conversion, that they would forget about the good things about their own culture before the missionaries came, that they dismiss that and turn away from it.

Thomas Mofolo, the writer of *Chaka*, the one who became a famous writer in Sesotho, in one of his three novels, *Pitsing*, he now and again, not so much as gets away from the story as, follows a certain line of development in the story to say:

> Look, we must not despise our own values simply because they belong to black people. Nor must we accept every value that is brought to us simply because it comes from people who declare themselves "civilized." We should know that there are certain things that we did that are of value and preserve them.

And he gives examples.

> The youth of today are not as well-behaved; for example, disrespecting parents who are not "believers" or been "converted."

This was peculiar to the latter half of the 19th century until, perhaps, into the first quarter or the first third of 20th century. Some missionaries were still saying that Mofolo's novel, *Chaka*, should not be read, should be banned, because it encourages people to believe in *witchcraft*.

They were saying this because the "moving" character in the story is what anthropologists would call or label a "witch doctor." Mofolo created him as "doctor." But they translated that as witch doctor. And his powers were just tremendous, in making things happen in the story, to the point that, eventually, he kills his own lover whom he loves dearly, and who loves him dearly. Like him, she too is of "royal" blood. Isanusi, this so-called "witch doctor," was begging Chaka to seek the highest level of power, as a king, so that nothing should stand in his way.

So he corrupted Chaka; corrupted him so that Chaka's attention was on Isanusi telling him: "Can you imagine if you were to be the king whose territory is such that if somebody were to start walking from this end of it to the other end as a young man, he would grow old before he even got to the other end." And Chaka is seduced by that. From then on, he is determined that nothing is going to stand in the way of achieving that power, all that territory.

Now, this takes us back to history, biography, fact and fiction, because the core of the story is true. Historically, Chaka was a military genius who created incredibly powerful armies. He even created vivid images answering such questions as "How do you attack the enemy?"

> Look, have you seen a cow's horns? When you approach a cow, it engulfs you with his horns. An "attack" is to be like a cow's horns. So, when the enemy comes, and they see only the front; it's like they see only the "chest" while they're being encircled.

These have been referred to as the "Wars of Chaka" or the *Mfacane* ("The War of Utter Destruction"). And the Basotho have taken that word and say, *Defacane*.

Chaka's notoriety comes from that. Nothing could stand in his way. He was a man who could say, "Bring that woman here. I want to see how a baby lies in the mother's womb." And he would have her sliced open right there. Again, we're talking about Mofolo's story—a mixture of fact and fiction. Mofolo gives us a Chaka who in the early years of his reign, when he sent out his troops to go and fight, called the armies when they came back, almost like the commandments, and, in a very strict voice, would say to those assembled there:

> "Those of you who have returned from battle without having killed an enemy warrior"—and the only way you can prove that is if you've captured their shield or spear—"any of you who have not done that to one side." Then, he would set his "enforcers" on them to kill them. "Now, those of you who returned without your spear, your Zulu spear, to that side" and they were also destroyed. "And, those of you who have your wounds in the back, which shows that you were running away, to one side" and they were likewise dispatched.

Again, let us not forget that this is Thomas Mofolo's reconstruction of character and events, as a very gifted writer. At one point, he makes Chaka's mother, Nandi, to think "This is enough." And she comes and kneels before her own son to plead with him, "Forgive them. Stop. This is enough." Now, this is creativity, because how did Mofolo hear all these things? But Mofolo makes him say, "O.K. the rest of you, just because of my mother you are forgiven." Mofolo says:

> From that day on, a Zulu warrior fought with the power of ten: one was equal to ten of the enemy. They were so determined: they didn't want to die a disgrace in the face of the community; they preferred to die on the battlefield than to come back and be exposed to ridicule.

Mofolo wrote his novel *Chaka* in 1909, in Sesotho. It is a genuine masterpiece that represents one of the earliest major contributions of Africa to the corpus of modern world literature.[1] The serialization of another book of his, *Pitseng*, spread over a year in the *Leselinyana*.

---

1   In an email dated 2/7/13, Dad writes:
    "Dear Clan,
    "Another piece of good news: I received an email from Waveland Press here in the USA who tell me my translation of Thomas Mofolo's *Chaka*, which was published in 1981 by Heinemann in England, is no longer available in the US and Canada, and that the Waveland Press, of which she is one of the editors, would like permission to re-publish it in this part of the world. I have responded to say I'm listed in the rights page as the copyright holder and that republishing is OK by me. I don't know where this goes for here. But it's in the works! As I said, it never rains but it pours!!! Much love to all of you."
    [The "Clan": that would be Liziwe, Sipho, Lu, Linda, Wandi, Somori, and Thiyane.]

JOHANNESBURG

After I moved to Johannesburg, I had to find a job and study by correspondence. One day as I was walking in the white area of Johannesburg, I heard someone calling me. I turned around and who should be there but a man from my hometown, Edenville.

"Big brother, Moisi!" I shouted.

Holding me tight, he said "Dan, what are you doing here? D'you want a job?"

"Oh my God, you are the last person I expected to see here! Of course I want a job, I'm looking for a job!"

"Well, there is a job where I work, at a white residential hotel. You can come tomorrow, and I will introduce you to the manager, and she will tell you more about it. You answer phones, carry luggage, tend the door, and generally be available as needed." That is how I got the job that I held for about two years, whose stories I narrate in my book *Kero Court Chronicles*.

Daniel, a Page: Kero Court Residential Hotel, Johannesburg (1944)

I was employed as a hotel pageboy in Johannesburg. Kero Court was a residential hotel. There were two of us. We were expected to carry luggage for residents arriving and leaving. In between that, we answered telephones. The residents did not have telephones in their rooms.

So, you answer the telephone and someone says, "Can I speak to Mr. or Mrs. So-and-So." You, of course, had to know the room number. There was a board inside the office with buzzers. The first thing you did was you go and buzz that room, of that person. If the person were on the sixth floor and the reception on the first floor, they had a buzzer. They had to come out of their room, and call the elevator, wait for it—slow moving elevator—get out and come to this little box where the telephone was.

You had to use your imagination if they didn't come within a certain time. You had to either assume they're not home or get in the elevator, go and knock on their door and tell them: "There's a telephone call for you." And, then they would come down.

There was the trauma of someone getting a phone call and they're at dinner. Dinner was at a certain time. So everybody came from their rooms and was assigned to their own table. Telephone rings, you answer it, "Can I speak to Mr. So-and-So?"

I remember my first experience of that. I open that dining hall and I see ALL these White faces look up at me. I didn't know where that particular person was, which table they were at; I just had to look around and spot them and say they had a phone call. It was traumatic. You're facing all these people, who are turning around towards the doorway where you just came in, and you feel like running away. It got easier as you began to know that Such-and-Such a family, sit at Such-and-Such table. The table wasn't numbered. You just had to know. Then, you went and whispered to them that there's a phone call for them.

Now, if you're not doing that, you're carrying luggage up and down or answering the telephone. Your station was at the front door. Stand there inside, there's a glass door. Open the door when a White resident is coming (there were only White residents). If someone is going out, then open the door for them.

There was one Englishman by the name of Mr. Penfold. That man comes walking up right to that door, the door opens inwards, and grabs that door and shoves it back towards you so that if you don't get out of the way you'll get that glass shattering on your face. So, when you saw him coming, either you had to rush for the door and pull it quickly before he got to it or get out of the way. Then he would walk right past you without a word. One had to live with those things, those daily indignities.

One day, one woman came down the elevator. I was in the elevator. She gets to the reception desk and realizes that the dress she had been carrying was missing. The next thing I know I am called to the office. I am told that Mrs. So-and-So said that I stole her dress. She said you were in the elevator with her and you stole her dress. I am absolutely dumbfounded, hurt, angry, and helpless.

What can I do? Here is a White woman saying that I stole her dress and talking to another White woman who is the manager of the hotel and she thinks a detective should be called to go and search my room. The detective comes. She and myself and the detective go to my room in the basement of the building. This is a White detective, a Boer; but he could see clearly, even from my demeanor, that I was outraged and helpless. He was not really interested, looking here, looking there, he was the one to give me some words of comfort. "Don't worry," he said.

He knew. He could see clearly what was happening, but he couldn't say no, he couldn't refuse to come: He's called, by a White woman, to come and find out where this Black young man, who stole her dress, hid it. The dress was found in the shaft of the elevator: must have slipped out of her hands. But they had created this story that "obviously the Boy took the dress and threw it somewhere until he could wait to take it to his room." That's what they tell the detective.

If you passed a day, a week, without being subjected to those kinds of indignities, it was a good week. That's where I was working: room provided, food, you ate from the kitchen. Some people who lived there were students at the University, White students. Black people, of course, could not stay in the hotel.

Another moment in Johannesburg still, was when the AME church held its "Jubilee." I featured in the church choir and also in solo singing.

Then, one day, I met Dr. Xuma, who had married a Black American woman, apparently while he was studying medicine in the United States. Mrs. Xuma—her maiden name was Hall—was very active socially among Black women, creating groups and clubs. One day I got a message from Dr. Xuma, who knew about my group. We called ourselves *Carpe Diem*, ("Seize the Day").

Dr. Xuma said he had visitors from the United States—a Bishop and his wife. Bishops of the AME church, at that time, were always appointed from the United States. There were four yearly conferences in Atlanta, Georgia, where Bishops for different areas of the African continent would be selected from among Black Americans.

The message said he had a visitor who was a Bishop and his wife, would we please come that Sunday afternoon to sing for them? We had some few days before that to get ready. I composed a song for the Bishop and his wife. I taught it to my group. It was one of the pieces that we performed that Sunday afternoon, "Wish You God's Speed," with words such as "Blessed messengers of God, wandering far from your home...wish you God's speed, wish you God's speed, may God bless you where'er you go."

Then I got an invitation to come back before the Bishop left. He was formulating a plan to get me to America for musical training. The Bishop virtually promised that when he gets back to the States he will raise a scholarship for me. I don't know who talked first about the possibility of having some of my songs published.

It was sometime before 1948, a very pivotal year in South Africa, because that is when the more conservative White group, the Afrikaners, the Boers, won the elections, in '48. The first elections after the end of World War Two. They are the ones who won on a platform saying: We're going to implement very strict segregation, which we'll call "apartheid," the Afrikaner word for "apartness." So "apartness" was going to be *the* policy of the country.

For a Black to get a passport was almost totally out of the question. Dr. Xuma and the Bishop, whose name I forget, were talking about how they might get me to what was then Rhodesia, where it would be easier for me to get travel papers to come to America. It was almost a done thing. My late wife and I were virtually engaged. It was a few years before we would get married.

Let me explain another thing among Blacks in South Africa. If two people like my wife meet—she is training for her career as a nurse, and I myself am busy training for something else—we would never marry before we were done with our education and reached our goals. This helps explain why our courtship went on for such a long time: she was completing her nursing studies and meanwhile I was doing some correspondence courses for a higher degree.

I was extremely excited about going out of this country that was denying me all kinds of opportunity and go and do what is uppermost in my whole being—music. In many situations, call it *fate* chose the direction for me, rather than me choosing the direction. At that time, it would have been a lot easier for me to go to the US because I wasn't married yet.

The Bishop left. He had my address, and he was in communication with Dr. Xuma. I never heard from him again. Never. Not one word. I had an address, which I think was in Alabama. When I saw that nothing was happening, I wrote to him, to remind him. I didn't get a response and then I wrote again: "By the way, any possibility? Shall I send you one or two of my pieces to be published?" Never heard from him to this day. *Fate* said "No!" Not me. I wanted to go to the United States to study.

The reality of it was I didn't hear from the Bishop and therefore my life had to go on as if that never happened. I don't know. Somehow, their circumstances might have changed. After I got to know more about the South, the Deep South, another thought that came to me was maybe they thought: "How can we take this young man from apartheid into this: land of lynching, the separateness, the hatred?" Alabama is certainly no improvement over South Africa, especially in the 1940s.

Back to Kroonstad Bantu High School. There I was, my first music composition in Zulu. It wasn't long before I formed a better-constructed choir, also from among the students. We used to perform at school concerts, under my direction. Then, at times, when the Director of the School Choir was not able to go and conduct at a concert, he would ask me to go and conduct the choir.

I was sixteen going on seventeen at this point. I remember on one such an occasion, I actually conducted the *Hallelujah Chorus*. I managed to pitch it just right, and it came out very beautiful. It was just something that I love doing. It was an integral part of my life.

There was a Student Organization formed called Orange Free State African Students Association, or SASA, that was statewide. Different schools within the Orange Free State would meet annually at an appointed town for a conference. We had some speakers, some debates, some sightseeing. But one thing that was later introduced was choir competitions, with a trophy to be won.

Now, this was quite a bit later into my being at Kroonstad High School. I was going into the year before my transfer to university, I was the one asked to train the choir for the coming annual competitions. There were actually two competitions: one was a full choir; the other one was double quartet. I was in charge of both, and I trained both. And we won both: a trophy for choir and one for double quartet.

As I mentioned earlier, A.C. Jordan was one of my teachers, starting with the beginning of secondary school and right through. He made a very, very great impression on me—and, I know, on other students as well—with his personality, his dignity, his competence as a teacher, and his mastery of the material. Above all, he had empathy with the students, something that many teachers really did not have (they were a bit distant).

We both respected him and liked him; we didn't fear him. He taught second-year English Literature; the woman who would later be his wife, Phyllis Jordan, taught the first year.

Now, at the school itself, something strange happened to me. I suppose it came from the Department of Education, a requirement: that whenever we students were on the school premises, WE MUST NEVER SPEAK OUR MOTHER TONGUES. We had to speak one of the two "official" languages, English or Afrikaans. And this was a punishable offense. And there were monitors who had pencil and pad, noting whoever broke this rule or that, and speaking "vernacular" was one of those rules. He jotted down your name and you were sent to the principal's office for a disciplinary action that the principal might decide on: physical lashes, or something to humiliate you, like pushing a box of sand from one corner of the classroom to another. Punished for speaking our mother tongues, our own languages!

We were being alienated, being deculturized in that process. We would get back home and our parents had this mixture of emotions and reactions. Sometimes they were happy that their children were learning English. Sometimes they would get annoyed. For example, if you happen to speak English in their presence at home, you would be scolded, "Never do that again!"

So here we are in that position, where at school we had to speak English or Afrikaans or get punished for speaking our native languages. I knew nothing of English before I went to school. I was able to read and write English by the time I entered high school. People like A.C. Jordan did see some advantage in learning English:

it's a world language, it carries so much written culture—Shakespeare, Milton, Tennyson—and so on.

Such topics speak to the importance of matters of one's identity through all kinds of things, including language, specifically language. This process of alienation, of alienating us from our languages had far-reaching consequences we'll take up later.

We had what was called *afternoon studies* at Kroonstad Bantu High School. We had our normal school day: morning classes, a break for lunch, then afternoon classes. Then go home for about two hours and come back to school for a more informal study period. We went into the classrooms, there was a teacher in charge; they didn't tell you what to do as long as you were picking up something that had to do with your schoolwork. Discipline was valued and important and that too we could not miss without consequences.

Another informal thing—I don't know how this one started, but one I remember with a great deal of nostalgia because it was so beautiful. We came often to school, in summer especially, quite a bit earlier than the school bell. From our school building, if you looked across, it was open veldt with green grass and trees, and we would grab our books and spread out here and there to read. The whole atmosphere was to inspire us, even just by being outside in a free space. We were not distracted to watch birds or trees; we were concentrating on reading what we had brought with us, silently or aloud…mostly, aloud.

All of this is another way of saying how much people valued education, how they considered it invaluable. We were self-motivated. Our teachers inspired us, but we had to carry the momentum after that.

One time, near the close of the semester, when our teachers were busy with all the paperwork that goes with that, one of the students brought a game called *Fiddlesticks* or *Pickup Sticks*. So, instead of having our books and doing something constructive, we went and hid in this little room and knelt on the floor playing *Pickup Sticks*. Suddenly, the door opened and it was Mr. Jordan.

He said: "Why are you fellows here and not busy doing your work? Now, you put those things down and go and do your work." He left, and in no time, we couldn't keep away from the *Pickup*

Sticks. We were back in our circle on the floor playing. The door opens, Jordan comes in and says: "What did I tell you?" And he grabs the *Sticks* and breaks them and throws them in the trash. That was the end of that.

I keep going back to comparing the facilities and privileges of Black children in Black schools with those of White children in White schools. The whole concept that there could be a place where you could go and borrow a book and read it and take it back, I didn't even know. I didn't even know the word *Library* until I entered high school; let alone be exposed to one. There was none attached to the school, there was none in the whole sprawling Township of Kroonstad. Eventually, there was a library installed in one of the rooms of the Catholic Church, where there was also an elementary school.

If we put that in the context of even the books that we needed to study from, we, as Black students, had to buy them. We had to buy them, while White students didn't have to do that. And, of course, they were exposed to books in libraries; and one mustn't forget too that more White students had the privilege of being in a home where there were books around them, where there was some tradition of adults reading books.

Now, in a place like Kroonstad, I don't think, even among Whites, that there were too many such, but there were some. Among us Blacks, your parents had a Bible, a hymnal, and a catechism and that was the extent of books in the home. You had your schoolbooks, which you carried to school every day and back. That was the extent of your contact with books. So, to have a place, at last, where you could go and not have to buy the book, but have it for a few days, two weeks, read it and then take it back, without paying anything, that was a very, very novel thing, highly appreciated. Needless to say, this was a very minimal facility, but it introduced to me the very idea of a *library*. Of course, we were not permitted to use the library in the White town, and I assure you we would have.

My first year at Kroonstad Bantu High School was 1938, but it could have been 1936 if not for our financial situation. In fact, one of the things I need to mention is the abject poverty we were in, be it poverty all around or just of your body. In a way, you didn't have to carry so much of the psychological burden around because you were not the only one in your community; there were so many others like you; there were some who were even worse than you. Still, there were scars: you're fighting against feeling ashamed of the way you look. Even though chores you have to do, schoolwork to do, that demands attention, there is this other thing, this burden of poverty that also preoccupies your mind, even subconsciously absorbed with this you have to deal with.

Primary School, Soweto 1960sRalph Ndawo

Secondary School, Soweto 1960s   Photographer Unknown

Some of us did survive these conditions. But there were *casualties*—casualties in the sense of people who had to drop out of school because of these conditions. So, in fact, going through school was a kind of *battle* that you were fighting, and either you won or you lost.

When I started teaching poetry, examining poetry written by African authors, I wrote a book called *Heroic Poetry of the Basotho*—heroic poetry which had to do with real wars: with victories, losses, casualties, with self-praise by returned warriors, and by the village poet creating oral poetry for them, in praise of them

A warrior was someone who was laying his life on the line for his people, for his community, so victory was something to be celebrated. There could be composition of praises, by the village poet, or by the person himself. There was once a king who was both an outstanding warrior and a wonderful poet. He would come back from battle and praise himself.

I found that teachers who started writing poetry very often devoted poems to successful Blacks who had careers—who became teachers, or later on, doctors, because of these difficulties, because it was a battle. You had gone through a war in your life that you had to win or to lose. By getting that education, by getting that diploma or certificate, you were like a *warrior* who went to battle and returned victoriously.

Even the metaphors that the poet used were *war* metaphors. Even the young boy called to read a letter, or come and write me a letter, or come and read this Bible verse for the church congregation before I start preaching, was a boon to the community. An "educated" young man or boy in the community was a "little hero" to everyone.

If you came back "Mr. Teacher," you were "Mr. Teacher" for everybody. You see, Black people had to go overseas for a long time to get even a *pre-university* certification they could not get in South Africa, to say nothing of medicine, studying to be a doctor; people had to go to Scotland, wherever they could get people to sponsor them. When you come back, you belong to the whole community, you are a blessing to the whole community.

We, as young people, trying to get an *education*, we were *warriors*. We were in a war. Either you became a casualty by having to drop out because the system you are struggling against had defeated you, or you persevered and you won. You didn't go to get grades; you went to get education, to get knowledge, not for grades. If you got the education, the grades came automatically.

In the time that we're talking about and for a long time after that—I don't know how it is today (2015) in South Africa, and this may seem trivial, but it's not—we did not talk about somebody coming out of high school as *graduating*. The term *graduate* was reserved for when one got one's first university degree; *then* one is said to be a *graduate.*

When you've got through high school and you've got your acceptance to a university, your beacon, what was pulling you forward were things like, "When I get my Bachelor's Degree I will graduate." That was a fantastic term to be used of you because you were now, B.A. or B.S.E., then it was the Masters, you were graduating again, then doctorate or Ph.D. Coming out of high school, we didn't have gowns and caps. No, in high school you are still striving to see yourself, one day, with a Bachelor's Degree, and being invested with this gown and cap.

Forgive me for saying so, but what I see with the use of these things in this (American) culture, I think there are even graduations from kindergarten. It's a trivialization. It is a trivialization of one of the magnets that was pulling you. In our case, there was no formality; once you were told you had passed, you had passed. Your certificate would come in the mail.

My junior certificate took three years and I received it in 1940. That was passing the equivalent of middle school and entering high school, which was called matriculation. When you finished matriculation, you were ready to enter the university.

It was while studying my first year in "Matric" that it was necessary for me to go to Johannesburg to find work because the lack of facilities was just too great.

But something I missed along the way, again having to do with A.C. Jordan, is that while he was teaching at Kroonstad High School, he suddenly was consumed with a zeal to study privately, while teaching. He had a B.A., a Bachelor's Degree, and decided to study for a Master's Degree. What inspired him to do this was having seen a book, an analysis of Zulu, analyzing the language linguistically, grammatically. This was done by a White professor, C.M. Doke, Clemens Doke, who was then teaching at the University of the Witwatersrand in Johannesburg. He was the son of a missionary and had grown up with people who spoke Zulu.

Jordan saw this book by Clemens Doke, who had decided that the way that was used to describe African languages, Bantu languages, grammatically, up to that point was highly defective. The terminology, the Latin structures of analyzing languages was being imposed on languages that had absolutely no such structures.

For example, *preposition—is* there a *preposition* in this language? Or, *Personal pronoun—is* there a *personal pronoun* in this language? And if there is, how is it used? So, Doke said, "We need a linguistic terminology that arises from these languages." In 1933, he came up with a volume called *Bantu Linguistic Terminology*, which was a watershed for the description of South African Bantu languages.

He applied this method to several languages, Lambda and Zulu, for example. Jordan looks at this and says, "I'm a Black person. I am a thoroughbred Xhosa person. And, if this White man can do such a beautiful job of analyzing our languages, I will analyze my own language and go one better than him." That was his inspiration for pursuing his M.A. by private study, in which he was analyzing his mother tongue, the Xhosa language.

It is another example that shows you who he was, what he was, what an inspiration he could be. It was also during my first year of matriculation that he wrote his first novel, in Xhosa. It turns out to be one of the best books ever written in an African language, up to that point. He wrote a marvelous novel based on places that people knew, where he himself had gone to school; his characters were familiar and in familiar environments.

This was such a fantastic book, in Xhosa, in his language. You heard stories of older people who didn't know how to read, gathering together and asking a young man, a student or teacher, to read it for them. And they were reacting like an oral audience, exclaiming, in a kind of call-and-response. The title of the book translates, from the Xhosa, as *The Wrath of the Ancestors*.

A really tremendous book, it was later translated into English. He wrote that book in 1940. This was still during my first year in matriculation, and we were visited by school inspectors who just came anytime, just "pounced" on teachers to see how they were doing with their classes (two Blacks and two Whites). They came to Jordan's class: he opened the door; we stood up, as we have to do when a dignitary comes in, until you're told to sit down. We sat down.

Jordan introduced himself; and one of the Black inspectors said to him: "I knew, the author of *The Wrath of the Ancestors"* and Jordan said, "Yes" with a kind of shy smile. And this man shook his hand almost out of its socket. He was so excited to meet the writer of this marvelous book.

This was the same year that I had to leave school to go to Johannesburg to find work. I visited Kroonstad a few times and never missed a chance to go to the school, just to be there. Jordan had used me as an example very often. I didn't know that, but he told me that.

You see, now, I had to continue my studies by private study. While I was working in Johannesburg, I decided that I must finish this University Entrance Certificate. Then I enrolled to study, by private study, for the Bachelor's Degree. One of the things that beckoned me was "You are going to *graduate*—for the first time in your life—when you get that Bachelor's Degree; in fact, for the first time in your life you're going to have a gown draped over you and a cap!" This was a very important incentive and motivation.

It's the knowledge that was driving me, to say: "I've got to study hard, I've got to study hard to pass in order to earn that place." I am mentioning this because, when I asked for papers to be registered with the University of South Africa (UNISA), as an external or private student who was going to write the B.A. first year exam, at the end of that year, and they sent me the forms, I filled in my name and other details... and there, where it said, "For What Degree?" when I wrote "B.A." next to my name, it was as if I already had it. It was such an exciting thought. "When I pass this, that's what I'll have after my name." It was thrilling. "This is a reward that is waiting for me. I'll be able to write B.A. after my name."

They send you the list of books for each subject that you're enrolled in, and the date of the exam at the end of the year. Between those two events, you're on your own. The University of South Africa was, at that time, a university that only dealt with *external students*. You were sent your information, your required books, and the date of the exam. You didn't know who else had enrolled. It would take three years of study, if you passed every year, to get your B.A., your Bachelor's Degree.

I was doing private study with UNISA (External). Jordan was looking for me. He wrote a letter to the magistrate in Jo'burg where he thought I worked. A letter from him did eventually reach me. In that way, we reconnected. He had been following my progress. He knew the exact time I was taking my exams for the B.A. He said to a class of students he was teaching at the time: "Right now, one of the students who studied here is writing his Exam for the B.A."

When you got to that end, and you were due for graduation, you didn't even graduate "on site" at the University of South Africa. You were delegated to some university that was affiliated. For example, what is now University of Fort Hare, which is largely Black, traditionally, when you studied there at that time, what was then Fort Hare College was affiliated with the University of South Africa.

So, when you graduated from Fort Hare, your certificate was going to read "University of South Africa Certificate: Affiliated College Fort Hare." I was working different jobs, living with different people, when one day I got a letter from A.C. Jordan. What had happened in the meantime, while I was in Johannesburg, was that he had got his Master's and successfully applied for a job as lecturer at Fort Hare College.

He got the job. Fort Hare was basically a Black college and he was there for maybe two years. While he was there, an opening occurred for a Black person to teach African Languages, specifically to teach Xhosa, at the almost exclusively white, more prestigious, University of Cape Town (UCT). Jordan applied for the job, was called for an interview, and was appointed. This was prior to 1945.

I recall that when I was in Standard Six, our teacher told us about a Black person who had been hired by the University of the Witwatersrand, which was an exclusively White university, to teach White students Zulu. Some White people were protesting about their children being taught by a Black person. Of course, at that time, the only Black person they saw was either their cook, or gardener, or nanny, or maid, who came in through the back door even to make their beds.

This is the only Black person they saw, and they had to be on time, serve them morning coffee or tea then, in late afternoon, disappear. They had no clue where he or she lived; that was the kind of Black person they knew. Then, suddenly, for one to come and be a colleague of the White lecturers and professors, and for their children to sit there and this man in front of them—"No! No!"" They were rioting.

Our teacher told us that, as a Black man appointed to teach in that university and teach White students, well, the protest didn't last very long, and the man stayed. I'm telling this in the context of A.C.

Jordan not being the first Black person to teach in an exclusively White university, that there had been this earlier experience many years before. This story links up with Professor Doke, who was the Head of the African Studies area, including African languages. And, it was he who engineered the appointment of the man, V.W.Vilakazi, a Zulu through and through. He had his Bachelor's Degree and was teaching somewhere in Natal, and was very proud of Zulu language, customs, and culture, the same way as Jordan was with Xhosa culture and language and customs. He was the right person to go and teach the language and culture of his people. He was also a terrific poet, writing his poetry in Zulu.

At the time he started writing his poetry, he was already appointed to the University of Witwatersrand. His story is another object lesson on race relations, starting with why parents were protesting him being appointed there, to the university itself, while continuing to regard him as a lower species of university employee. For example, people who were teaching were called either *Junior Lecturer* (for those just beginning to teach), then *Lecturer,* then *Senior Lecturer*—basically, three steps on the way to becoming a *Professor.*

For Mr. Vilakazi, they created a new term to describe his position, which was not applied to anybody else, and that term was *Language Assistant.* Professors were getting quite embarrassed by the fact that this able man, over several years now, had proven his capability, his expertise, his knowledge, his excellence in teaching. He had, in addition, the ability, which Doke would ask him to do from time to time, to stand in as an administrator of the department when Doke had to be away.

Doke fought with the University to get Vilakazi's position regularized, to be like everybody else's. The university balked, at first, and then they got to the point where they said, "Alright, we'll call him *Senior Language Assistant.* How about that? And we will increase his salary." Doke was not satisfied. In the meantime, Mr. Vilakazi had enrolled for the Ph.D. Degree at the university itself. He was teaching with a Master's.

Doctor Vilakazi, an author, a poet and teacher that he was, unfortunately, died prematurely. He may have been only thirty-seven when he died. I don't know of what. So, this situation never got resolved. Would the university ever see the light and do the right thing? Institutions often hide behind some law: "It's not us, it's that law there, preventing us from doing this or that." And when that law is not there any more and they have to face the issue, head on, then their racism comes to the fore.

For A.C. Jordan, when he started teaching, there were no protests. Later, after he had taught there for a few years, two White female students confessed to him that, when they had originally joined his class, they were sent there as *spies* by the government. It turns out, they fell in love with his class and his teaching and began to wonder, "Why are we spying on this man? He's a good man and an excellent teacher." And they confessed all this to him at the end of the class.

At the University of Cape Town, only in this department where African Languages were taught was there a Black person teaching. No one in Psychology, no one in the Science Department, no one anywhere—which really meant that it was an act of desperation by the university to hire Jordan. If they had a White person who knew Xhosa as well as Jordan, who knew the Xhosa language and culture, they probably would have employed him or her rather than a Black person.

There were brilliant students, Blacks and Coloreds, who graduated in the English Department. Would the Department of English ever consider them as lecturers? No, never, at the University of Cape Town. The University of Cape Town and the University of Witwatersrand were almost exclusively White. White liberal, I might add, because liberal Whites always wanted to be seen to have some kind of *sympathy* with Black movements.

I don't remember when UCT opened its doors to Black students or when the University of Witwatersrand opened its doors. Those doors were only slightly ajar, suggesting that Black students can go in and attend classes, write exams, but, besides that, any kind of social life was out of the question. They could not go to the swimming pools; they did not play in inter-varsity sports like Rugby or Football; even an annual event that was between UCT and the University of Stellenbosch. The University of Stellenbosch was all White, Afrikaner, and very apartheid-prone and they would never have a Black student or a Black teacher.

The University of Cape Town did have a kind of "open-door" policy, but unwritten, a sort of gentlemen's agreement: that the Blacks would exclude themselves because it would not be comfortable for them.

Another university that had started to admit Black students, which was also a predominately White university, was the University of Natal. It had several campuses, including one in Durban and one in Pietermaritzburg, Blacks were restricted to the Pietermaritzburg campus; there were White students also on that campus, but that is where the Blacks *had to go*. Worse still, the students did not meet in the same classroom for a lecture while taking the same course, from the same professor. They could not be there for one lecture. The professor had to give his lecture to White students, who would then leave and then Black students would come in and he would repeat the same lecture to them.

It was ridiculous. It was amazing that the White professors would tolerate this sort of thing; they themselves were being exploited ("Teach this class twice every time you teach it"). I remember, while at UCLA, meeting a professor who was teaching there, a White Jewish man, Professor Leo Kuper, said to me: "When I got fed up with teaching the same class twice, I didn't go to the Administration, I didn't go to anybody, I just said to my students: 'Anybody who is taking this class, come at such-and-such a time and that's when the class is going to be'." Everybody came at one time and there wasn't anything the Administration could do.

But you can see to what ridiculous lengths these White universities would go. Kuper's actions started a movement that spread to other campuses, and other professors started doing the same thing. These universities—University of Cape Town, University of the Witwatersrand, and the University of Natal—became known as the "open universities."

Stellenbosch, which absolutely did not want to see a Black face on campus, had a White person as Head of the Department of African Languages, similar to Dr. Doke, for example, whom I've mentioned before, at Witwatersrand.

I was speaking with this man, Mr. Gideon Manwala, who said: "I find it so insulting because I'm there to teach students as a Teaching Assistant, but I'm not allowed to step in the classroom." He could not stand in front of the class. He had a little office, virtually a closet, where students came one by one and stood outside and talked to him through an opening. They were demonstrating so openly with so much disregard for even their own decency, as if to say: "We just want your voice. If we could do it without seeing your face, we would do it. Your presence on campus is being tolerated and you're being paid." That's what Stellenbosch did.

Another thing about Stellenbosch I remember, when I was a student pursuing the Master's Degree with a friend of mine, we had attended high school together in Kroonstad, pursuing Master's degrees in Bantu Languages. Here was this graduate student, a Boer, an Afrikaner, who was doing an analysis of languages that we spoke very well, our Mother Tongues. And he came to the University of Cape Town and asked us if we could help him and he would record what we said. We said we could come there, we could come to Stellenbosch, and he said, "No, oh no, no. I'll come there." Now, he wasn't being considerate, necessarily, as if to say "I don't want to trouble you"; it was more like "I don't want you to be subjected to indignities when you get there." In fact, if they saw any Black person on campus, short of their life being in danger, they were absolutely made to feel unwanted and uncomfortable and had to leave.

Daniel Kunene, Cape Town, S.A. (1948)

APARTHEID

Then came apartheid, introducing total university segregation. This would be around 1950-1952. The strictly apartheid government had come into power in 1948. They were making such drastic changes in people's lives, professional and personal; they created pigeonholes where everybody had their space, and you did not interfere in somebody else's space. There was the Group Areas Act, which affected people living in urban areas.

These liberal universities passed the Extension of University Education Act. What it did was stop Black people from attending White universities anymore. Instead, the government was going to establish "colleges" for them. These "colleges" were also tribally oriented; so, there would be a "college" for the Zulu people, a "college" for the Xhosa people, one for the Basotho, one for the Venda, and so on and so forth.

This thing is so methodical that it's frightening—to think that, after they remove you from the predominately White universities, they still split you into further fragments among yourselves as Black people. Thus, at a Zulu "college," all the students would all need to qualify as Zulu students; at the Xhosa "college" they had to qualify as Xhosa; etc. And geographically, they were placed so that, where they were, that particular language group was predominant.

The two "liberal" universities—University of Cape Town and Witwatersrand in Johannesburg—as well as maybe the University of Natal took this action. The faculty organized protests against the exclusion of Blacks. I should qualify that; it was not protests over the exclusion of Blacks, it was protests that challenged the government, or drew the government's attention to, or made loud noises about the fact that, up to this point it has been us, university administrators, university councils, who determined what students could be admitted and what students could not, and you're trespassing on that right.

Implied in this was that the University of Stellenbosch had made its decision to exclude Blacks. And, according to these protesters' little booklet called *The Open Universities*, it actually said: "The government should not interfere with our right to decide who may or who may not be admitted." They went on to say: "We (government) will defend the right of the University Stellenbosch to exclude whomsoever they wanted to exclude." So, it was not the welfare of the Black students at all; it was the rights and privilege of the university to do whatever they damn well wished.

Many times it was either total apartheid, like Stellenbosch, or very, very minimal integration in the classrooms. Many political organizations were against this. There was a big demonstration, a march—people wearing their academic gowns, the Chancellor of the university wearing his colorful gown, leading this procession; there was drum beating and I joined that procession. At that time, I thought, "Well, it is doing something." But I hadn't fully analyzed it to say, "It's not doing something for *us*; it's not doing something for Blacks. It's doing something for universities, which are White controlled anyway." Therefore, they can say, "We don't want to see you on our campus." That is their (so-called) right and that is what is being defended.

At this time, I was a student at the University of Cape Town. I entered the university in 1950. But the hollowness of it: There were political organizations, the ANC (African National Congress) included, that boycotted these "protests." They said, "That is a sham." It was not saying, "We would like that Blacks and everybody else should be free to come to our universities." It was really a protest about freedom of action by the faculty; it was not a direct commitment to equality or social justice.

When we think about these protests against these so-called "open universities," against the so-called University Extension Act—with their big marches in Cape Town, with academics in their gowns, with the High-Court Judge of the whole country leading the procession (since he was the Chancellor)—remember, their main reason for marching in protest against this law was that each university had to retain the right to conduct its own internal affairs, including, of course, appointing new people, including admission of students; saying, in effect, "Whom we admit and whom we don't admit should be our own business as universities and not the government's."

It became clear that the university was not concerned with the welfare of students applying to be admitted. In other words, they were not going to say, "We are going to admit any student who is qualified, Black, White, Green, Blue." They were going to say, "If we say we are going to exclude Blacks, we should be free to do so." That was the hollowness of this protest. It was protesting against what they perceived as the government taking their right to have their own interior laws that said if they decided not to accept Blacks, they should be free to do so. They even said that since Stellenbosch does not accept Blacks, Stellenbosch should not be forced to accept Blacks. So, it was all a sham.

These universities, knowing full well (another thing they never touched) the inadequacy of the preparation of Black students—very inferior high schools, inferior equipment, teachers not adequately prepared (not their fault), and just not giving the Black students the same quality of preparation for university admission as White students.

There's a total social context within which the Black students were raised, even in their homes: there is no incentive, there're no books around, no parents sitting reading a book for pleasure, always just the Bible. You didn't have the environment for reading in your family.

Also, a really bad situation came with the Bantu Education Act in 1952 (first enacted in 1953). That really deteriorated education throughout the country, made a bad thing worse. They created a special syllabus for Black schools that started from the premise, stated by Dr. Veerwood:

> We must remember we are dealing with a child born by Bantu parents, rocked on a Bantu knee, and we must reinforce that. We must have them taught in their Mother Tongues.

Considered the architect of apartheid, Veerwood had asked: "Why should we train Blacks for occupations they will never occupy...for jobs they will never have...that will not be available to them?"

Of course, somebody might ask: "What's wrong with teaching a child in his mother tongue?" The problem here was that this was done with a view to cramping their thinking, so they wouldn't be exposed to a language like English, a language that opens up the world—you can travel, you can discuss with scholars outside your country, outside your culture. These students were to be taught exclusively in Bantu languages. English and Afrikaans were to be taught as *subjects*, never to be used as mediums of instruction. Of course, another outcome was people thinking "I'm a Zulu" or "I'm a Xhosa" and so forth.

Interestingly, Walter Cronkite, the American newscaster, did a series of interviews in South Africa during the Bantu Education era , and produced a video done while visiting several schools. One of the subjects that was compulsory in Black schools was manual labor. Verwoerd, in arguing for this, said "They have to be taught the dignity of labor." Well, this begs the question: "Who had been laboring for them all along—washing their dirty clothing, cleaning their children when they soil themselves, digging their gardens?" *Now*, suddenly, they have to be *taught* the dignity of labor? If anybody needed to be taught the dignity of labor, it was *them*—Verwoerd and his Boor flock.

One of the scenes I remember from Cronkite's video was in the classroom, where a teacher was teaching a girl how to wash a piece of clothing. Also, because all farms were owned by Whites, many cases of a White farmer coming to the school and telling the teacher he has work for students to do—mending fences, digging, or whatever—became part of the syllabus. The children were taken out of school to do free labor for a farmer, yet it was part of the syllabus.

Take a child who comes out of that school and let him or her compete for entry into the University of Cape Town or Witwatersrand with a White child who comes out of first-class schools... obviously, there's no comparison. Black political organizations also argued that with Bantu Education crippling the minds of Black children, universities did not have to worry about competition from

Blacks; you were not going to get Black children who qualify to be in university.

Of course, at this time, Blacks did not vote. So, either way, it was a White group winning elections. One group may be promoting a "liberal" agenda promising "limited" integration; the other may be one saying, "We're not going to tolerate any kind of even the smallest integration." Instead, we're going to formalize what is already there and make the boundaries more strict and visible.

This was their mission. And this apartheid went into every aspect of the lives of the South African people. One phrase that was used by Verwoerd when he was advocating Bantu Education was that:

> Their [meaning Africans'] education, that they've been getting so far, is preparing them for careers that they cannot get. We don't want to prepare them as if they are going to graze in the same green pastures as the Whites.

What is the point of giving them the same education, and then using this metaphor of "cattle grazing"—that we're going to "graze in the same green pastures as the Whites"? Prepare them for their *place* in society. Now, who had defined that place? Of course, apartheid has defined that place. It says, in effect: "Let's now reinforce that by creating an education that will make them accept that status of inferiority."

It was not even as if they were looking at individuals like myself and Jordan and saying, "We can tolerate this." It was: "we have a mission. And we're not going to look at those little details. What we want is apartheid. A Zulu child will go to a Zulu school; a Venda child to a Venda school; a Venda person will live in Vendaland; a Zulu person will live in Zululand"—that kind of thing was absolutely crazy.

It is not surprising, then, that they co-opted education. Because, in education, you capture the children's minds when they are still very impressionable and that's when you can begin to make their thinking move in the direction that you want. That's what Bantu Education was all about. It was part of the Bantu Authorities Act, part of the University Education Extension Act, part of the Immorality Act (no Black/White touching each other across the color line)—it was incredible.

At first, the Immorality Act would find a couple—Black man and White woman or White man and Black woman—in the sexual act. They would be taken to court, go through a trial, for contravention of the Immorality Act. Then came the time when it was not just sex but what they called a "compromising position," and for that too they were taken to court. Even if they were just *necking*, they were taken to court for immorality. It's another *crazy* thing. If you try to control people's natural instincts and passions, you're just asking for trouble.

There were "transgressors" who were in high places and were White. Like a Minister of the Dutch Reform Church, the State Church, who was in the habit of taking his housemaid, Black, at night, outside of town, onto a hill somewhere, and having sex with her. This didn't sit quite right with her but she was unable to say "No" in the beginning: here was this White man with authority over her.

It got to a point where she decided, "I'm going to get him caught." And she asked some Black men to go hide in that area on the night he said he was going to take her there. They were hiding there when he arrived: he began to undress. When he was in his underclothes, they came out and pounced on him, and took away his clothes. Then said to him, "Now, you go back home. We could do some bad things on you, but you just go back home." "Oh, please, give me my clothes?" "Go back home. Go away."

He goes to the highway, dressed in his underpants, and starts thumbing a lift. This White couple stopped when they saw him – of course, only Whites had cars – and asked him "What happened?" "Well, you know the Bantu, they robbed me. They took all my clothes and all my money. I'm lucky I'm alive." "O.K. we'll give you a lift to the city." When they get to the city, they ask him, "Where do you live? We'd like to take you there." "Oh, no. That's all right. Just drop me here. "It ends up with these people being suspicious: why doesn't he want them to get to his house. He ends up being divorced from his wife and defrocked and disgracing the church.

There was another one, again a White man, who was the Secretary of the Prime Minister, who also had a Black woman and was caught. He was pleading with the police, "You can't do this to me. Don't you know who I am?" And, of course, the newspapers, especially the liberal ones, would splash these stories all over the front pages. So, the government got embarrassed. They virtually told the newspapers: "Don't make these stories so prominent; tuck them away somewhere."

In the police force, they had a special branch called the Immorality Squad. This squad were a whole bunch of Peeping Toms, *legal* Peeping Toms, because, if they suspected that a White and Black were sleeping together in some apartment, they were required to go and look and see through the cracks in the drapes, people having sex, then arrest them. Well, arrest the Black person and tell the White person not to do it anymore. The police loved that job. An indication of just how corrupting this ridiculous law became.

The Immorality Act shows the extent to which apartheid was insinuating itself into every fiber of society, every institution, not just that you can't get married to a White, but you can't even *touch* a White person in a suggestive way.

I was still at the University of Cape Town at this time and, by 1953, when I had finished my Master's and took another year to do a Teaching Diploma, a University Teacher's Diploma, at UCT; I was then appointed as a Junior Lecturer at the University of Cape Town. At this time, they were forcing Black students out of universities, not teachers. I knew, however, that it was just a matter of time before they did that. So those laws did not affect Jordan and myself.

I could go on talking about apartheid's madness and how it affected so many things. One thing that does stand out is the hypocrisy of the University of Cape Town and Witwatersrand, and even more so the University of Natal, in terms of the claim that "We are all open universities, we're integrated universities."

A.C. Jordan got a one-year sabbatical from the University of Cape Town. You were not required to do research while on sabbatical, but you were expected—not required, but expected—to go visit other institutions, maybe overseas. After all, you're on sabbatical, you're getting your full salary, for that whole year. Universities were very generous; for example, there was something called "Holiday Pay" that every teaching employee got during Christmas time, over and above their usual pay.

Daniel Pule Kunene, Cape Town (1953)

Jordan was going to go overseas, starting in London. He was going to stay in London for half a year and then come to the United States and visit several universities. Of course, this is all on an *honor* basis; you expect, just as a matter of integrity, that in fact the faculty member will go visit some institutions and colleagues, and literally broaden his or her own thinking.

He applies for a passport from the apartheid government and, after some delays (and sometimes they did these on purpose to try and disorganize your plans, as a Black person), they then declined. They refused to give him a passport. Now, he had been involved in some political movements, the same as I was. Nothing radical that says we want a revolution, we want an armed insurrection, we want to remove this government by force—nothing of the sort.

At that time, there had been enough people wanting to go out and being refused that the government introduced what they called an "Exit Permit." *Exit Permit* meant: if you insist on leaving, and we're not giving you a passport, then get out of here and don't come back. *Exit* Permit meant that you were being *exiled*—legally.

Jordan tried to get the university to intervene to get his application approved for a passport; the university did, but the government refused. That is when Jordan applied for an *Exit Permit*. Knowing that they could not really refuse an *Exit Permit*, unless they wanted to put you under house arrest or something, they were going to give it to him; but they just kept delaying on purpose, to disorganize his plans.

Until he decided to leave the country at night, to virtually escape, without even an Exit Permit. By this time (1960-1961), there was a secret escape route more or less like the Underground Railroad in the American South. He had his two sons drive him, at night, to the border, where he was met and had to cross the Limpopo River. He went to Kenya. It was not long after Kenya had got its Independence from British colonialism, and Jomo Kenyatta was then the President of Kenya. Jordan told me when I finally got here (US) how he and Kenyatta were so emotional when they met.

Even I didn't know that he was leaving. By then, it had become a secret. I had known when he was going to leave *normally*, that is, get a passport and get on a boat. The first time I came to know was when the head of our department, Professor Lestrade, called me. He had read in that morning's paper that A.C. Jordan was in England and had been interviewed by the press in London. It was news to me.

Then, he calls me into his office, and he's absolutely angry and says: "Look at this." I look at it. "Did you know that he was planning this?" I said, "No. I didn't know." And he's more concerned with Jordan having "betrayed" him: "He left us in the lurch. Now, what can we do about teaching Xhosa?" In other words, like someone who was so totally insensitive to what we go through, even though we were teaching there, how our lives outside of that institution, even *in* that institution; but more so when you left there and you didn't even have the protection of the hallowed halls of the University of Cape Town. You were just another Native, another Bantu. You had your *Pass* to show when they demanded it or go to jail.

This man sitting there and being not just hurt, but fed-up about Jordan having left without him knowing—if he were to go through all that, would he? Somehow, the hierarchy of authority stops you short of just telling off this person, because you may lose your job.

After all, Jordan had run into some trouble (described below), under the State of Emergency that was declared by the government in 1960, in order to break a national strike called by the Pan African Congress. One of the *provisions* was that a policeman, of any rank, could stop any Black person seen walking in town and ask him or her, "Where do you work?" If you said, "I work for such-and-such bookstore, or shoe store," then the next question would be: "Here, where you are, where I meet you, are you in the process of carrying out your duties for your employer?" If you said, "Yes," you had to prove it. If you said "No," you were immediately arrested. You were arrested also even if you said, "Yes" but could not convince this policeman that in fact you were telling the truth. You were immediately arrested *and* the policeman had the power to administer punishment on the spot. In other words, the policeman starts assaulting you, beating you up. And, you still go to the judge.

When a liberal member raised the question in Parliament, Helen Sussman, she asked: "Does this punishment on the spot include a punishment that can result in death?" the answer was "Yes." Giving a "license to kill" to policemen who already had the power to come and disrupt people's lives at any time. Now, it's "legal" if you're murdered in the process.

One instance involved a Black Minister, collar on, who was asked that question, which is absolutely ridiculous: "Are you doing your job as a Minister?" When his answer did not please the policeman, he was chased down one of the main streets of Cape Town and beaten with a sjambok by the police.

Now, as to Jordan's "trouble," during a break in classes, he goes down to Rosebank, to his bank, to do some business, and is ready to go back to campus, to his office. He lights a cigarette and is about to go, when a young (maybe even teenage) policeman stops him and asks him, "Where do you work?" Jordan says, "I work at the university." And the policeman goes through this thing about "Are you doing your work right now?" Jordan is smoking and answering his questions. Then, he slaps his hand that's holding the cigarette and says, "Don't smoke while you're talking to me." The cigarette falls to the ground.

Jordan becomes incensed, insulted; the rage that was going through him could not be described. After reporting the incident to the university, they did follow up. Jordan got an apology from the Chief of Police and the young officer was reprimanded. The editorials in the liberal newspapers were very angry over such a dignified, professional person being treated like that by this little nothing of a White boy.

This was all brought back by this man, this White professor and head of the department, sitting there; he needed someone to ask him: "If you were in Jordan's place, if you had gone through these indignities, wouldn't you think of leaving this country? Wouldn't you think this country is a police state?"

At that time, there were so many laws that restricted the movements of Black people. Among these was one that said: outside the limits of Western Cape or certain cities like Cape Town, one had to have a permit to come in prior to actually coming in. So people had to have permission to travel from where they were into Cape Town, for whatever reason. University of Cape Town, knowing this law, was very nervous when they did their recruiting.

They needed two people to fill Jordan's position, two younger people. One of them said later to us, the university sent urgent letters to them, "Don't come. Don't come. Don't come until we've got *Permits* for you from the government." One of them got his "Don't come" message, the other one did not. By the time he got there, he had not got the Permit, and the university was extremely nervous. They had to approach the Department of Bantu Affairs to ask them if they could get a Permit for this person, who was already here, after all.

It was to me a very shameless and weak-kneed response to the government's interference in what the university should be free to do. They should be free to bring in whomsoever they consider suitable.

So we ended up having two younger people doing the Xhosa that Jordan did and I was back with my own section. This was well into the period when apartheid was in effect, around 1958.

South Africa at the time was a Police State, certainly for Black people. The Pass Laws, the Pass System made it very much of a Police State. That law committed the police to invade your privacy anywhere, anytime, and demand that you show them your *Pass*, your papers. They could stop you anywhere and so you had to carry this thing on you. By then, it had been made into a book of about sixty-four pages, because there were so many different little pieces that said you had done this, or not done it. There was a receipt to show that you had paid your Poll Tax. At that time, Poll Tax was enforced and it did not depend on whether or not you were working, had been working, or whatever; you had to pay your Poll Tax once every year. People were taken to prison if they didn't have that one pound to pay that *Poll Tax*.

You had to have that piece of paper that said you had paid your Poll Tax. Another piece of paper said if you had permission to stay in this area; one said that you were employed legally, which meant a White person employed you. Before leaving home, you had to grab this whole bundle of papers, which had become a whole book, and look to see whichever one they want and give it to them or get arrested.

Another deceptive law passed called the Abolition of Passes and Coordination of Documents Act. It didn't abolish the passes at all. What it did was accumulate all these separate pieces of paper into a little booklet, with a color-coordinated cover to indicate one exemption or another. Of course, the irony is that you had to produce it to show that you're exempted.

With the Population Registration Act, it was a matter of neighbor spying on neighbor, neighbor reporting on neighbor, especially as a result of the Race Classification Board. If there were any doubt, especially between a Colored person, whose hair was not as kinky as mine, and who might have light enough complexion to pass for white, many of them would do that. On the other hand, the thing that was so crazy was that some Whites would go to the Race Classification Board and say, "I suspect that my neighbor isn't really white." That immediately started the gossip about them; suddenly they find their children at school being shunned by other children, and life becomes terrible for this family. The man is called before the Race Classification Board. He's asked about his lineage. I don't know how many generations back they had to go. But another way to prove this person's race was to take a pencil and run it through his or her hair. If it stuck, that was something to create suspicion. This form of Race Classification was a form of Nazism. In fact, that's what Archbishop Desmond Tutu would call it.

The police would come right in the middle of the night—2 a.m., 3 a.m.—and bang, bang, bang on the door, flashlights on the people sleeping: "Where are your *Papers*?" And people have to grope and find their *Papers* and show the police. If there is anything more inhuman, I don't know what it is. Where you can just walk into people's homes, in the middle of the night, when they're sleeping, and demand *Papers*. And if you did not produce them, produce what they wanted, they had the van waiting outside for you to be taken to the police station. Women were taken in their nightclothes.

If you were across the street from where you work—maybe it's a break and you go to buy a sandwich or something, and you forgot your jacket across the street where you work, and your *Pass* was in it—the policeman demands it and you say: "Sorry, I left my jacket there; we can cross the street, go to my employment place, that's where it is." They say, "No. You can tell that to the judge." They really like saying "You can tell that to the judge." They handcuff the person.

GETTING MARRIED

My wife was a nurse. When she came to Cape Town, she was what here (in the US) is called an RN (or Registered Nurse), which, in South Africa is called a Staff Nurse. I met her when she was training as a nurse. She lived away from her home, Potchefstroom, to be nearer to the hospital where she was training. There was this woman, a very political woman, who had accepted her to live with her, and she was staying there. I came to live in the same Black Township a few blocks from where she was living.

In the meantime, I was studying, privately, even as I worked there. Some of these students, when they heard I was studying, and if I were doing something within their line of study or expertise, would offer to help; some of them not even really knowing how to teach, but offering still. It was wonderful to have people like that, especially in that context.

When I did pass the Matriculation, by private study, still being there, an Army General, who lived there, when he heard that I had passed Matriculation, asked, "Did you pass Matric?" And I said, "Yes, sir." And, he took out his wallet and gave me ten shillings. At that time, that would be about a dollar and a half. It was a good gesture.

Then he asked me "What career, what line of profession do you want to pursue?" I said, "I want to be a Medical Doctor." He said, "I'll talk to the Medical School Superintendent. I know him, personally." You have to put in what may seem strange terms that, you want to go and help your people. You don't just want to help *humanity*. You want to go and help *your people*.

The Medical Superintendent's answer was negative. He said I would need a scholarship and they didn't have one. But, if I wanted to help my people on the health side, I could become an ambulance driver.

Some of these liberal White students who met me by being resident in this hotel established a program at the Black hospital for students whose studies were interrupted by illness, but who could still be helped along even as they were lying in hospital. This was open to anybody who wanted to study, could be an adult, whatever level, and people were needed to teach at that hospital.

They approached me because they knew of my interest in education. After considering this, I decided "Yes, I'm leaving the job at the hotel and taking up this job at the hospital." Then, I had to find my own accommodation; and again with help from people who knew people, I ended up at that place, which I mentioned, a few blocks away from where my wife-to-be was then staying as she was studying towards the completion of her nursing degree.

The two women were very close friends, it turned out to be. They did things together. Her landlady was a very powerful politician in the ANC. She was a born leader—a powerful voice, kind of tall, a wonderful person, and very aggressive. She died when my wife and I were in Cape Town, so we couldn't be at the funeral; but we saw a picture of her at the funeral with Winnie Mandela as one of the pallbearers for her.

That's where Selina lived. Also, these two women went to the Anglican Church—Black Anglican Church, of course; it's in a Black Township. Selina use to sometimes be sent by her landlady to my landlady, to carry some message or on some errand or other—that's what we did as young people, we were sent. Sometimes she would get there and my landlady wouldn't be there. I may be reading, and she called me "teacher." "Oh, good morning teacher. I've been sent for Mrs. Magow." "Oh, she's in the backyard" or "She's inside" or "She's not home." And, I'd just go back to my reading. Showed absolutely no interest.

Then came a big occasion at the Anglican Church in Sophiatown. A Bishop was going to be *consecrated* at this Church in the Black Township Sophiatown. There were tickets issued to official members of the church, each one was given two: one for himself or herself and one for an invitee, anybody they'd like to bring. My landlady told me about this. At that time, I wasn't going to church, in spite of my background.

"Oh, Kune [she called me "Kune"], we're going to have a big service. I'm sorry I don't have an extra ticket. I gave my extra one to my sister. You know Kune, the Archbishop of Canterbury is going to be there." As the time gets closer, she says, "You know, Aunt Ida [Selina's landlady] has an extra ticket because the person she was going to give it to cannot come. Are you interested?" "Oh, okay." So, I get that ticket.

The day the Sunday comes I am in my landlady's bedroom that was the only privacy I could get to change. And then I come out of there and there is this young lady so well dressed, the hat and two-tone shoes, I can see her right now. Right away I thought "I think I would like to walk with this lady." And who was it? This girl who used to be sent here and I didn't even pay attention to—Selina.

We were going to walk. We had no cars; we really didn't miss them; just allow enough time to walk. Here I was walking with Selina and her landlady and getting anxious about when I would get the opportunity to be alone with her. I said, "Well, let's make sure that after the service we don't get separated and we go back together."

We get in there and she's sitting some distance away; but we can see each other. Not long after the service started, she realizes I don't have a hymnbook, and she passes on a hymnbook through different hands until it gets to me. I was so thrilled! Oh, my goodness. The service went on. The consecration took place, and the service ended.

We all met outside to walk back home. The adults, my landlady and her landlady, made friends and started talking. So I say, "Let's just walk ahead." We walk slowly back to Western Native Township, which is where we stayed. When we're parting, I asked: "Do you play cards? Can I come later for a game of cards?" She said, "Yes." "Alright."

Well, one thing led to another as they say.

We didn't rush things. I didn't kiss her. I just know the thrill I felt when we were playing and I touched her hand. I was in heaven. Her landlady invited me to come for supper. I agreed. After that,

Selina has to go and get on the bus, to go back to the hospital where she's training. Her landlady asked me if I would be kind enough to escort her to the bus. Oh boy. It was hard to suppress my excitement. When the bus comes, she gets on and sits by the window. I wait for the bus to go. As the bus starts to move, she waves, and I wave back. "She *waved*! At *me*! She *waved at me*!" I walked like blazes to go back and tell my landlady "I'm in love! I'm in love!" It was 1946.

We had a kind of rule that was understood between young people planning to marry: If they met while they were still studying for their careers, they waited for each other to finish first before they got married. She was still studying but getting close to completing her studies as a nurse. We delayed our marriage so that Selina should finish studies for her career.

Selina a nursing student

Then came the Jordan invitation. I was working at the Magistrates Court, I received this imperfectly addressed letter—a letter that had just the bare information that either it could have been sent back for an incomplete address or could have been "address unknown" or whatever, but enough information that the postman was able to trace me to the Magistrate's Court building. I received that letter. That was a letter whose handwriting was so familiar, once the letter got into my hands. It was the handwriting of my mentor, A.C. Jordan.

He had been following my career, knowing that I was studying, using me in his classes as an inspiration of an "ideal" student, knowing when I was writing my exams, he would tell the class: "Right now as I'm talking to you, he is sitting for such-and-such an exam." Now, he was inviting me. He had managed to get some funds for me to come to Cape Town where he was now. I had by then got my Bachelors' Degree, in 1949, by private study at the University of Cape Town.

When I was contemplating leaving Johannesburg to go to Cape Town to go and do the study that A.C. Jordan was inviting me for, many people—because I had stopped going to church and I was becoming *political* about these things—said, "Why don't you just go to church and become *confirmed*... so you have a certificate that says you are a member of the AME church. You never know when these things might stand you in good stead."

So I did go back. This, again, was in Sophiatown, the same place the Odin Cinema was. I sat in the front row. The choir director, who was also the pianist, sat there at an angle to the choir so that he could sort of conduct with his head, and facial gestures and so on while the choir was singing. Then, there was just a tad of "off-keyness." I could hear that the harmony was off by so slight a measure that many people might not have noticed. But I was noticing. I heard this and I just looked down: my hands on my knees, and very, very slowly, gently shook my head. Lifted my head and found the choir director was looking at me. He smiled a smile that said, "Yes, I also notice it."

We met after the service. He introduced himself as Bartholome Pache, and it didn't take much for him to convince me that I ought to join the church choir. We became friends in music for all the time that we were in Johannesburg together. He moved to Cape Town and our relationship continued there, musically.

When this Church Jubilee was taking place, Pache and I had known each other quite a while; I was in the choir, I sang a solo at a concert in a large community social center, where dignitaries were there—ministers, teachers, visitors—*my mother* was there. I sang a solo accompanied by Pache this time. It was *Sewanee River* ("Way down upon the Sewanee River...").

Later in the show, Pache came to me and said: "You know I also have a double quartet here. But our bass did not show up. We're going to sing one piece, *Sweet and Low*. Do you know it?" My voice range was very wide: I could sing tenor, high tenor, mid-tenor, and low; I could also sing bass. I said, "I know the tune, but I don't know the words." So he said, "Let's try something." And, we went into the wing, the double quartet is there. We hummed the melody of the song. I was and still am able to harmonize quite naturally: once I hear something, I can put in bass or tenor, maybe even some alto where it's needed.

Knowing that I was able to actually hum the bass, the question was: "How do I sing the words?" Then somebody came up with the idea that, "We'll write the words on a slip of paper, and we'll pin them on the back of the person in front of you." And then, when we're finished, we'll take it off quickly, before we bow and then leave the stage. That happened and it went perfectly.

At that point, Selina agreed that it's a good thing that I go to the University of Cape Town and do my Master's Degree. I had to leave for Cape Town at the beginning of 1950. We agreed then to let each other finish what we were doing:

> March 7, 1950: My dearest Selina, my journey was splendid, darling. It had never occurred to me that I would indeed leave Johannesburg, and my acquaintances, and, above all things, that I would ever leave you so many miles behind me before our marriage materialized. It has happened, darling; and I must say how proud I feel at the fortitude and courage with which you bore it all.

In fact, I must say that that collapse of mine on the Saturday on which I received Mr. Jordan's last letter proved to me beyond all doubt that the woman I am to marry is not only pretty and dainty, but that she can rise to an occasion when circumstances demand it, summoning up courage to stare facts in the face and laugh at fate.

In the afternoon, after we had been back home for lunch, Mr. Jordan and I went back into town to purchase some books and stationery. He then took me to the museum, the public library, the famous Cape Gardens, and he also showed me the Houses of Parliament. This year I am going to do Xhosa I and Shona I in addition to advanced phonetical work in Southern Sotho. We have also to learn the rudiments of German, to be able to read something in it. Well, that's a lot, darling.

The university itself is on a very lovely spot, just at the foot of Table Mountain. It is considerably elevated above the rest of the town, and from it you look down upon the roofs of the houses below, with misty mountains bordering the far side. The buildings themselves are so artistically arranged, that to go there for the mere sake of sight-seeing would indeed be worthwhile. They are roofed with red tiles, and green creeping plants on the walls add more color to an already attractive scenery.

Meanwhile think of me, sweetheart. Think of your Dan who is thinking of you every minute of his waking life. Absence from each other, instead of weakening the bond that holds us together, let it rather strengthen that link.

Now, Cape Town became more than just a place I went to study. It also became my first real initiation into *politics*—politics of resistance, politics against oppression, and so on. With A.C. Jordan's encouragement, I joined a movement called *Non-European Unity Movement* (NEUM), which was structured to embrace other organizations that were all affiliated with it. This was my initiation into politics.

I didn't just wake up one morning and say, "I want to be a revolutionary." I went into this by degrees. Especially after reading the "Aims and Objectives" of the movement, and their affiliated organizations, and the vision of the South Africa that they wanted, I felt this was, if ever there was one, an organization, a movement that I wanted to join.

It was so exciting, their Aims and Objectives, their vision of a new South Africa, I saw this as something really close—as long as you worked hard, were committed—we're going to be "free" soon. It was good to keep us in the *movement* but was also, in a sense, naïve. Very similar to when we were here (in Madison), on my sabbatical, and the first thing we thought that apartheid had got to its climax, its peak; and that from there on out, things were going to get better and better, and we would be going back to South Africa.

Later on, another, smaller group, affiliated with the Unity Movement, was formed that was called the Society of Young Africa (SOYA). I became the first chairman of that organization. The politics of South Africa were and still are, to a large extent, very complex, especially when it comes to places like Cape Town. That's where the Colored People really congregated, in Cape Town and the Western Cape area. Historically, that's where it all started, with the Dutch settling there to have Black women.

Cape Town was a city which had many surprises for us. It was a more "liberal" city. The commuter trains were mixed, the city buses the same thing; buying your ticket—same line. On Sundays we'd go to the City Hall to listen to symphonic orchestras. Sipho recalls, years later, returning there to play with legendary composer/pianist Abdullah Ibrahim to perform in that very spot. There seemed to be a determination by the South African government to root-out this liberalism from Cape Town. They started introducing separate seating in the buses and commuter trains, eventually making Black people sit at the back, mimicking the American South.

When I first got to Cape Town, there was no SOYA. There was nothing for the youth. Complications arose, especially in places like Cape Town, where there was a very significant group of Colored people, who regarded themselves—and were encouraged to regard themselves—as superior to Blacks. Segregated by schools, by residential areas, by employment, many became materially much better off. Some tried to fight off being *seduced* by this bait that said: "You are better off. You are superior to the Black people."

Those who tried to fight it off were in movements like the ones mentioned. SOYA grew out of tensions in groups like the New Era Fellowship (NEF), which were dominated by Coloreds, who were mono-linguistic(they spoke only English). This put them at an advantage: many of them had gotten better education, many of them spoke English at home, and here were African youth many of whom came from rural areas, who were too self-conscious about their English to participate fully in discussions, and who were sort of browbeaten by these people who get up and rattle off something about how they understand what oppression is all about, what the laws are all about—and they have the language ability.

After this thing had gone on for some time, the elders, including my mentor, Africans in the movement, decided it was time to form a separate group that would not only have Black people as members; like there was the *New Era Fellowship,* which was basically a Colored group. So let's have a Society of Young Africa, which will be basically Black, and which will use Xhosa, if necessary, but which will also, by having Blacks by themselves, would make them less nervous, less self-conscious, less afraid to participate in discussions and political debate.

That created a lot of tension because I, as one of the first officials of SOYA, had been told by senior members of the movement who engineered this that "Coloreds should not be allowed in," that "they would attempt to inundate and control too much. We should not let them in." It was very awkward because they got to know that they were being excluded from this organization. But, again, if we were to speak Xhosa in the meetings, they would feel excluded the way that many Africans felt excluded having to speak English, which they could barely speak.

I also formed a SOYA choir. At that time, I now found myself composing songs that were supporting the struggle. Earlier there were the "religious" compositions; now, I am aware that all the arts, especially by Blacks, have to express something for the Movement and against the oppression. My SOYA choir performed in different situations; our meetings to practice took place in all kinds of places. One venue we could only reach by going on two buses and a train.

It was a hospital that was isolated from the city. About two or three nurses were members of the choir.

In correspondence ("Love Letters"), beginning May 25, 1948, a letter dated February 10, 1952, inter alia, says:

> My dearest Selina...I am sorry that I have kept quiet so long, darling. My intention was that I should write when I send the ring. But since I'm likely to take a few more days before I procure it, I thought I might as well drop you a note so that you are not kept guessing as to what is happening.

April 8, 1952, Selina, writing from Boksburg Benoni Hospital, Boksburg, South Africa, replies:

> My dearest Dan, Thanks a million for your letter which I received on Saturday morning. I was surprised when you still asked me about the letter which you had addressed to Potchefstroom. I had also mentioned something of great importance in it, concerning our affair. We should be knowing how far our parents have gone; it's only then, that we can know what to start with. We should forget about a *special license* and work hard for a white wedding in December. For I feel we will be very unfair to ourselves; after all we are both still young and bright. Why should we really marry by *special license*? Let's show the world our pride. It only happens once in one's life, so let's do it correctly.
>
> Let's be an example to many others younger than us, that it is not impossible to wait for a young lady or a young gentleman for several years and still marry each other after a long separation due to reasons.

I answered on May 6, 1952:

> My dearest Glory, "thanks for your last letter my dear. I thought that by now I would have taken a picture to send you, but unfortunately, I have not yet done so. I haven't seen such bright and beautiful winter days in Cape Town before. Usually, the rains begin pouring almost endlessly from the middle of April throughout the winter period up to October and even November.

But this year we have had a glorious May, and June seems to be no exception.

Then, a small cut on Selina's finger got infected leading to the following "small" tragedy. On August 4, 1952, Selina writes:

> My dearest Dan, it's Monday morning 9:30 AM. The Bone Specialist has been to see me. He also tells me that there is absolutely nothing that he can do for me, except amputation. You know the main thing is that the pathology has gone into the bone and that it is still very active. He says the sooner I go for amputation the better.
>
> Sweetheart you have no idea how troubled my soul is, that I have to lose my finger, but still I cannot do otherwise: if amputation be the only remedy, then I just have to take it the way it has come. I know very well that you are just as hurt and sorry as I am.

Undeterred, on October 8, 1952, I responded:

> Now, darling, first I must express my deepest sympathy with you in the ordeal that you are going through. Sometimes things that seem unimportant at first end up seriously. Who could have thought that a mere cut of the finger with a knife could lead to the amputation of that finger? P.S. just give me a rough estimate of what you think the wedding expenses might come to.

Finally, as the need to finalize a wedding date intensified, Selina wrote to me on December 5, 1952:

> My dearest Dan, I arrived home on Wednesday night and I found your letter waiting for me. Darling you have no idea how excited I am about the radiogram. I wish it wasn't so heavy then you would bring it along absent the electricity. Concerning our affair, I would really like us to marry and get finished this very month as we have said. Even if we marry now and arrange for a party next year July or any suitable time, because time is already very short especially that our people have not come together again...All we know is that we love each other and that we are marrying as soon as you come to Johannesburg.

Selina and I got married January 23, 1953, in Boksburg; a small town east of Johannesburg and south of Pretoria, a small wedding. I went back to Cape Town, then came back again to fetch her.

Professor Daniel and Selina Kunene, Cape Town, S. A. (1962)

We built our house while staying in different places. Some people would give us some accommodation. We found accommodation in a backyard room—you know, people used to build rooms in their backyard and then rent them. At that point we bought a plot and had our house built.

Now, there's something about that too. The government had started as far back as 1927—or even earlier, 1923—to restrict Black ownership of landed property in urban areas. What they did from 1923 on was, they *froze* land that was in the possession of Black people by having a law that said you could not, as a Black, buy land from somebody other than another Black. Which meant, also, that if a Black was selling his property and a White bought it there was less land in the hands of Blacks altogether. So, it was just a matter of time before Blacks would have absolutely no land.

They didn't even wait for that. The Group Areas Act came to take care of that. For example, I became a *disqualified person* to live in the house that we had built.

First of all, when I knew that that plot was available, I could not go to this Black woman who lived right next door, and owned another plot. I could not go directly to her and say, "I want to buy it." I had to get permission from the Governor General's Office: a Black wanting to buy from another Black according to this 1927 Act, I could not just go and buy it. By the way, this is what Jordan had to do too—build his house where he did, which isn't very far from where I built my house. He also had to apply to the Governor General for permission to buy that plot.

I bought it. Then there were low-interest loans available to people employed by the state, which I was, by being employed by the university. But the office that controlled these loans was trying to be difficult, just because they wanted to make it difficult for Blacks to buy land. I went to a White attorney, who was very liberally inclined, who had his office in a Colored area. All he did was to go personally and say: "I want to talk to the person in charge." "Well, we can help you." "No, I want to talk to the person in charge of all of this!"

Eventually, he got to that person. And that person said, "Of course he qualifies. Who said he didn't?" Well, it was these people at the lower echelons who were actually implementing apartheid on their own initiative, not waiting to be prodded from above. That way, we were able to get our loan and purchase the plot.

Can you imagine the day we got there, and they had dug the foundation? It was very exciting. But the Group Areas Act, in the 1950s, meant that, in the urban areas, the government was going to apply strict apartheid in residences so that there would be areas for Coloreds only; areas for Whites only; areas for Asians and Indians only… and none for Blacks.

The whole attitude that Blacks were only in the urban areas *temporarily* was being carried on. You're there as long as you worked for a White person; that was the only reason that you were there. One of the laws made you liable to arrest if you were in the urban area without a job. Either you had a Pass showing that you worked for some White firm or some White person, or you had a Permit showing you were, maybe, admitted for two weeks to perhaps to seek a job or what have you. You had to have some Permit that allowed you—that permitted you—to be there.

Blacks were not given an area under the Urban Areas Act. They belonged to the rural areas, where they were recruited for labor and after their time they had to go back. It was sort of like an ostrich burying its head in the sand. There were so many Blacks who were living in houses, even though they were renting them from the municipality. Schools were there for Blacks. It was just a pipe dream to think that Blacks could be shifted all out and only come when they're needed. It was just incredible—no such areas for Blacks to buy property. I had been able to buy mine under an earlier, 1947 law.

We had a new house, a new child, Liziwe, and a new car—a Ford Zodiac. I applied for a phone, and it took a year or more before a colleague wrote a letter to the Department of Communications—then we got a phone. We were one of the first families to have a car and a phone. There was communal pride, but also probably envy.

Then comes along the Urban Areas Act. This area where my house is, is declared a Colored Area. I am clearly not a Colored. I am not even pretending to be one, quite happy to be what I am, who I am. But I start then getting these slips, these little notes from the

Group Areas Board, from their office. First one: "You are hereby informed that according to the Group Areas Act you are a disqualified person to live where you are living."

That's my house, but suddenly I am a *disqualified person*. I think, I'm not going to become a party to my own displacement, by them taking away my property, by responding to this sort of thing. To start responding to this would mean I am co-opted into uprooting myself. Next thing, a note that says your house has been evaluated at so much. Your house is worth such-and-such an amount for you to sell it. You had to sell it, of course. They were not asking, "Do you agree that you're going to leave? Do you agree that you're going to sell your house?" They were telling you: "You are disqualified. Your property is worth so much. And if you sell your property for more than this evaluation that we've given you, half of the extra money that you make from that will be taken by the Group Areas Board."

Now tell me, what is the sense of that? What sense did it make? Let's say they evaluated your house at $50, 000 Rand, and you get someone willing to pay $70, 000, that's $20,000 more, then you have to take $10,000 and just give it to the Group Areas Board. No reason assigned for this: Why? On the other hand, if you sold *under* the amount of their evaluation of your house, they would give you 10% of that difference. When you make a profit, they want 50% of it; if you sell under, they give you 10%.

There was a professor who was actually a Communist, openly, and was being victimized by the University of Cape Town by not being given the promotions he should have, and one of the most brilliant minds there. As if he had read my mind, he said: "Dan, don't respond to any of that. Don't respond." I had already made up my mind that if I'm going to be removed from this house, they are going to have to carry me out physically. I am not leaving on the strength of these little dirty pieces of paper they're sending to me.

This must have been around 1962. It was during the process of this harassment that I got a sabbatical. I needed to have a passport. Passports, for Black people, were virtually unknown. We carried Passes to say we have permission to this or that. We didn't have passports because it was not something we were expected to do—to travel overseas.

Remember, A.C. Jordan, himself, had to go through an ordeal when he applied for a passport, which the government refused him. As I've noted, when it was clear that they had rejected his application, he decided to apply for an Exit Permit.

A.C. Jordan

The university decided to help me get a passport. And they did. I got a passport that covered the whole family. We left by ship, Friday the 13th of September 1963. The journey by ship to England was going to have us sailing for two weeks.

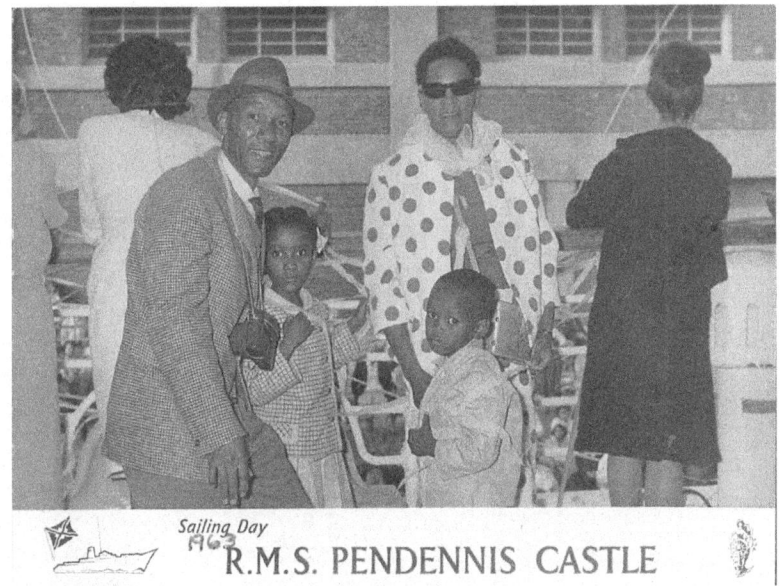

Sailing Day 1963
R.M.S. PENDENNIS CASTLE
Dr. and Mrs. Kunene with Liziwe and Sipho (1963)

We got on the ship and there were streamers that we held, that were held by us on the ship and by friends and relatives…down there, on the dock. Kind of like a final handshake. When the ship started to move, the streamers became taught, then more taught, and eventually they snapped. That was saying, symbolically, "You're gone."

For us it was more symbolic than that because our coming back was indefinite. At that time, I must admit, we, my wife and I, thought apartheid had reached a point of badness and evil that it couldn't get worse. So, we're coming back at the end of my sabbatical year and we're going to see the new South Africa emerging. How naïve we were we would find out soon because once we started subscribing to an overseas version of a South African *liberal* paper, we realized how in those few months we had been gone, how much worse things had gotten.

Sipho and Liziwe in route to London (1963)

Selina, Sipho, Liz dining on ship

Getting Married

After ten days on the ship, we stopped at Las Palmas Islands and we were taken on small boats to waiting buses to have a quick tour of the island. We got back to the ship and there was a cable waiting for me from the University of Cape Town. It was asking me to represent the UCT and there would be another representative who would come directly from Cape Town, and we would meet at this conference in Venice, Italy.

That would be during the three months we were going to be in London. It turned out it was going to be soon after we arrived in London. I don't know how I learned to find my way in that city. We arrived on a Friday. The trip to Venice was the next Wednesday, less than a week. I had to go find the Standard Bank, in Haymarket (whatever "Haymarket" meant, I didn't know). I had to look for the Italian Embassy to get a visa, then buy a ticket. Things I had never done in my life. Then, having to study London in such a hurry.

I did get to these places. I did find myself on a train to the airport, an Air Italia flight. I did find myself getting onto the plane. Don't ask me how I did it, I don't know what was carrying me through that in that short time that I was able to do those things.

That very Friday that we arrived in London, from South Hampton, by the boat-train, we ended up in a small hotel where we were going to stay while we looked for accommodation, by Victoria Station. We went to look for a restaurant. We ate. On our way back to the hotel, our daughter, Liziwe, was about to turn seven, on Sunday the following week; our little boy, Sipho, was still little. He was on his legs and could walk. We stopped in a shop where we thought we might want to buy another piece of luggage. There in the shop is a Bobbie, a Policeman. Sitting with his helmet on his knee, chatting away with the person behind the counter.

We put our little boy down. He starts to call him, in a very fatherly way, call him towards him, pick him up, put him on his knee, and of all ironies say to him: "Are you afraid of the policeman? Are you afraid of the policeman?" I could not help but think: If you only knew where we came from what a policeman means to Black people, that would be the irony of ironies to your question.

Moma and Papa Kunene with Sipho (front) and Liziwe (1963)

In Italy, in Venice, we had this conference, which was on Native Law. I didn't know much about Native Law, hardly anything. Perhaps the university planned to save some money by not flying two people all the way from Cape Town, I don't know. I found out my co-delegate was a woman I knew, a White woman from the University of Cape Town.

Now, if the university wanted to give an impression of how liberal they were by having a Black man and White woman sitting next to each other as delegates from the University of Cape Town, many people's idea of apartheid would get shaken: "They can't be coming from an apartheid country. They certainly aren't coming from an apartheid university," quite clearly.

She knew Italian and that was one of the reasons she became my co-delegate. Then there was this Italian reporter, a woman, who knowing that I was from South Africa, so badly wanted to interview me. Quite clearly, it was going to be all about apartheid: How is it to be a Black in South Africa under this system? I knew it would be all about that. She didn't speak English. She was speaking through my co-delegate who spoke Italian.

My co-delegate told me what she was after and when she noticed that I was inclined to agree, she said, "You know, Dan, I wouldn't do it if I were you. It's going to get to South Africa. It's going to be in the papers there. It doesn't matter if you say she should not mention your name; they'll know it's you because they'll know it's not me. You are one of the two delegates from the University of Cape Town, and who would be saying those things? It's you." Even at times when I was inclined to say, "I want to…let me talk," she would say, "I wouldn't do it." And I was very thankful to her for having done that.

I had had two visits by detectives, security police, at my house in Cape Town. At separate times, two men came to the house and, strangely enough, on both occasions they found only my wife; I was not home. "What shall I tell him?" she would ask. "Just tell him we were here." If I had talked with this reporter, this is what would be waiting for me when I went back. At this point, I was still planning to return to South Africa.

We stayed in London for about three months. It was for the last quarter of 1963. One day, we lived in a duplex, an upstairs-and-downstairs duplex, and upstairs lived our neighbor. She was from the Caribbean. She heard us coming in. This was nighttime. We had been to a movie. It was the days when England was still cleaning itself up to prevent this Pea Soup, this mixture of fog and smog that was a very serious problem in England. They were using ways of controlling what fuel was used in what part of the city, on certain days of the week; to avoid the whole city using the same kind of polluting fuel for heating and for cooking.

Here we were returning from this movie. Our neighbor from upstairs hears us at the door, and she comes running down the stairs. She meets us at the door, and she says, "Have you heard?" We say, "What?" "President Kennedy is dead." "What? Was it an accident?" "No, no, no. It was not an accident. He was shot dead."

She had a T.V., which we did not, and she said, "You can come upstairs and watch on the news. They are talking about it right now." We went upstairs. The story was coming over and over again. The pictures. It was shocking for us. We remembered that before we left South Africa there had been the attempted assassination of the then Prime Minister of South Africa. This was apartheid South Africa, so one could understand that there might be attempts on the life of a leader who endorsed apartheid. "Kennedy?!" That was quite a surprise. Why would anybody want Kennedy out of the way?

They talked about the suspect, Lee Harvey Oswald, and how he had been in the book repository and so the shots came from there. The first report had been that the entry was from the front and exit at the back; and that pointed to that infamous Grassy Knoll. By the afternoon, they had switched that around completely; now it came from where Lee Harvey Oswald was. We were beginning to think, "What's going on here?"

And what was it? A day, two days after Oswald was arrested he was himself assassinated, by this guy Jack Ruby. We were just amazed. Oswald was supposed to be sealed off, in the protection of the police. It was then that I said to my wife, "I don't think we should go to that country. I think we should not go to America. It's a very violent country." At that time, it would have been easy to do that, to not go. The University of London wanted me very much in their African and Oriental Studies Program.

I did not change my plans. We came to the United States at the beginning of 1964. I flew from London. My wife and our two children, Liziwe and Sipho, followed two weeks later by ship. I had an obligation.

My sabbatical included a visit to the United States. I had a Carnegie travel grant from here that would finance this itinerary of going around to various universities. If I did not go, it would have been breaking faith with too many sponsors of my trip.

EXILE TO AMERICA—UCLA

My first impression of London when we arrived was the chimneys; you could look and one house may have eight chimneys. I arrived at Idyllwild Airport in New York, which became the J.F. Kennedy Airport, after his assassination. What struck me, my first impression as I got off the plane, was the number of wheelchairs, so many wheelchairs. I had never seen that number of wheelchairs in my whole life. I wondered, "Has this country got such a large number of cripples? What is the matter here?"

New York was my first US city. I was to meet the people from the Carnegie grant there. My hotel was on 8th Avenue, not far from Central Park. First, I go into the dining room to have dinner. I'm given the menu. I look through the menu and one of the items I see is "half-broiled chicken." I thought, "Well, I don't know what it tastes like when it's half-broiled, but that's what I'm going to have." To my amazement, for the very first time in my whole life, I'm served half of a chicken, in the plate. I couldn't believe that. So it wasn't half-broiled, it was a half-chicken broiled. That was a revelation. I lost my appetite. Just looking at so much food on my plate was too much.

At that time, these chickens that are raised in captivity, in these large feeding coops, must have been fairly new, I'm not sure, because chicken was one of the most inexpensive items of food, of meat. Which was the very opposite of South Africa, where I had just come from, where chicken was the most expensive; that's what you gave your honored guests. You gave them chicken. That was the best. And here it was, now, you could be given half of it: Half of it, on a plate, for one meal. That totally knocked me backward.

Also, the salad came before the meal. I just sat there, with the salad, waiting for the rest of the meal to come. I was going to eat them together; that's what I was used to; or, for that matter, eating the salad towards the end of the meal. I was the only one in the restaurant at that time until the waiter came and whispered, "Sir when are you going to eat your salad?" "Oh, am I supposed to eat it now?"

After dinner, walking back to the hotel, I was shocked to see so many people walking around late, past midnight, so many people. At a news-stand I bought a Sunday *New York Times* and, when back in my room, decided to count the pages—every page! There were over 600 pages! Can you imagine?!

More serious things happened in that hotel. Coming from South Africa, we did not use interior heating, heating that was automatic in the house. We were used to not having that much heat. If it were a good winter day, like today, the sun is shining, you might just go and find a nice corner where you could sit in the sun and read. Going to bed, you had to warm those blankets with your body heat.

I went to bed that night in that hotel and I could not breathe. I tried to sleep. I was choking from how much heat there was. The window, I couldn't open the window, I tried. I started calling the desk, telling them: "I need this window to be opened. It's too warm. I can't sleep. I can't breathe here." I guess they were surprised. They said, "O.K. sir, we'll see what we can do." Then time went on, an hour or so, and I called again, and said: "Look I'm not able to sleep in this room. It's over-heated." When somebody didn't come for quite some time again, I called, I was very angry, and said: "Look, I'm going to sleep in the corridor. Maybe I'll get more air there. But you have to come and open this window." Eventually, somebody came, with a huge crowbar and ranked the window open. When that air came in, it was so good in my lungs.

In L. A., I remember, there was such an overuse of energy. Overheating in winter, over-chilling in summer. You go into a building in summer, in short sleeves, dressed for the heat outside, the extreme hot weather outside. You get into the building. You sit for a half hour or so. You have goose pimples from the cold. There's this attitude that, "There's plenty of energy and we're going to use it. We're not just going to cool a room just to be comfortable."

That first evening in the hotel, I turned on the TV and a report was announced of the findings of the American Medical Association linking cigarette smoking to cancer. Now, it had been known even in England way back in the thirties, but they had suppressed it too. Eventually, England came out with a connection of smoking and lung cancer, many, many years before 1964.

That is not really what surprised me. What surprised me more was that the announcer kept breaking this story of this findings by the American Medical Association with a comment about how much taxes are collected, how much revenue is collected from selling cigarettes. After he said it a few times, I realized that he's saying, "All this money will stop coming into the economy if we stop selling cigarettes." It's an amazing comment about values—to sacrifice human lives to make money for the economy.

I was only in New York for a few days, visiting universities, following the Carnegie itinerary. I did part of that before my family came. The Carnegie Corporation was hosting me in New York. I went to Washington, D.C., then back to New York, then taken to the ship where my family was coming in. I met them and it was a wonderful reunion. The remaining visits to universities were with my family. We went to a university; I think it was in Cincinnati, Ohio, which was run by the Quakers. It was not so much giving a talk as "Here's a family from South Africa. Students gather round." Apartheid, at that time, was on everybody's mind. We were people to converse with to find out whatever we could share about being a Black person in South Africa.

There were sessions like that. Our last city would be Los Angeles, where I had a one semester teaching arrangement offered to me by UCLA. Carnegie funded my sabbatical for a year. The last six months I would teach at the University of California, then return to South Africa.

That is where we had to do a lot, a lot of soul searching about the advisability of going back to South Africa. Again, breaking faith by not going back... with Carnegie, yes; but, also with the University of Cape Town was financing me; I was getting my salary even while I was away. This was very hard to decide: to break faith with my institution, my colleagues. Yet, the UCT itself, though it was partially integrated, was largely still segregated. The integration of universities like Cape Town, Witwatersrand in Johannesburg, was so minimal it was really integration in the classroom—you go to the same classes. Socializing, even institutionalized things like swimming pools, rugby teams, no Blacks. It was all White. Functions, dances, what have you were ALL White.

In a sense, it was: "Do we go back to that situation of apartheid getting worse and worse, just so that the University of Cape Town could be happy we came back?" Or, do we ask: "If it had been you, if you, president of the University of Cape Town were me, a Black person, or oppressed by the government in which you lived because of your color would you go back?"

In addition, at this time, the University of London School of Oriental and African Studies was an option. They had made me an offer to stay in London. They were saying, "We want you…stay here… you can cut off your trip."

My wife and I agonized over this for several weeks. In the span of a semester, we had to decide. My decision was also being influenced by UCLA offering me a permanent job. If I chose not to go back, they were offering me a permanent job. I had to go through quite a bit to have my visa changed. At that time, my wife and I had not been experienced travelers at all; we didn't know about work visas, visitor visas, permanent visas and all that. UCLA knew that if they could prove to the United States Government, I don't know what level, that if they offered me a job, that there wasn't any American in the whole country that had the qualifications that I did, who could take that job. They had to prove that I was so unique, the government should agree to change my visa status.

Being that naïve, we hadn't thought that this would be a problem. We had even thought that maybe I could go back to South Africa alone, leave my wife and children here and see how it is, and then come back. It was as easy as that in our minds, little realizing that this thing involved so many legalities. We struggled with this. One day we're going back. The next day, "No, we can't go back to that." It continued on and on like that until, in the end, we decided not to go back.

I came to know later, after I sent my Letter of Resignation to the University of Cape Town, that there had been some anger in the meeting where my resignation was discussed—something about how I should pay back the money the university had paid me during that time. I understand that even some liberal Whites said, "For goodness sake, would you come back to a situation like this?" They took a very strong stance and I didn't have to pay back that money.

At that time, there were alternatives. One was to ask for an exception to be made for me by the government so my visa status could be changed. Another one, which UCLA was advised legally, that the government did not want to make an exception. "We don't want to create a precedent here. You're going to have to apply for a *special law* that applies to Daniel Kunene and his family. It will be a one-time-law; nobody can refer back to it and say there is a precedent." I should apply to Congress to get a copy of "My Law."

I had several interviews with the Immigration and Naturalization office. My background was being checked, including my political activities in South Africa. First, I'm given a form to take home and fill out. One question was: Have you ever belonged to a political organization? I said, "Yes, I have." Then, "Give the names of all the political organizations that you belonged to." I gave the name of a Federal organization that I belonged to, and a few of the constituent organizations that were a part of this federation.

I'm called in for an interview with an interviewer with a recording machine. He says, "I'm going to record this interview, and everything you say may be used against you in a court of law." My whole defensive mechanism was at its highest.

He starts by asking me: "Have you ever belonged to an organization one of whose aims was to remove the government of South African by force?" I said, "Of course not." These were organizations that wanted a round-table discussion. He then asked questions about organizations that I had written down, then about ones I had not written down, so I knew that a lot of background research had been done about me.

He knew a lot more than what I'd written down. He asked me, "Have you ever belonged to the Society of Young Africa?" "Yes. In fact, I was a founding member." "Did the Society of Young Africa have as one of its intentions to remove the government of South African by force…by violence?" "No." "What were the aims and objectives of the Society of Young Africa?" "The aims and objectives of the Society of Young Africa were the same as the aims and objectives of the Unity Movement, which was a federal organization."

The one question that made me angry, because he would not accept the answer that I gave, was: "What do you think about the government of the United States of America, good or bad?" Just like that. I said, "I cannot give you a simple answer, *good* or *bad*. I'd have to add qualifications to my answer. I can't say 'good' or 'bad' I'd just have to describe what I feel about the government of the United States of America."

Mind you, this is a government which it had become quite clear had been implicated in the assassination of their President. Leaving out all those details, he wanted an absolute "Yes" or "No." I said, "No. I cannot give you that." Then, I stalled on that until he stopped the recorder from running. He looked up at the ceiling, clearly at a loss what to do, then said, "Off the record. What do you think of the government of the United States?" "Just as I said, I cannot give you an unqualified answer. It would have to be a descriptive answer, and good or bad can be worked out of my description of it." "You know, it's really simple," he said. "Well, no, not to me, it's not simple. I have to give an answer that I can stand by."

After the discourse not running for some time, he turned the recorder back on, and repeated the same question: "What do you think about the government of the United States of America, good or bad?" I repeated my answer, and in the ensuing silence I said: "Well, you know, the government of the United States is *not as bad as* the government of South Africa; that's why I'm here." I had to give him a comparison. He accepted that. You don't have a *perfect* government here and you're trying to make me say it *is* a perfect government. It is not.

UCLA offered me a position to teach a South African language. In that year, 1964, when my wife and I were agonizing about going back, when, eventually, my status had changed, my mentor, A.C. Jordan, was here, at the University of Wisconsin, in Madison. He was part of the formation of the Department of African Languages and Literature, which is still there today. Which remains the only such department in the United States.

The trip to Los Angeles was a bit adventurous. We flew from New York to Chicago. When we got to Chicago, we were very cold and hungry. So, we got off the plane to get something to eat and missed our connecting flight. We took a later flight but, by the time we arrived in L.A., the people who were going to meet us had left. We called them and they came right away.

Arriving in Los Angeles, and not long after we got there, we learned that were guests of the university. We were housed first in married student housing. Then, once we were going to stay and not go back, we were looking for permanent accommodation, places to rent. I would talk to someone on the phone about a place they were renting. UCLA had a list of places to call. UCLA also said, "If you feel you are discriminated against in terms of getting or not getting accommodation that is listed with us, you've got to come and report that and we will take that up."

And it happened so many times: On the phone, the place is available, "Yes, you can come tomorrow or whatever day come, we'll meet there and I'll show you around." I get there and the attitude would change completely: "Oh, oh, I didn't know that my husband had already rented it when I was talking with you."

Another such experience. "Children are O.K. You can come. We accept children." I get there and the attitude has changed again. Of course, we realized that in South Africa you wouldn't even go to an apartment building because they were all for Whites—they were in the White areas. And you wouldn't be exposing yourself to this kind of humiliation and embarrassment and rejection. It became obvious to us that we were being denied these places because of our color.

Because you think that apartheid would never be practiced in America, you expose yourself to these situations of being humiliated, of being reminded that color also matters in America. This was a shock. But I was to have an even worse shock when I took one of these cases to UCLA to the Housing Authority, to report what had happened. They said "Alright, we'll get in touch with the person." Which they probably did or didn't, I don't know. When I came back, those in charge of this Housing Authority, all of them White, had changed their attitude: they were not going to be aggressive with this person who had discriminated against me. Until I began to feel "Now I have a complaint against this office." And I took it to the Chancellor at UCLA. The Chancellor was very embarrassed. I think he made some calls to that office to intervene.

A week before Christmas, 1964, Luyanda (Lu) was born at Queen of Angels Hospital in Los Angeles. "Luyanda" is a sentence in Xhosa. It means, "It (the family) is growing." Themba Lu's middle name means "hope." Any ironic connection to our current circumstance was purely accidental.

Two years and a few months later, in 1967, Wandile (Wandi) was born at Good Samaritan Hospital in L.A. "Wandile" is also a Xhosa sentence, "Umzwandile," meaning, "It (the family) has grown." And, "Pule" (Rain), Wandi's middle name, is my middle name as well.

This was 1964. The Civil Rights Movement was on the ascendancy. For one thing, we soon realized, my wife and I, that once they met you, and once they knew you were from outside the United States—we were from South Africa—then you were more embraced by White liberal society, than if you were a Black American. Quite clearly, they didn't feel you were someone in contention with them. African Americans, who were then called Afro-Americans, were automatically considered the people who were in contention with them about jobs and rights, who might look at them with some hatred.

Whereas you come from some place outside of the United States, from Africa—South Africa, Nigeria, wherever—you are no threat. All that I could think of was that I am not a threat. I am not going to fight for Civil Rights here because I don't belong in this country. Not being in a position of someone who might be a Black Panther, who might belong to the Student Nonviolent Coordinating Committee, I was not considered a threat.

There were African Americans, Black Americans, who were in the same position I was, professors and managers, but who were a threat to White America's power—you know, determining rights and privileges, where you may live or you may not. It wasn't said in those terms, like in South Africa. It wasn't like when I was threatened to be thrown out of my house, because there was a law called the Group Areas Act. No Group Areas Act in America; but still there are "Group Areas." In effect, it's basically the same thing. You get people clustered there, and of course, Blacks are usually confined to the worst kind of accommodation, the worst part of a city. One has heard of stories of Whites "fleeing" Harlem as there were more and more Blacks coming in, until Harlem became virtually a Black suburb. This is that "White Flight" that one got to know.

You can have "White Flight" or you can have "Black Expulsion"; it comes to the same thing—expulsion of Blacks by the law, in South Africa, creating these pockets of racial groups, or creation of racial groups by continuous "flight" away from Blacks as they get more and more into the area. To describe what I taught at UCLA, I have to also describe the context, how subjects were departmentalized. I taught an African language and later added some literature in African languages. UCLA, however, did not have a department like the one here in Madison, and still does not. There is still none like the one here in the whole country.

When I first arrived, it was the Near Eastern and African Languages Department—"Near Eastern" being the dominant concern. Then they moved me to Linguistics. So I taught the same courses I had taught under Near Eastern and African Languages, but in the Linguistics Department. There is, of course, *literature* written by Africans in English; *literature* written by Africans in French; *literature* written by Africans in Portuguese, etc., depending on who colonized what part of Africa.

So people absorbed quite a lot of the culture of their colonizers. Some of the people colonized by France ended up in Paris at the Sorbonne—just a few at the top who were being siphoned off to eventually help oppress the masses.

The languages of these occupying countries—colonizers—were acquired to the degree that they became second nature and people wrote in those languages—novels and poetry.

At UCLA, African literature written in African languages is put in the Linguistics Department; literature written in French by French-colonized Blacks in Africa, in the French Department; literature written in English by English-colonized Blacks in Africa, in the English Department. There was no way that we could feel that we were doing things that belonged together; that can be taught in a sense of one body and different specializations—as was done at UW Madison.

Dr. Jordan, when I was teaching at UCLA and he was teaching at UW Madison, tried to have me recruited to Madison so we could reconnect. It would be, basically, like how it was at the University of Cape Town, where, after I finished my studies, we became colleagues. That didn't happen. I was not offered a job in Madison. I was eventually recruited here after Dr. Jordan died.

Dr. Jordan and I had seen each other from time to time, especially at an African Studies Association conference, which is an Anglo conference. And on a few occasions, at least twice, I drove from L.A. to Madison with my family. We spent maybe two nights on the road, sightseeing, having car trouble, all that.

At UCLA the African Studies Center was building a constituency of students having to take African Studies courses. Graduate students were being offered big money to go to Africa and do research; some of them needing to study an African language precisely because they were getting ready to go do their research; hence, it was a requirement that they have an African language as one of their courses.

Then there was a problem about how to admit Black students from downtown Los Angeles, from very, very terrible high schools, where by no stretch of the imagination would they qualify if strict standards were applied. They did not qualify to be there. They were coming from the Watts neighborhood.

UCLA had an admission plan that bypassed the regular admission. They had a program called "High Potential." Students were admitted under this program because they had the "potential." You got some students who shouldn't have been there. They're supposed to be given special tutors and training to try to bring them up. Then, I come to UW and they have the same kind of stuff. They had Black professors in charge of a program designed to bring Black students up to a level where they qualified to be at university.

The same kind of determination of the quality of the student by their economic and social background, their neighborhood, that I experienced at UCLA was here and is still here to this day. So it's very difficult to answer the question about Black students coming to take your courses. For the first time I became aware of students trying to bribe their professor, indirectly. There were students, some from very well-to-do families, White students, having picnics for their professors on the beach.

I was shocked that students had not had the same quality of preparation I had had. Also, they did not have the same motivation. I regard motivation and dedication as saying, in effect, "I'm going to make the best of this bad situation. I know what I want. I must get what I want. To do that, I have to suffer. I have to accept that part of it is a lot of sacrifice; it's a lot of inconvenience." Remember my describing (above) how, when I went to high school, mothers would be walking the street trying to find a family that would take you in because there were no dorms and you were away from home. You were pretty young because this would be Junior High. Whites, meanwhile, who could better afford it, did have their Junior High at home at this little town where I was born and raised.

So, we're punished in a lot of ways, directly and indirectly, and that is what we have to go through to get our education. Now, you get here and not only Black students, but motivation becomes a factor. As if students are saying, "O.K., I'm here. I want a good grade. I want an A." That attitude that says, "Between entering the institution and exiting, these courses are irrelevant. I want an A. There."

After I gave my first lecture, in Literature, on a novel written by A.C. Jordan; translating portions of it from Xhosa into English for purposes of my class. My first lecture. I finished and some students came to the front and I thought they were going to remark on how they enjoyed the lecture or ask questions. They were not doing anything of the sort. Here we were at the very beginning of the semester. I wasn't even used to the semester system because we had a year system in South Africa, a calendar year, an academic year; but here we have this limited space of time.

And the students are here not to say, "Could you explain this or that?" No, they ask me "What kind of exams do I give? What kind of questions?" I was shocked because I saw them skipping this entire space of time, when we're supposed to be going through the material, and thinking of exams at the end of the semester. This for me was quite a revelation. Here they are thinking of exams: not about what they would be learning, or what I would be teaching in the space between.

At that time, it didn't occur to me that there was such a system as "multiple choice," which I became aware of later, and that was another initiation into the American educational system. The person setting the questions, especially in the Humanities, where you're trying to get people into the art of writing, and you're trying to get them to know how to think, just the process of thinking, should proceed as follows. "Here's a problem. Take that problem. Think through it and take whatever number of steps it takes for you to come to a resolution. Or, here's a problem, this is Humanities, all the answers need not be the same, but you have to go through the process of thinking."

But, to me, *multiple-choice* means the person setting the question thinks for you... and has the squares: "Am I right? Am I wrong?" Let's say that there are three possible answers given and you have to choose one that is right. The very fact that these possible answers are juxtaposed, are next to each other, means that there is some kind of *trick*. Each one has a possibility of being right; but which is the most right of them? The person who chooses the two that are not right is given a zero for that multiple-choice question; doesn't get any credit for having recognized that there is some truth in their answer, but that's not the one that I decided on.

Also concerning education is the automatic promotion, the idea that they have to be with their peer group. So I wonder, "What do they come to school for? Why do they sit in a classroom and listen to a teacher? If school is a kind of daycare where their parents shove them off when they go to work in the morning, then let them be there and just have a good time, then bring them to the university for us to cope with that?" That really riled me.

This lack of appreciation of getting educated, of getting your brain enriched, your whole being enriched by knowing today what you didn't know yesterday—just appreciate that, not thinking, "I need a grade." Sometimes students are going to do some little quiz in class, and it's happened in my classes, you get some students who would like to know if they are going to get *credit* for this particular thing. It makes it very difficult to say, "These students are here to learn, they appreciate just having knowledge."

One time a student complained because "the quiz did not include this, so why did they have to learn it?" I said to the student: "Are you sorry that you know that you have that knowledge? Is it a waste of your time? You have that knowledge. You possess that knowledge. Why should you complain that it didn't come into the exam?"

Also, there were students who were clearly trying to bribe me, trying to buy my favor. A colleague of mine, Professor Joseph Applegate, an African American, was teaching African American Literature. We went to lunch and got to talking about this poor quality of students from downtown L. A. I said to him, "You know I really sometimes think one should take that into account when grading them. Give them a higher grade than you think they deserve because it's not their fault that they grew up in those circumstances." And he said, "No. Never." My sort of introduction to the American education system.

I'll never forget that. It gave me the resolve also. Because you're only creating problems for them in the future, when they are expected to *apply* this knowledge—when they're supposed to take a job and they don't know how to add, they don't know how to spell, they don't know how to read. What will be the advantage? It doesn't matter what disadvantages they've had, they've got to learn.

Suddenly, I saw myself, back in my childhood, having gone through those kinds of hurdles and pressed on to overcome them the best way I could. I would not be truthful to that history of my struggle if I were to say: "O.K. You have problems, social problems, economic problems, bad homes, drugs, therefore you get a good grade that you don't deserve."

My problem with programs that try to bridge the gap between what students should have gotten in high school and what is expected of them at university was and still is when they become a permanent part of the institution. Then, you're in danger of the standards going down. Now, you are incorporating a program that doesn't belong to the institution, to the university, which is at a lower level, and you're making it a permanent part of the institution.

We arrived in Los Angeles, at UCLA, in 1964 and left for Madison in 1970. In those years, the mid-'60s, I was shocked by what I saw on the lawns—warm day and students are lying around on the grass, some of them *necking...* really, really getting into very, very compromising positions, kissing and hugging and doing things that belonged to the bedroom and daring anyone to say "Stop." Professors just walked on by. And then I heard afterwards, this was called the *sexual revolution.* It totally amazed me: this *sexual revolution* thing.

My wife and I became aware of how children were never restrained from doing something that was clearly wrong, that must not be done. Later, we were to learn that this is a permissive society: just let them be natural; let them do what they want. Then, later in life, there's no doubt in my mind, in many situations, people who have been brought up like that, who are now young adults, regret that they were never given the guidance of what is right and what is wrong, at a time when it would have done them the most good.

Professor Daniel Kunene at UCLA (1964)

About two years after we arrived here, a Black man by the name of Dead Wyler was driving his wife to hospital, his wife was pregnant and going into labor. Suddenly, police, a patrol car, stops him. He's told to show his license and told he was speeding. Not only that, but suddenly there are about eight other police cars surrounding him. The next thing, he is shot dead by a policeman while he is still in his car. His excuse was: "The car lurched forward, that's why the gun went off." I say to myself, "Why was a gun pointed at him to begin with? If he had been stopped for a driving violation, speeding, why does the policeman leaning into his car have a gun at the ready pointed at him? Ready to shoot?" Obviously, that was a lie.

It was a short step to asking: "My God, suppose that was me driving in that area and I'm stopped by police and they shoot me, kill me?" Wouldn't it be ironic, having left apartheid South Africa to come and be shot for the color that I am, here in America? In Los Angeles? I had the same thought when the so-called Watts Riots were taking place, in 1968. We were living on the West Side, near Westwood Boulevard, an area insulated by the presence of Whites. It was not as if police would come and raid the place—unlike Watts and East Los Angeles, where there's a concentration of Blacks, a concentration of poor, of poverty, where the easiest thing is for police to virtually invade the area.

That takes my mind back to South Africa. In South Africa, we were, by law, segregated in our residence. You were in Western Native Township, you were all Black; you were in Orlando, you were all Black; you were in Soweto , you were all Black; you were in Sophiatown, you were all Black. So police raids were easy for the police. They knew "There are no Whites here."

While the Watts Rebellion was going on, and on reports we heard that Blacks in downtown L.A. were being stopped at random by the police, spread-eagled on the pavement, cars searched, people frisked and just being totally humiliated. We heard that there were even some Black film stars who found themselves in the same situation: "I'm a star!" or "I'm an actor!" "Yea, yea…spread-eagle there."

Another situation that made me feel, "Is it different here than in South Africa?" Look at the marches in the South led by Martin

Luther King. The police would confront people with water hoses and dogs. Those things made me feel very uncomfortable about the South. If I were there, I know I would be always looking over my shoulder.

It is so important to realize that America is as racist as anywhere you might go. So, in America you have the same effects without laws that required those effects.

Also, when we were in L.A., that was when my wife, Selina, discovered that she had breast cancer. Being a nurse, she discovered it on her own. We were visiting a friend in Colorado, in a very small town. While we were there we would drive and there are all these healing springs, just by the roadside. We could get into an enclosed place where there are natural waters, healing waters coming through.

We were in one such pool, dipping our bodies in there. Suddenly, my wife concentrated on a spot on her breast. She got rather alarmed. Indeed, when we did go to the doctor and they did further exams, and a biopsy, they determined that it was in fact malignant cancer. That was very devastating. We had four children at the time, the youngest still in infancy. This was 1966-1967.

Another thing I could not understand was that the doctor would come out to where I was sitting and, in this public place, with everybody around just talking, telling me about my wife's condition. "Surely," I wondered, "this should be between me and the doctor." But he comes out, into this public place, and just talks about my wife's illness. To this day, I still don't understand how and why that should be the case.

By then, we were aware of a healthy style of living. We decided we were not going with conventional treatments. There was a support group, and there were places to get organic food. At that time, there was a medication that could largely be purchased in Mexico called laetrile, which was illegal in the States. We used to have to go to Tijuana, Mexico and be seen by a Mexican doctor who was also practicing there, a natural approach.

Once we were through the crisis, around 1968, and doing these juices and sticking to her diet, she began to live a very, very full life, without any bother from the cancer. Eventually, it came back, around 1992. She passed away in 1993. She had lived with the cancer for about twenty-six years. Most of that time, as long as she did some of the basic things that the natural-cure doctor suggested, we were happy. We traveled.

We traveled to Germany, we traveled to Zambia, spending a year in each place. We traveled to Holland, the Netherlands, and spent a year there. The trip to Zambia was paid for by UCLA for the entire family. Another of those first impressions, I noticed: in Lusaka, mangoes grew everywhere, it seemed, even in the middle of some streets. That may be a way of saying that the natural way of living and eating and natural medications had a very good effect on her.

I got in touch with people in Switzerland. So, we flew from Zambia to Geneva and the World University Service helped us find a place, a chalet. It was a beautiful train ride from Geneva to Interlocken to Bern The owners of the chalet met us there.

We rented a beautiful chalet in the German Alps, in Switzerland. Surrounded by these tall, tall, tall mountains; some peaks would go through above the clouds...incredible. We took a trip to the Schilthorn and rode a funicular and cable car to a slow revolving restaurant. A James Bond movie was filmed there.

A field away from the village we were staying in were Lake Thun and Lake Lucerne; where the two lakes connect is called Interlocken. We attended an Interlocken Festival.

There's been a kind of unplanned pattern of my following in the footsteps of A.C. Jordan: Cape Town, London, UCLA, and Madison, Wisconsin. I did get an invitation after he died, in 1968, to come to the University of Wisconsin. January 20, 1970, Phyliss Jordan wrote us the following letter:

My Dear Selina and Dan,

This was to have been Selina's Christmas greetings but I was late in sending it off. Now, it is a wish for a prosperous 1970. *Pula! Khobso!!* We are very sorry Dan to pressure you about the Wisconsin affair. You will have to bear with us; it is because we want you so very much to say: "Yes". As I said to you over the phone, everybody, other than mfundisi, wants you to come and those in the department are already planning things on the assumption that you will be with them some-time this year.

I may be wrong, but I think there are greater possibilities for academic growth and career-making in African Languages & Literature in a place like Wisconsin, where the department exists as a department in its own right and not tagged on to Anthropology, History, Political Science, Linguistics or whatever as is the case in the other American centers. Here, you can make your department whatever you wish it to be and you are free to put your ideas into practice. This, in fact, was what decided for Joe (A.C.) to come here as against U.C.L.A. and London: You can here, as the popular saying is: "Do your own thing," within *your* department. This, to me, gives one unlimited scope and I think it is an advantage.

Forgetting about the extreme winters in this part of the world, Madison is a very healthy place to live in for those with young children. The schools—judging them by American standards—are good; the environment is good and life is not hectic. There is a lot of cultural activity geared to the University; though, I must say, it is not of the standard of Cape Town. But, for all that, one is not in a desert and other things compensate for lack of cultural life. In New York, this aspect of life is there, but only those who have money can afford it. So, for the most people it is as good as not there.

Mfundisi came back and told all those he spoke to, that you were not at all keen to come here. This is as I told you and I hope you have by now written to him as you said you would. He is a snake and perhaps this is why he is a Mfundisi. And he goes on to say (to his students)—"I do not know why, he should not come here, for the head of his department is not satisfied with him as a linguist? *Nyuye kanye ke lowo nangaleyo yokuthetha* about other professors to his students. And suppose the head of your department had told him this, was this not said in confidence? What right has he to repeat it to anybody and of all people—students? That is he, all over!! A mean, malicious man!!

Selina, seeing you may be coming this way, do you think I should still send the shoes along? They are still as they were when you left them—too small, no one can use them, unfortunately. What is what about the Magubanes? I hope, they are on the way, if not in L.A. already.

Kunguma kuthi, hi!! Keep well, we are well too, surviving the cold winter—the coldest in years.

Love to you both and the children,
Phyl

Daniel and Selina discuss Zambian Art

AT UW-MADISON

We got here, UW-Madison, in July of 1970. Less than a week after we got here, we were woken up by a loud BOOM, which rattled the house. This was around 3 a.m. My first reaction was that this was some sort of sonic boom—if sonic booms were still happening, I didn't know what happened to them—or, whether it was the beginning of the big earthquake that everybody had been talking about. My mind was back in Los Angeles. It was only the day after that, that my neighbor told me: "That was a bomb that exploded in one of the buildings—Sterling Hall."

At that time, the anti-war protest, against the Viet Nam war, was at its peak. That is what I sometime refer to as my ONE BOOM SALUTE on my arrival here. Ironically, for my first class, I was given a room in Sterling Hall to teach in there. I didn't like it. I asked to be transferred. After the first couple of weeks, I was transferred.

On campus, Van Hise Hall, where my department was and still is, the glass panes and doors had boards on them. Even across University Avenue there were buildings that had had their windows blown out.

I was not sorry I had come to Madison at that point. I thought a campus that's lively on social and political issues is where I like to be. I used to think that UCLA was very docile and nothing was happening there, while Berkeley was very active. But at UCLA, nothing; until, one time police came on campus. That was about it. I don't even know why they were there.

A.C. Jordan, my mentor, went to the UW campus during all this upheaval. There was still tear gas in the air that he inhaled. He went to the doctor, and in the process of examining him the doctor found he had lung cancer. Since they knew about my wife's experience, he took some time off work, and came to L.A. to go to the same doctor and try the methods that my wife was using. He stayed with us in Los Angeles for several weeks. Then returned to Madison.

Another thing that I was happy about is there was activity here concerning apartheid in South Africa; concerning the participation of American businesses, which had their subsidiaries in South Africa; about the flow of American capital to South Africa; about investment of pension funds—all of which were very helpful to the apartheid regime in the sense of giving them economic security.

Obviously, American businesses that were operating there were benefitting from the exploitation of Black labor that was taken for granted in South Africa. The people who dug the gold did that under circumstances that no place in the world should ever tolerate. Namely, trade unions were illegal; employers or businesses did not recognize them; they had no power.

Strikes were absolutely illegal. Strikes brought out the army in no time; especially strikes in the mines. You didn't have the bosses, the owners of the mines coming to bargain. Oh, no. Immediately, you had, not only the police but the army coming there to force people to go back to work. There were automatic fines for strikers in the mines, over 1,000 rand for someone who is earning next to nothing.

America, the US, officially, was participating in that exploitation. Some European countries were as well, but not to the same extent. There was a group here that I automatically joined. I had been with one group at UCLA, on that. The dynamics here were: protests against the Viet Nam war and protests against American involvement in the oppression of apartheid in South Africa. These things energized each other. We had marches, made public speeches. For all these reasons, I was not sorry I came to Madison.

Shortly after we got here, we heard reports of an upper-middle-class Black family buying a house in a White area in one of the nearby towns and having their house stoned by a group of Whites at night. Who wants to be subjected to that?

The subjects that I taught here, at first, were mainly languages—Zulu, Xhosa, Sesotho—and some literature. At that time, there was such a concentration on Africa by the United States. I came to learn that this was a part of the "Cold War Strategy," where you had America wanting a foothold, wanting to capture the favors of young people who might become President of Nigeria in a few years' time, President of Congo, and so forth. Especially with Political Science, that's what they did.

Languages were also important for people who were going to go and do research. It turned out that not all languages were as attractive as languages like Swahili. Swahili had always been an appealing language, I'm not sure why. I know Swahili is spoken in a very wide area—Kenya, Tanzania, Uganda—and a wide area across that part of the continent. Yet, it is a Bantu language, like Xhosa, Sesotho, and so on.

But the ones that I just mentioned, people say, "What? Where is it spoken?" So, we didn't really attract many students in those languages. I got to learn that because of the disproportion between the number of faculty and the number of students in the languages, our department was in grave danger of being closed down. It was too expensive. I moved, not necessarily because of that, but also because of numbers, more and more into Literature and Poetry, which I enjoyed tremendously, much more than teaching languages. I got more and more into Literature and Poetry until those were the only subjects that I taught.

In my first year here at UW, 1970, the Dean of Letters and Sciences, was Dean Cleany. Cleany immediately roped me in with a few other Blacks to be in a Steering Committee that was created to help the then-fledgling, first year of Afro-American Studies.

I was on this Steering Committee for one year. That year, the Chair of Afro-American Studies was a meteorologist, Charles Anderson. I would go to meetings as a member of the Steering Committee, and meetings of the department, and there were so many tensions and shouting. It was a place where power was still trying to find its center for the department and where people contested not only positions, but also: "How dare you tell me to do that? I know this is the best way to do that?'" Several people were in a very antagonistic mindset.

When Charles Anderson decided "I've had enough of this," there was no Chair. I was pulled in as "Acting Chair." I had a rough time. I sort of played it so that I did not impose authority that people might rebel against. At the same time, the negative side of that was that there were things that I should have stood up against. One of them was Black Americans, African Americans, those who were now teaching there; there was a lot of recruitment to be done for faculty for that department. They determined and decided that nobody could tell them who was qualified. They were the ones who knew who was qualified to teach. All those things like you've got to have a degree, a PhD, or you've got to have experience. "No, no, no, no. We are the ones who know." And, that way you did get a lot of people who had no business being there to teach. It was more like, "I know Miss So-and-So; she's a fine person. She knows Black History and we're going to have her hired."

The university was going along with this. Looking back, I realize that the university was just giving them a long rope. In the end, that's what was going to hang them—that rope: "We know. And that's that. The Dean's Office said it's all right."

At that time, there was not only the Afro-American Studies Department formed, but also an Afro-American Program. "Program"—a very, very undefined term. It had its own office. The Afro-American Studies Department was housed in the Humanities Building right from the start. This Afro-American Program was housed in a little building on the university near the corner of Park and University. Its Director was Kwame Saulter.

He took the name "Kwame" from Kwame Nkrumah, the first President of Ghana. That was a time when people did all kinds of things to try to project their African origins: men wore dashikis; women braided their hair. He had a sort of whisk made of a horsetail. The sort of thing that Jomo Kenyatta, the first President of Kenya, was known for—always having this flywhisk on a little stick. So Kwame Saulter had one and now and again would flick it—a symbol of authority, perhaps, as if to say:. "We are in now. I'm the Director of this place." What was its function? Very undefined. Any Black person could come there, relax, play cards. There was no definition of what that thing was doing.

We had the Department of African Languages and Literature and the African Studies Program now, whether it was modeled on that I don't know. But functions of these two are very, very clear: the function of Afro-American Studies, was so-so at the beginning. They really had to struggle to give it its own identity, apart from the general university. Less so the Afro-American Program, which was an absolute waste of money. The administration seemed to have decided, "Let's let them disqualify themselves, by doing things that are not going to sustain the department."

The Program itself was very short lived. It didn't go on for long. There were some protests when the administration decided they were going to stop that program. But, again, if there was no substance, there's really nothing to hang on to except to accuse the university of racism by closing this "white elephant" (or should I say "black elephant"?).

"We know who's qualified to teach" also came back to haunt the department. Before you get to the end of the academic year, the Dean is waiting for you to make any suggestions for promotions, such as:what have the people published? They have to face that, because it's a rule. They don't make the rules. They might decide to ignore the rules for a time, but that's going to come back to haunt them; and, that's just what happened. Many of the people who had been recruited like that had to go. They didn't meet the requirements for promotion or even merit increase. I found it difficult, as Chair, to justify that So-and-So deserves a merit increase, because you had nothing to show this is what they did, this is what they're doing in research, or this is what they published. There is nothing that you could show.

One person who stood out was Frieda High, who taught Art and Art History, in the Department of Art and in Afro-American Studies. Frieda earned herself respect. One of her sisters took her class and did not do the work. Frieda failed her. Failed her own sister. Everybody was thinking, 'Whoa, whoa, how do you fail your own sister?' She had done it on principle: "If you don't work hard, if you don't earn a pass, you fail."

I was "dragged" into this position of being Chair of this department. Maybe I corrected the position too far to the other side:

instead of avoiding this contentious relationship with the faculty, I tended to be a little more lax than I should have been. I should have stood against employing people who really were not qualified. It was a time when a phrase like, "To relate" was being used a lot: "You don't relate"—meaning you're out of it, you don't understand.

I tried to bring people together both professionally and socially. If you didn't speak the "lingo," like young people from South Madison, if you spoke a different kind of English, so to say, as I did, as I do still, you didn't' "relate." Some of these people using this language and using it cleverly, were getting applause. They "related." I was really tired of it, but I went on as Acting Chairman for two years, from 1971 to 1973.

Other stellar faculty, in the midst of all this, were Nellie McKay and Richard Ralston.

At the end of my second year as Acting Chair, I said to the Dean "That's it. I'm not going into that again." There was a friend, a White guy, and he was teaching Literature in the department. I used to tell him about these things, and he use to sympathize so much. When it was the very last day of my being Chairman, the next day I was going to be free, he'd invited me to his apartment, and we opened a bottle of champagne at twelve midnight to celebrate my freedom.

The Department of Afro-American Studies, through this period of growth, eventually got to be the respectable department that it is today. When I said earlier that "It had to find its identity," what I meant was: you have a Department of History, in the whole university; you have a Department of English/Literature; you have a Department of Psychology or Sociology, or Art; all kinds of things that were duplicated by having the Afro-American Studies Department—"duplicated" even though Afro-American Studies was concentrating on "Black" History, "Black" Literature, "Black" Psychology, "Black" everything that you could think of.

Their "complaint" which I fully understood and supported, was that in the "regular" departments these subjects are hardly ever taught. If they are, they're just given very slight attention. To major in History will be to study the history of Europe and the history of

America; "Literature" will be *English* Literature. So you did not get the concentration on these subjects that they needed.

For instance, African Americans distinguished themselves even during the days of slavery. But we are the stepchildren. Our subjects there are worse than stepchildren, they are "given a nod" and then we go on with the more serious business. So there was very good reason for Blacks to fight to have a "Black" department, an Afro-American Studies Department. I'm so glad it survived its growing pains and ended up being the department that it is today, with excellent faculty like: Frieda High Tesfagiorgis, Richard Ralston, and Nelly McKay.

As I said, I tended to move out of language teaching into literature and poetry. I was writing poetry myself and for several years I formed groups of students to extra-mural readings of poetry, for those who were interested in poetry. They didn't have to be students in my department or my class. But mostly they were students who were in the Department of African Languages and Literature. Mostly, they were from Africa.

Similar to what I said about teaching African languages, it was "Cold War Strategy." Another "strategy" was to bring in groups of Africans: you suddenly realize that most of the African students, here, are from Ghana. Later, when that group goes out, you suddenly realize that most of the African students are from Nigeria, then Zambia.

My own sense of what that meant is that if diplomatically, or in terms of intelligence, America was concentrating on a given part of the continent of Africa, that's where they would make scholarships or fellowships available for students to come from there. That's the most plausible explanation I can offer.

I formed a group and it got to the point where we met frequently—weekly—at each other's place, such as my house a student's apartment. We had a very good time doing this. The African Studies Program, at that time, started by having an "Africa Day" and we'd be on the program to read poetry and short works. Then, it grew and became an "Africa *Week*," with activities throughout an entire week, and we would be part of that as well. Students were very productive in terms of creating the works that we used.

One of the things that they did, they started this experimentally, they would take several African authors, and take excerpts that would make it appear that these authors were talking to each other and responding to each other. Also, they would take a story written by an African author and create a little skit, a little play based on that story, and act it out.

One time the "Play" was set in Nigeria; and the people were in a bus. This may have been an original Nigerian play. The driver, when an attractive looking girl comes in, wants her to sit next to him, as the other passengers are talking loud, as we do as Africans, conversing, complaining loud to the driver, the driver turning around, "What's going on?"

This is something I found I missed once it stopped happening. It stopped happening largely because we stopped having these *batches* of African students coming. The group was simply called "The African Poetry Group." It was also a wonderful social coming together every week. And it encouraged creativity because these were our poems; you came and you read your own poems.

We decided one evening that we would sit in a circle. We would then create a sentence by the following process: first person starts, then, it goes clockwise, then counter-clockwise; you say a phrase that gives an idea; the next person picks that up and develops it by adding something else; and the next person likewise; and when we finished the first round it was just so great that there was a lot of excitement and yelling over the result. One such result was the sentence "Wait, I have to go to my apartment to get a tape-recorder, I've got to record this." We did things like that. And that was one of the highlights of being in the department.

Another high point for me was that, in my research, my most well-known book, which was used for many, many years and may still be being used was published in 1971. I had already been working on it before I left UCLA. It was titled *Heroic Poetry of the Basotho*, referring to the Basotho people who speak the Sesotho language that I mentioned earlier—my Mother Tongue.

I took poetry that had been previously collected, that was praising warriors, praising warrior kings, praising rulers, poetry that was very ingenious in the use of images from the culture. That book got so many excellent reviews when it first came out. Oxford University Press published it. They had actually asked me if I would do the book. At that time, they had a series they were creating called the *Oxford Library of African Literature* (OLAL). The first two had been written already and they said, "We would love you to contribute to this series." I took that on. I was at UCLA when I started it.

There was a Professor of History from South Africa at UCLA at that time whose work concentrated on the history of the Basotho. As soon as he knew my research plan, he tried to take it over by telling me how to proceed with my research, what to do—a White liberal South African. In fact, what he was trying to get me to do was to research it as a historical document. These praises, what part of the history were they? I immediately realized this man wanted me to do his research for him, so he could write another history book. I said, "No, that's not my intention. My intention is to *analyze* this poetry. I want its features to stand out as poetry, regardless of whether the things it says about kings and warriors are true are not. I don't care. I care about how they're structured. "

He didn't give up. At one time, another White Professor of History, from London University, was visiting and he suggested we go to lunch together and we did. This professor was putting the same pressure on me, and I realized that he had been set up to do that. Again, I said, "No, no, no. You cannot tell me how to proceed with my research. That's not what I'm doing. I 'm not doing history. I'm doing literature." He wasn't too fond of me after that. But precisely because of the fact that I concentrate on the structure of the poetry, the imagery, the linguistic and stylistic parts of the poetry, it really made it into a classical piece.

Oxford stopped publishing it in 1983, and then one of my alma maters, the University of South Africa, bought the rights from Oxford. They produced it in soft cover for the use of students of UNISA. I met people in Lesotho years later who, when they heard my name, asked me, "Are you the author of *Heroic Poetry of the Basotho?* " and when I said "Yes," they would respond with "You know, that book at UNISA it is our bible. It is our bible." I really felt happy about those reactions. Which would not have been the case if I had yielded to the pressure from my liberal White South African historian.

This is, undoubtedly, the book that made my reputation. Years later, I would meet somebody from South Africa who'd say to me: "I'm at last meeting the author of this book, *Heroic Poetry of the Basotho*." It happened many times. I have, of course, written other books since this one, so I can't say that it played a particularly significant role in my obtaining tenure.

At UCLA, at the time of my recruitment, I was Assistant Professor. UW recruited me as Associate Professor. So I was recruited to a position with tenure. That's when UCLA did a counter-offer. But I said, "You don't have a department here that is comparable to that one, where all these subjects are taught in the same department.' I said, "If you are considering establishing such a department I would certainly consider not going to Wisconsin." Well, they just shook their heads and said, "No, that's not in the cards."

Shortly after I got here, I visited Harvard University to discuss some of my work. I sent the manuscript to Professor Albert Lord, a very well-known scholar of traditional poetry—not African, but traditional European. I spent a weekend there and we had wonderful discussions and he was very supportive of my work. The book did help me move toward full professor.

One of the things I'd like to emphasize has to do with the subject of African Literature in Translation. That, perhaps more than any other thing, kind of challenged me to challenge the students to suspend their judgments, to know that they were going outside of the American culture; because most of them were American, and most of them were White. I tended to fear this notion that everything American is the best, everything that's not American needs to bring itself "up to scratch," needs to become "American."

That is an unfortunate state of mind. And not only in my African Literature in Translation courses, but also in the others, like Poetry, I had this challenge all the time: Can you suspend your American thinking and American self-centeredness that might say: "The world has to look like us"—which is not only demeaning to other cultures but also dangerous, "dangerous" because how long will it be before you move on to "If the world, on its own, voluntarily, determines to be like us, maybe we'll help them along." We'll do an Iraq.

The subject of African Literature in Translation gave me that sense of challenge: "How do I make students not to giggle at some of the cultural norms and behaviors of other people?" So, I decided to add a dimension of the class that I called "Cultural Partners." Each student was to find a student, didn't have to be in Literature, didn't' have to be in African Literature, just had to be somebody who was not American; who was clearly from a culture preferably from somewhere in Africa; even more preferably from South Africa, if they could. Here was a body of literature, written by the Zulu, the Xhosa, the Basotho, all concentrated in this part of the continent, all having shared the inconveniences and evils of colonialism. Colonialism, in a place like South Africa, had become transformed into "settlerism."

I wanted an American student to find an African student, South African even better; if not, if you can't find anybody from Africa, by all means go anywhere else: India, China, wherever it's not America, and get a student. Tell them that you're taking this class and that I have assigned you a task, which is part of the class: the two of you are to meet at least once a week, more if possible, and exchange your experiences about your cultures. But I want you, as an American student, to learn more about the other person's culture. European culture, American culture, most of us are simply forced by circumstances to know it. As an American student, I don't expect that you will teach your "partner" about America; rather, I want your partner to share with you what he or she knows about his or her culture.

I thought this would help students get past some of their cultural barriers and prejudices. I used to make a joke, thinking of some kind of transgender partnership: "If a marriage comes along, don't forget to invite me." Many students took it seriously. I would sometimes have them invite their cultural partners if they were free during our class time to come to the class. Then, I started having this meeting, on the 19th floor, for poetry, what I called a "Reading Festival." I would take my class to this beautiful lounge on the 19th floor of Van Hise, you can see all around, and say, "Today, you're going to share what you've written, doesn't matter what. Or, what somebody else has written that you like."

I began to take my translation class there too, twice a semester. They would have to bring their "cultural partners." Their "cultural partners" were going to share, now, not only with them, but also with the entire class. It was fantastic. I liked it very much. It's something that, at one time, I thought I might propose to the university to take in some modified form and try to see if it could be applied at least to the Humanities and the Social Sciences, but especially the Humanities, and see if they might be able to put a dent in some of these cultural walls that are really keeping people apart.

I did want them to look at other cultures as if they had a *right* to exist, since they had "evolved" just as much as American and European cultures. When I held these meetings on the 19th floor, I said "Let your 'cultural partners' bring a dish from their culture, to share with the entire class." So we would have a wonderful *potluck* thing as well as reading excerpts from translations and poetry. It was such a beautiful thing. I would have some music in the background, CDs from South Africa.

One time I had this meeting, with food to share. One student from Italy said, "I love cooking, and I love cooking for crowds. I will bring food for the entire class. I'll cook it at home and I'll bring it here." And, by golly, she did. She had to come by cab, she told me, to bring all the food; and she had this *spread* and actually gave this "mini-lecture" on where each item came from, from what part of Italy. It was just beautiful.

Of course, there will always be students who will try the easy way out, who think maybe something like "a 'cultural partner' you've got to meet once a week, oh, well I'll just take my time, I'll find somebody; maybe they'll write something for me to read to the class to say who they are." There were people who did that. But most of the students took it seriously and found partners.

In poetry, as well as in fiction, short stories, and plays, African writers mostly found that their political status—being under colonial rule—automatically meant oppression and exploitation, because the colonialists would find some natural products like diamonds and gold in South Africa; or soil that was good for planting coffee; and they would simply undermine the local agricultural culture and devastate the soil as long as it produced their cash crops.

All those were things that people wrote poetry about. They wrote poetry about their struggle and efforts to get out from under colonial rule. But definitely, the whole continent of Africa had, basically, the same experience. And poetry that addressed itself to colonialism and its effects was very common. Black poets had to deal with racism, racism all over the world. You could go to any part of the world and find poets like Claude McKay (author of "If We Must Die"), like Oswald Mtshali and Don Mahera in South Africa, or like myself.

We imposed it on ourselves, maybe helped by the pressure that we felt from our colleagues and our fellow sufferers to write poetry, short stories, and plays that addressed the issues, life issues of the day; to the point that you found that you did ask yourself: "To what extent could I make this to be another stone that we throw at the oppressor?" In many cases it compromised the quality of the writing. The intent, the situation that you're writing about mostly took over more than fifty percent of the process of writing. Writing of that kind did not come out as the best *art*; it came out as works that were part of the struggle for liberation.

Social segregation, poverty, people living in sub-human conditions were problems that people had to deal with. In all of this, the Blacks were carrying the burden of oppression and exploitation and being degraded into sub-humans. And so they wrote—those who did write, those who could write—as they were inspired to write about these things.

There were White people, White liberals, whose humanity brought them over to be very sympathetic with the struggle; to be more than sympathetic with some of them; and some of them, difficult though it was, to be empathetic. Even more so, some of them went to the point of getting actually involved in the struggle, risking a lot. They were few. Not in the sense of "Hey, I'm a White person, I know best how the struggle should go" but in the sense that "I'm joining this and I'm going to follow the leader of this movement. I submit myself to this movement and its goals."

The majority of sympathizers, as writers, also had something in their writing that addressed these issues. They did not address it as directly as the Blacks did. The Blacks had to cope with things like, "Here, our comrade has been shot dead by the police [or] has been murdered in prison by police. Here, at his funeral we're going to read our poetry that defies our enemy."

Poetry was given back to the *oral performance*. You had a crowd there. You had to proclaim your poem to the crowd. So, oral performances of poetry became a major part of the poetry of struggle. People who really did it right and combined poetry and music and dance attracted huge crowds. When people were reading on street corners in the Black Townships, whoever wanted to stop could listen. A very *military* style dance was developed by the youth that they called "Toyi-Toyi," where they *high-stepped* and chanted at the same time.

All that is *art*—art that is shaped a great deal by political, social, and economic pressures such as segregation, invasion of your privacy, pass-raids for the Pass Book, police brutality, the police actually bringing their brutality lower and lower by age until now they were brutalizing children and thus, politicizing the children. All this was being expressed by a kind of military, but also artistic performances.

Since the poetry we were studying was so issue oriented, was so much a part of the people's struggle for human rights, for a better life, then, I would say to the class: "Let's find out how many of you have had issues to face that might have led, if you were a poet, to writing poetry similar to this? Poetry that would help to carry your struggle forward."

Women? "Yes, of course. We have gender issues. We're fighting for women's rights." Of course, Africans, as a people: "We are fighting against colonialism, segregation, racism, and sexism the world over."

Then, White males: "Nothing has ever really bothered me. I just never had to bother about anything." Now, the first time I heard this, it took me off-guard; I wasn't sure how to react to it. But then suddenly, I knew how to react: "O.K. maybe you were sealed off from these irritants of poverty and racial prejudice and profiling, you never had to face them. But, since these things were happening all around you, did you ever observe other people having to cope with these conditions? Did you ever observe that? Did it ever make you think, 'Why should other people live like this?'" Most of them would say, "No. It's never occurred to us."

It was upsetting. It was also a revelation. That there could be people around whom there's squalor, there's hunger, there's violence, lynching, people dragged behind trucks until their heads were severed from their bodies, police beating somebody—eight of them or twelve of them around one Black man on the ground. They're not aware of these things?" There's something wrong there. I can understand if they themselves, personally, have not ever had to cope with adversity of this kind. But I cannot understand how these things could be happening around them and they're totally unaware.

It reminded me also how South African Whites, who were either indifferent to what was happening to Blacks or supported it, suddenly found themselves criticized by an American intellectual—by an American, maybe a graduate student who gives a talk; after being in South Africa, studying the situation, going to Soweto and other Townships, and virtually knowing more about where the Blacks live and how they live than their madams and bosses; who are happy just to see them show up in the morning and then leave in the afternoon or evening. They didn't care where they went, as long as they showed up again the next morning.

They would then claim, "We live here. You can't tell us about conditions here." And, the retort would be, "Do you know where Soweto is? You, who live here in South Africa as a White person, can you point to where Soweto is? Can you tell me about it?" Then, they wouldn't know what to say. This was triggered by the fact that people who are very comfortable and imagine that they are not affected by what is affecting lots and lots of their fellow citizens, never ceases to amaze me. This sense of security from such isolation is such a false sense of security. There are many things that are happening to the people who are suffering these terrible conditions which can and sometimes do have an effect, and sometimes a great one, on the very people who have been ignoring it or do not even know it's there. You can have an epidemic that starts from a condition of squalor. There are things that always blow through the borders that you thought were protecting you.

I have both enjoyed teaching American students and been frustrated by their shallowness. Some, very few, sad to say, did show that they came there to learn, to receive what you had to give, to share, to talk about it, to get as deeply into the subject as possible; who showed great interest in their intellectual development through your teaching. Of course, they also wanted good grades and, mostly, those are the ones who did get good grades.

But there were too many, I'm afraid, who for some reason had a sense that they came to this institution just to get a good grade. "Good grade?" "Sure. You can get a good grade, but you have to earn it. Nobody can get it for you. You've got to get it for yourself. Don't ever think of me, your professor, as someone who doles out grades, who looks at you and says, 'Oh, this guy he's ugly. He'll get a D.' or ' Oh, this pretty girl, here's an A for her." or 'So-and-so did me a favor'." I'm not doling out grades. You earn them.

Every beginning of the semester, after explaining the syllabus, I would say, "Now here's my grading system. At the top of it is an A at the bottom is an F, and everything in between those; and you can get any one of those. You can get an A. You can get a F. And don't think I'm kidding when I say you can get an F. If you deserve an F, you're going to get it. If you deserve an A, well of course you're going to get that too."

Just about every time I'd start the semester, very good students are happy, we're on good terms. When I grade my first quiz, we begin to have this friction that is brought to education by something called a *grade*. Some students don't care if they learn something or not. Give them a good grade and "Ah, that's it." And maybe they'll go have a beer that weekend to celebrate. But that's all they're concerned with. One hears of students who "graduate" and then can't even read the menu at McDonald's.

I wasn't going to be a party to that. I did fail students who needed to fail. Students in class did accost me. One time, giving out papers with grades, this female student went out of control and shouted and screamed at me because she had received an F. I got those kinds of reactions. It's people like that who made it difficult to continue to believe that people who come and sit in front of me at the beginning of the semester are there for the right reason, the right reason being to get an *education*; to leave that class at the end of the semester knowing more about South African poetry and *why* it was the way it was; knowing more about the literatures from *colonized* countries, and knowing *why* they were the way they were.

Setting aside the mental framework of America for a moment, let us go to Africa. Let's go to South Africa. Follow me. Let's go together; through this story, through this novel that I have translated. Few did, but those who did, got a sense of comfort that there could still be students like that.

Trying still to make students involved in the subject, I would say, "Look, after I teach a segment of the poetry or literature in translation, I'd like each one of you to write a list of what I will call 'talking points.' If you were learning what I have taught so far and you were to talk to somebody about what you've learned, this would be a good point to talk around: Maybe the poetry? Why is there so much poetry that sounds like military poetry, with images of war— even though they're not about war? Good point to talk about, these images of war praising a teacher, a lawyer, a doctor. Why? What war is he involved in? What war has he been involved in? "

I would ask them to formulate points like that. Just give a subject. That way I would know whether they were thinking critically and that they were, sort of, crystallizing ideas in their minds.

It was not easy during this time, the 1980s, to maintain communication and connection with former colleagues in South Africa. The struggle had also defined the term *boycott*. "Boycott South Africa!" Boycott it at all levels. It took a "racist coloring," which was unfortunate. With the boycott of South African intellectuals, for example, they were not to show their faces on our campuses. Students would go into big protests. The good suffered just as much as the bad. Now we were, as apartheid had taught us so well, judging people by their color. White is bad: Black is good. Very dangerous: Very dangerous.

I know, for example, some of my colleagues, White colleagues whom I've met since the '90s, when surface apartheid was gone, whom I had refused to see when they were here visiting: people who admired my work. It was what I had to do at that time. Also, invitations that I declined to go and give talks in South Africa during apartheid, that was the price we had to pay as well.

When I visited South Africa, I always say the 1993 visit with my late wife, Selina, was the *actual* "Return." I had returned briefly in 1991, when then "citizen" Mandela, later President Mandela, who had been released from prison in 1990, had asked that all writers in exile, Black writers especially, should be invited home for a conference, to come and present at a conference at the University of Witwatersrand.

I remember traveling with Lewis Nkosi; we just happened to meet in Frankfurt, and we were on the same flight to South Africa. As we flew overnight from Frankfurt to Johannesburg, and we got there, morning, maybe around about 10:00 or 11:00 a.m., a beautiful day. I remember Lewis Nkosi looking outside and looking at me and saying: "Do you feel anything?" I said, "Well, no." I knew the meaning of his question. You feel as if you *have to* feel something. This is a moment. You feel like Pope John Paul, that you've got to kneel down and kiss the ground. "No." But there we were. We were back home after many years of being away.

The occasion of black people voting for the first time in the history of their country is an extremely important event. As I saw people going around advising the voters—particularly the elderly people—it just seemed to me that this was a wonderful thing. I would say that while we won the battle, we may have lost the war. So much of the victory was lost. So much was given away in trying to accommodate the other side—the conservative white element.

The danger lies precisely in this euphoria—the raised expectations. I shudder when Mandela, in campaigning, says, "We are going to give you houses and jobs." I know every leader who seeks power makes promises during the campaign and then backs away from them after the election—we have a recent example of that in Clinton. But in South Africa it is more dangerous. In South Africa, people are expecting a revolution.

There is in Mandela an element of almost the messiah who came to lead his people to freedom. The people, by the sheer weight of

At UW-Madison

their numbers, are going to bring about change. I think it will happen in spite of the political leaders.

But the real "Return" for me was 1993. On our way to South Africa in '93 with my wife, we got to Heathrow, in London. As we walked into this area to wait for our flight, I started hearing clear, clear Afrikaans accent of speech. They were speaking English but with a very clear Afrikaans accent. That made me cringe. I can't pretend that I like hearing this accent. It reminds me too much of the Boers, the Afrikaners, and the cruelty of many of them. Again, here, one tends to generalize; there were good people who were Afrikaners. There were some like Reverend Abraham Fisher, a lawyer who disguised himself in order not to be incarcerated, sufficiently that he lived in South Africa and the government didn't know it was the same Abraham Fisher. Until, as almost always happens, somebody betrayed him, and he was arrested.

Just as not every White South African was a supporter of apartheid or had prejudices against Blacks, not everyone.... Even so, we had it drilled into us that "the Boers, the Afrikaners they are really the cruel ones. The English are much better." That was my reaction when we got there to wait for the plane to South Africa, hearing that accent.

The Boycott of South Africa extended to boycotting South African intellectuals. Students here would just rally. There was a time when a White South African happened to visit the Geography Department. He was warned by university security that they could not insure his safety. He was cloistered there and had to leave without having given the talks he had come to give.

Students at Guttenberg University in Meinz, Germany, when I arrived there to spend a year at the university teaching and doing research, I walked right into a demonstration by student activists, opposed to the university's hosting a conference of the World Archeological Congress that had been kicked out by protesters in South Hampton, England. Seeking another venue, it turned out that they were invited by the city of Meinz as their guest, including the university, because that's where they were going to meet.

When my wife and I first got there in 1986, one of my White colleagues in Germany had invited us and driven us to show us part of the country where they made wines and so forth. At the same time, he was saying things that, at that time, having just got there, I didn't understand, that they were trying to nudge me in a certain political direction. I could not resist when the students realized "Here is a South African who is an activist, doing this kind of work at his university. We want him to be part of our struggle here, our boycott." The reason this group, the Theological Congress, was kicked out of South Hampton, was that it had one or two South African scholars. That was the reason.

When the students approached me and told me what was happening, that the city of Meinz had accepted these people who had been kicked out of South Hampton, with the university supporting that, I did join the students. I wrote a position paper that was published in the World Archeological Congress' Bulletin.

To one of my hosts in particular, apparently, I had become not a very good guest. He didn't do anything negative, but I do recall a comment made by his wife one time at a New Year's Eve party in a little suburb outside of Meinz. Suddenly, during a lull in the conversation, she said: "You know, my husband is a racist."

I thought "Whoa." This goes to the fact that the students found themselves in opposition to him. I wasn't' going to be with him in that regard. So, this was meant for my ears, that her husband had been defined as a racist, and I'm on the side of the people accusing him of being a racist. Well, I survived that; but that told me what the situation was.

Between that period in 1964 at UCLA to the announcement of my retirement from UW in 2003, I knew that in order not to fail everybody in the class, or in order not to fail ninety percent, fearing that my classes would die because nobody would enroll in them anymore, I had been compromising my standards. Compromising and compromising until, most recently, I found myself using a new word, maybe a technical term in literature. Simple terms like metaphor, alliteration, rhythm, to say nothing of oxymoron. I would find myself pausing to ask, "Does everybody know this word? How many of you know what this word means?" Maybe a few hands go up. "Now, how many of you don't know this word?" Everybody looks around grinning. Nobody raises a hand. Then I say, "How many of you want to take the Fifth?" More giggles.

There we are. I should be lecturing. I should be assuming that these people have vocabulary of this level, knowledge of technical terms at this level, so that I don't have to stop and ask "Is there anyone who doesn't know this word?" Most recently, before I retired, I heard some students complaining that I called them "high school material." And I can't say "No." Sometimes I have. Sometimes I feel that I'm teaching high school here. They didn't like that, but that was the point that I had arrived at.

I've had colleagues, for instance in the German Department, one of them an Italian, who had retired before me. He said, "Hey, Daniel. The students here are such low quality. They're just so incredibly under par, under-prepared, that I can't go on anymore. I'm just leaving." This was some years before I left. I was already feeling that way myself.

There is no doubt that there were students who made me feel rewarded for my efforts by their attitude, their study, their seriousness, and the quality of their work. But the majority were like this woman who screamed at me because she got an F on her quiz. One time there was a class incident that I felt was threatening. I had to write to the Dean of Students. One thing I would absolutely criticize the Administration of UW for is the extent to which they are nervous about getting the students to be responsible for their good manners, good behavior, respect. It's a subject that has bothered me.

We once had a visiting Professor from Nigeria who came with the idea of the dignity of the professor. The professor teaches. Students come to see him in his office if they want to, but not to demand "Why didn't I get an A?" He wasn't used to that. His reactions to these things were such that these students became very unruly, even in class. It ended up with some students calling him names along the corridors; one of them having the audacity even to write him a note that called him an "asshole." This is a student communicating with a visiting professor who's here to teach him; who deserves respect; whom the student has the audacity not even to say it orally so he could deny having said it. He wrote it: "You're an asshole."

The university is really nervous about bringing the students to account for their misdeeds. The university is nervous about being named in the newspapers. A student complains; immediately the sympathy is with the student. "O.K., what did the university do to him?" The university is very nervous about that.

I remember, again, I used to have these Reading Festivals in connection with my Poetry Class, on the 19th floor of Van Hise. One time, I was having this and I would have the names alphabetically. We had things like music. I'd have somebody from the Video Center to come and do some videos of what we were doing.

Then, having arranged names alphabetically, as I went through, it was clear that day I wasn't going to finish, that not every student was going to get a chance. Sometimes, they could read next class in the "regular" classroom to finish the list. When I was in the C's or D's, then there was this girl student who was in the W's, just got up and said, "I'm going to read next. I'm going to read. I must read my poem." I said, "Alright. O.K. Come along. If it's burning you so much inside, come on. Come and read it."

She introduced her poem by telling a very sad little, actually disturbing story. That she had been at a party. She walked away from the party back to her dorm in Elizabeth Waters Hall, walking with a young man, a student also. They were chatting away and got to know where each other's dorm was. Apparently, it was supposedly just a friendly chat. They separated. It was a very warm night. She got into her room, turned on the radio, stripped and lay on her bed. After a while, suddenly, she heard the radio blaring like heck, the volume going so high. She looked. And there's that young man who had walked with her. And he comes to attack her. With the radio blaring so loud, her screams are going to be swallowed; nobody is going to hear.

She tells about the struggle that she put up to ward him off. She tells about how she gave up...and he raped her. Then, she wrote this poem. She said, "I had to write this poem." And, it was so touching, so moving. She said in her remarks that the rape had happened almost two years before and the university was refusing to do anything about it. She reported it and they were always beating about the bush. And that student was still here, still on campus after she had reported it. The university didn't do anything about it.

I know it's hard for the image of the university to say, "Well, you know, girl students are sometimes raped there." If that is the case, you need to stop it by exposing the people who do it and letting them know that they will always be exposed; there will always be consequences for that kind of behavior.

She read the poem very full of energy, very full of emotion and passion. Other students were in tears. Afterwards, I talked with her. I said, "You know, you must have this poem published. In the student paper here, let it be known. With your introduction about what happened." She did soon have it published by the *Badger Herald* and so the story got known.

This is both about what I taught and about how, sometimes, it brought out the most unexpected reactions from my students. It depended on what kind of students you were dealing with. Some students were just there like a millstone dragging everybody down and being happy to do so. But there were times when I would give them a topic, perhaps a current topic. One such topic was "Clarence Thomas and Anita Hill" and the controversy about his Supreme Court nomination. It had issues of gender and race about it. I would say, "Try to write on that. You don't have to if you can't and are prepared to write about something else, but that would be the general topic."

I did not have many American students of color, specifically Black students, taking my courses. In fact, that was one of the surprising things. Partly, it might reflect the percentage of Black students on campus, who perhaps were so few that they were spread out thin, taking Psychology, or Sociology, or what have you. But in spite of that, I would have expected a higher percentage of African American students than I was getting. Black students that I got mostly were from Africa—Ethiopia, Kenya, Ghana, and so forth.

It is good to remember that the Afro-American Studies Department was established at the demand of Black activist students. It wasn't a long time before the majority of the students were White, and you didn't see many Black students. What's wrong with this picture? Well, there's certainly nothing wrong with White students taking a course in Afro-American Studies, but these are the places you would expect Black students to be even though they are so few.

There has to be a reason for this. I cannot begin to second-guess them, how they were thinking, what it was they had in mind. One thing I do know: if my reputation for being strict with my grading went around, that might have been a factor. But I really don't know. I don't want to put words in their mouths.

How education is valued is a subject that touches me so deeply that I guess I could just keep talking and talking about it. From the time that we arrived in this country, at UCLA, and the student after the first lecture wanted to know about the exam questions, I want to add a little bit to that.

We went out on a rented fishing boat, a peer group, more-or-less, and older students doing graduate studies, some of them having already graduated. We went a little way out where we dropped our fishing gear. We had a long, very unfruitful, or shall I say "unfish-ful" day. It was hot. We caught a few, but not enough to even share among ourselves. One of the young men who had recently graduated from UCLA with a PhD was married to a young woman from Beverly Hills, apparently from quite a wealthy family. He told us how his in-laws talked down his achievements, telling him: "You've graduated from the university, but you have not *made it*." "Made it" to me, having just come from South Africa, would have included earning your degree. If you've earned a degree, never mind whether you've got a big job from that and earning lots of money or not. Simply, by virtue of reaching those heights of education, you had "made it."

I had to come to terms with what "made it" might mean. The only conclusion, and indeed I was right, "He has not made it" means he has not got into a position that pays big money. I don't deny that, ultimately, getting a good job that gives you a decent living is one of the reasons young people come to university. But the other side, too often, the thinking is that "the education that is being offered here is worth nothing if it doesn't make me rich." The content of these courses from the beginning of the semester until the end of the semester is not important. "I need to have a grade. I need to have a degree." By skipping the content between Registration and Exams, they are saying, in effect, "Give us good grades, that's all we want."

It can't be overstated that education that results only in letters after your name, that have no substance in themselves, is not education. That whole attitude is underlined by the fact that there are diploma factories, where they say, "Send us so much money and we'll send you any diploma for any degree you want." That is really very cynical, but that is what it has come to.

I've got to say a final word about the administrators and administrations of these institutions of higher education; that they're doing no favor to the youth, the country, the population, and ultimately everybody by emphasizing how many people graduate, without emphasizing the content and saying, "The people who have graduated here can hold their own with any scholar from anywhere in the world." That was one of the foremost things about Oxford University Press in Oxford, England. A scholar from Oxford has bedrock knowledge.

Administrations here should begin to give a lot of attention to high schools, and question high schools: "Why do you pass to us material that is really not fit to come to us? What are we supposed to do? Are we supposed to be always creating stopgap, supplementary, complementary programs to make the students even worth getting into our institutions? That's your job. You at the high school, that's your job." The admission standards should be set at a level where they would really sift and winnow these students. Don't be afraid. You're not supposed to accept students simply because they've reached a certain age, because they have been automatically promoted at high school. No. That is so totally unacceptable.

I wouldn't say that I regret coming to teach in the United States, but it's far more complicated than that. I didn't come here *only* because there was a teaching job at UCLA. I came for a whole variety of reasons. I couldn't disentangle having got a job at UCLA and UW from the rest of my tangled life. If I separated the education by itself, I wouldn't use the word "regret." I reached my retirement age and surpassed it by many, many years.

It's so complicated. I also enjoy teaching. I do enjoy teaching. I enjoy having a student who receives and gives back to me also, where I know I have made a mark. I resent students who are there to waste my time, to annoy me, and who shouldn't be there; who, some of them, as time went on, and they were getting dumber and dumber, some of them coming to the university still pulling the pranks of high school kids. I can't say "regret" because that would disqualify a lot of things.

About The SOWETO Poem

Another event in South Africa that really hit home to me, to my wife, and to the student group here was the police shooting of school children who were in a peaceful march to go and meet at the Orlando Stadium in Johannesburg and discuss problems that the government's educational policy had created for them. Of course, in South Africa under apartheid, while your day-to-day life's problems were created by the politics of apartheid, once you protested that, you were accused of *bringing* politics into this whole arena. But it is not the case that they had brought in the politics and that you're reacting to that, but that *you* were bringing politics into whatever it is—in this case education.

In 1963, a new educational system was introduced by the then fairly new apartheid government (which came to power in 1948) and they lost no time in making huge, huge changes. One of them had to do with "Education for Blacks." When a division in Parliament was created, "The Bantu Education System" was introduced as a bill and discussed. The basis of "Bantu Education" was that a Black child (I'll use "Bantu" here because that is the term that they used)—a Bantu child—"was raised by a Bantu mother, on the knee of his Bantu father, etc. etc." And the "education" that then existed, during the period of segregation (segregation was its own kind of apartheid but was not as stringent nor as clearly defined as apartheid), differed only in that apartheid just created those absolute margins, boundaries—where you may live, where you may go to school, what kind of education you may receive, and so on.

The apartheid government decided that we were going to define things very, very clearly. One of the things is this government that we just replaced—which was White, liberal—made Black students study from the same syllabus as White students and that was unfair to the Black Students, because (to use the metaphor that was used by Dr. Verwoerd at that time) "Blacks must not be made to expect that they were going to graze in the same green pastures as the White people."

That metaphor, "green pastures" may have made the education that was being given seem much more liberal, but, I must repeat, you could say again, "O.K. there's the syllabus. It's no different from the White school children's." You're still dealing with people who live in so starkly different worlds. We're talking about schools, for example, that have no libraries; about schools whose teachers had not the training equivalent to that of White teachers; where the school itself was not inspiring; where the families could not, just by being parents, be an inspiration by having around them books; by having around them images and symbols of success they could aspire to—photos of university graduates, framed graduation degrees, photo albums of college life, anything challenging, anything saying: "You should be aiming at such-and-such goals."

No. Our parents, on the contrary, encouraged us by sheer pushing and sacrificing and saying, "Whatever it takes you're going to get that education." Even during the more "liberal" time, even though the syllabus was the same, eventually, you were never going to get students who are qualified to go into White-dominated universities. They wouldn't have the qualifications.

The government then said that Black students cannot expect to be trained to go and "graze in the same green pastures" as the Whites. They said, in so many words, that Black children should be taught the dignity of labor. We're talking about people who are laboring every day for every single one of those Whites. *They* were the ones who were supposed to learn the "dignity of labor"? Because they hadn't a damn clue what "labor" really meant? Now, suddenly, they have an item in the Black syllabus that says: "manual work."

There were *farm schools* for Blacks. Every White farmer had several Black people working for him. Most of the time, Black students from these areas walked many miles to come to school in the Location, the Black Township, and walked back home after that—and were still to be available if the White Boers wanted them for some chore or other. They carried their bit food in billycans. Now, that was something that was so discouraging to the students.

Under Bantu Education, "manual labor" came to be so abused by White farmers, who would come to a school and say to the teacher: "I have a fence to be fixed; I have some weeding to be done; I have some ploughing," whatever is done on a farm, "and I need your class: or, maybe your whole school"—because they were small schools—"they need to go there. It's a part of your syllabus, 'manual labor'." That was how abused the system was. Apart from the fact that it already, in itself, was a total degradation of the meaning of education: doing work for a White farmer.

In a 1964 CBS videotape; Walter Cronkite was talking about South African stories. One of the topics was about education and about manual labor. It was so pathetic. So insulting, really, to see a little tub (this is in a classroom, mind you) with a washing board, with pieces of clothing—shirts, blouses, whatever. The teacher, a woman usually, was supposed to teach the class how you wash a piece of cloth with your hands: "You put it like this. Then you put some soap and then you do like this…now you come and show me."

That was just incredible. Incredible. But I think this abuse by the White farmers at the school was one of the worst features of it. They cut down on the use of English. They were saying that Afrikaans was not getting its fair share of time in the Black schools. So they had to cut down on how much English not only can be taught but also can be used as a medium of instruction.

Also, at that time, Black teachers, most of whom did not know Afrikaans, did not have to know Afrikaans, now were required by a certain amount of time—a year, six months, whatever amount of time—that they should be proficient in Afrikaans to keep their jobs. Classes were held during school holidays and teachers had to go there and learn Afrikaans.

That's what they called the fifty-fifty rule. As medium of instruction, subjects that were not taught in the mother tongue of the students, and were usually taught in English, now had to be split in two halves—one half to be taught in Afrikaans, the other half to be taught in English.

You see, from this, just how much politics had been introduced into just this area of people's lives—the schools, the teachers. How much politics had been brought in to interfere with and redefine and totally debase the whole idea of education. So strict was this definition of education for Black children that, up to that time many of the schools, perhaps all of the schools, had been built by missionaries, by missionary institutions, church-related in that sense. At that time, White schools were under the government and there were many, many advantages, including: higher salaries, better facilities, better supplies (such as books!), just from being a government institution rather than a missionary institution.

Indeed, ironically, there was a time when Black teachers, politicians, and political organizations were clamoring for Black schools to be taken from missionary control to government control, in order to "enhance" things, they thought. Then comes Bantu Education. Black people protest against this and the government turns around and says: "Haven't you always been wanting government control of your education? Well, here you're getting it. Now, you're griping." You can never beat the devil for finding all excuses for doing the evil that they do.

When some churches, White churches, like the Anglican church, decided they were going to create private schools, then the government decided that "Yes, private schools are o.k. provided we give you what to teach." Private schools would have to use the Bantu Education System. In other words, nullify the whole idea that the private school would counter Bantu Education.

"Hands are tied." How can you go and sign that you're becoming a part of the Bantu Education System? One of the most ridiculous things that happened in Johannesburg was this: an older man, who had an old Singer sewing machine and who knew a little bit about sewing, decided he was going to collect some children—their parents being at work, they were aimless—and he said to them: "Children, come here if you like and I'll teach you sewing during the day." It didn't take a week before the government was right there breathing down his neck: "This is a school. It has to be registered under the Bantu Education Act. To register you have to fill out this and this and this...." So, they destroyed it. It did indeed have the functions of creating little skills, but also keeping the children off the streets and giving them something to do.

Then came the crisis of 1976. The apartheid government decided now they were really going to push for Afrikaans to be a very big percentage of what was done at the schools. They picked up that fifty-fifty rule and said, "From now on Afrikaans will be fifty percent of all instruction." Both students and teacher, seeing what Bantu Education was doing, were in the process of having meetings to protest, to try to see how they could redirect this whole thing. They had school boycotts, where students would not go into the classrooms, but would sit on the lawns and "talk politics"—talk about what they should do.

Teachers were very nervous because they could not be seen as being part of these things without being dismissed. At the same time, many of them connived at what the students were doing. They said, "Well, we can't stop them. We can't make them come into the classroom if they don't want to." Political organizations—ANC, Unity Movement—to which I belonged held protest, upon protest, upon protest.

When this was first implemented, the ANC made a blunder. "As a protest action," they said, "we're going to encourage every parent to withhold their children from school." The apartheid government, well, they laughed. They said, "Well, O.K., let them stay at home. Let them be in the streets while their fathers and mothers are at work. We don't care a damn. Keep them away from school. We'll just fold our arms and watch."

It didn't take long before this became a crisis for the Black communities, with children roaming around aimless. It got to such a point of crisis that the ANC, who had called this strike, said, "Alright, now the children can go back to school." And the government said, "No. You've got to negotiate with us for them to go back to school." It was a matter of humiliating the ANC, saying, "You've got to come on your knees, to come and beg us to reopen those schools. We're not reopening those schools until you beg us and tell us that you're never going to do this sort of thing again." They had to swallow their pride and go to the government and say, "Yea, we're sorry." And then the doors were unlocked and children could go back to school and continue their Bantu Education.

The children were doing all this and sometimes asking their teachers to go to the government, to the Department of Bantu Education, as a delegation to say, "We can't live with this kind of education. Something has to be done." "Nope." Nothing happened. Until, on the 16th of June of 1976, the students from many Black Townships, as a whole conglomeration of Black Townships, serving Johannesburg as a Black labor reservoir, all clustered on the same side of the city, which eventually were called the Southwestern Townships—it didn't take long before the people created the anagram SOWETO.

The students in those Townships decided that they should march away from the school, go and meet *en masse* in Orlando Stadium, go and decide what is to be done. What are we to do with this problem? As they were marching toward the Orlando Stadium, suddenly they were confronted by fully armed police—not a riot squad, not a crowd-control squad, but armed with firearms at-the-ready. They stopped the students and demanded that they immediately disperse. And, without really giving the students time to do anything, they opened fire. One student was killed. There's a photograph that went all around the world with this student, Hector Peterson, carried by another student, with terror in their faces—two students running away with this dying child in their arms.

About The SOWETO Poem

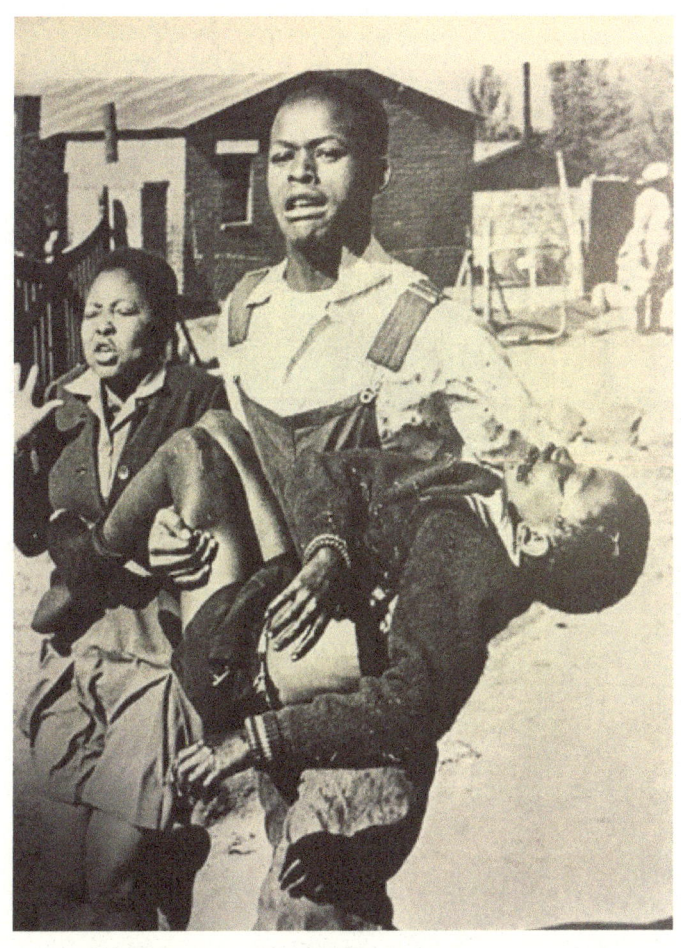

Hector Peterson, the first child to be shot dead by police in Soweto on 16 June 1976 (Sam Nzima)

SOWETO children killed while protesting the use of Afrikaans as a medium of instruction - 1976: Photos by Liziwe Kunene Pointer

That first confrontation opened up an ongoing harassment of Black children, with police and army going to the schools, being on the grounds, and sometimes, in a strange attempt to be friendly, getting into the classroom and trying to "help" children with schoolwork—in uniform and carrying a gun. What child would relax and listen?

About The SOWETO Poem

This was an extreme invasion of education, being right there in the classroom.

From then on, it became commonplace for the police to invade schools, and then, later, just to shoot Black children in the street. To be a Black child in the streets was a dangerous thing. The police would shoot you for sport. Children were attacked on playgrounds; children were chased, sometimes, riding to their houses. There's the story of a child who ran and crept under the bed and they pulled the child out and they shot him. A woman would send a child to the store: "Go and buy me bread. Go and buy me sugar." The child goes. Then, suddenly, some adult comes to the house and says: "We saw your child lying on the street. He's been shot by the police."

When it started, this first confrontation, the activist group here, in Madison called a meeting to march from the Library Mall to the Capital steps. When we were at the Library Mall, before we left, this was such a hastily put together event... there were some speeches made and then we were to march up State Street. There was some hesitation. It was clear people hadn't thought, "Who's going to lead this march? We can't just walk as a mob." Then Selina, my wife, and I, seeing this, I just grabbed her hand and we went to lead that march. We were the "natural" leaders of that march at that time in 1976.

1976... the year of the massacre of children protesting the use of Afrikaans language as a medium of instruction. In the aftermath of that incident, schoolchildren have been shot down on playgrounds, in their own back yards, and the police have gone into the schools, killing anything that moved.

Nothing is more disturbing to me than what's happening to the black children. They are targets (of police action), in much the same way that college students here were targets during the Vietnam demonstrations. Children of South Africa never experience childhood; they are adults much too soon.

The atrocities that go on in South Africa are for the most part unknown in America. Police killings of black children are so common there that they aren't reported in the media. News blackouts also are common. A state of emergency exists.

I want people to actively support the South African investment divestiture bill currently in the State Legislature. People must realize that the American government and big business are helping apartheid and the ensuing violence continue. We must withdraw our share of what makes the South African system work.

I must say that many students here were very active. We got to the capitol and made speeches denouncing the South African apartheid government, police action, and Bantu Education. There were other protests, but there was always me going to give talks every place you can imagine here in Madison. There was a time when we spoke to the State Legislature, here, the State Assembly, and various committees.

Sometimes I was amazed: "Am I really hearing right? This Assembly person... is it that they don't know?" They would ask: "What happens if this change you're advocating leads to *revolution*? I asked in return, "What do you mean?" "Revolution, revolution." I said, "The State of South Africa, being as it is, the change that we're looking at *is* a revolutionary change; but, if you mean by 'revolution' bloodshed, no, that's not what we want. By 'revolution' I understand something being changed in a revolutionary manner, in a very drastic manner... we don't need bloodshed for that."

Another thing that I noticed about some of those legislators at those meetings: they wouldn't even be looking at you, they'd be maybe two of them chatting, here and there all around the chamber. You got the impression that they were saying, "O.K. you could talk your head off, we're not bound to listen."

Coming back to SOWETO itself, the whole movement that started on the 16th of June, 1976 was called the SOWETO Movement. The students now began to really, seriously become activists in a physical way—confrontational with the police, acts of sabotage if they could get away with it. That's when the students created a slogan that turned out to be most unfortunate, that they never should have done. That slogan said: "Freedom First, Education Last."

That means dedicating themselves to being soldiers in the physical sense, in this war, not being students. Rotten as the education system was for Blacks, you'd have rather seen them there, in the classroom, than in the streets, where they were not under any disciplinary control. It was one thing for them to have won protests, as they did on that day. It was quite another to dedicate themselves to full-time soldiering. "Freedom First, Education Last." They were so optimistic. They thought it was going to happen in no time: "Freedom comes and we go back to school." But clearly, this was going to be a protracted war. In that time, they were growing older, and older, and older. It wasn't as if they could say, "Education, wait for me here. I'm still going to war, and then I'll come back and be the same age I was when I left you here and pick you up." No. They were growing to be young adults, an age when coming back to school was going to be difficult, a problem. Where were they going to pick up?

Those who have stayed in school (thankfully, they didn't *all* leave) have been making some kind of "progress," even under Bantu Education, while the "activists" had no measure of discipline imposed on their actions, no structure—unlike ANC or the Unity Movement or the Pan-African Congress, each one of which has a document that spells out its aims and objectives as well as its methods of struggle, documents that impose discipline, that will continue to have meaning even if you go into exile.

So the children, when it came time to save themselves, went into exile—encouraged by their families in some cases, others just sneaking away into neighboring Black states like Lesotho, Botswana, Swaziland, Tanzania. Once they were out of the combat zone, they truly didn't know why they were there, why they were not with their mothers and having their food at home. Life outside of "control" was now very pathetic, very tragic indeed for them.

After our march, I wrote letters. At that time, I was president of a recently formed organization called the African Literature Association, of which I was one of the founding members, founded in 1974 in Chicago. I wrote these letters both on my own behalf, personally, as a South African, and as president of this organization. I wrote letters to the UN Security Council, saying that "apartheid is something that undermines security." I wrote to the ANC in their NGO status at the UN. I wrote to their leadership there. I wrote to the Pope. I wrote to President Ford. I just sent out these letters to say, "This cannot be allowed to happen, this killing of children in South Africa." Of course, I got only formal responses. I don't even begin to think the Pope or Gerald Ford read my letter.

Before the SOWETO Movement, the Colored People (not Black, not White—mixed) had started to increase on their own. They were strictly the descendants of Black/White unions. Remember, Asians were not Coloreds. Under the Group Areas Act, Asians were given their own area and Coloreds were given theirs.

This Colored increase started in SOWETO and began to spread. Before that, the tendency was to think "It's a Black fight, especially in a place like Cape Town, where there is the greatest concentration of Colored people. We're not involved. We have some privileges that they don't have." We're looking at apartheid here.

The apartheid government, having succeeded in crystallizing divisions and making certain people feel more privileged and others less so, those who felt more privileged also felt that they had some stake in the status-quo. It didn't take very long before the police, way down in Cape Town, were going into Colored schools and children were running out, there was teargas, dogs, clubs, teachers jumping over fences. Everyone who had thought "As long as they don't treat me like a Black" now thought "I have something at stake here." Right at that moment, they were no different from Blacks.

The term "Black"and the phrase "We are "Blacks" started to be bandied about; the Coloreds, the Asians, the Indians, everybody was now claiming "We are Black," shouting slogans and holding demonstrations. In context, these were people who, prior to this moment in history, would never, never admit that they had anything that connected them with Blackness, with Black people. No, they would rather have been linked to "Whiteness" (to the extent that it were possible). They claimed that. They wanted that. Now, all of a sudden, everybody is black.

I didn't think it would last, and indeed it did not last. But, for that moment, you begin to see people who had been placed in a position of indecision as to where they belong, what they should claim to be. "Are you claiming that Colored is a legitimate status and that you are Colored? Are you wanting to shift toward White? Want to creep under the fence maybe?"

About The SOWETO Poem

At this point, being "Black" was convenient. They knew that if and when liberation came and there were a universal vote, Blacks were in the majority and they would inevitably get a Black-controlled government. So they were nervous, in that sense. That's why, when this thing about "Blackness" came along, they'd be shouting all over the place.

It was at this time that I read a report that a little girl, twelve years old, had been shot dead by the police in Alexander Township. Alexander was, and still is, inherited by the current Black government from the apartheid government as one of the most neglected of the Black areas—lots of crime and unemployment.

This little girl was in her school uniform, carrying her books, walking back home after school, and was shot dead by the police. I read the report and the police explained their action by saying, "She was looting." I thought to myself, "These police, these big men with guns, parents too, perhaps, could say, in loco parentis, "Hey, little girl, what are you doing there?" Even if it was true that in fact this child was looting, which I doubt very much—in fact I think it's a lie—even if it were true, whatever happened to spanking? To just saying, "Come here" and *pop, pop, pop* and "Never do that again. Go home." No, just take a gun, point it at the child, and shoot her dead? I couldn't get past that, it just stuck with me.

And I knew that one day I was going to write something, most likely a poem, about this. Indeed, it took some time, about a month; but, when it did happen, I started to write with the girl's voice. In the poem, I depicted her lying in the dust, in the street, to dying slowly. And in the process of dying, she's talking. Her mind brings back vivid images of her life and her involvement with the activism of the students. Then those tender moments when she's calling her mother. But it doesn't take long from the beginning of her mind talking, before a voice comes in. I don't know what made me create this voice. It was disembodied. There was no physical person there: A voice that responded to her, and comforted her, as best it could, telling her, "You don't know what is happening to you, but just lie there and rest." Calling her mother, and the voice saying, "She cannot hear you, child."

After a certain amount of this, I said, "Ah, I have created the voice of death. This is death." And "Death" is very sympathetic, very empathetic; it is saying "I will sit here and simply be with you at this moment while you're dying." When she speaks to this voice and says "Who are you?" the voice says, "Fortunately you will never know who I am." Then, it gets to a point where she is feeling some pain, some discomfort, and she says to this voice "Please touch me; I am hot?" And the voice says "No, I cannot." She pleads, "Oh you *thing*." The voice says "I cannot. Yes, I am *thing* and I am no thing." She's thirsty. She calls her mother to bring her some water. The voice says "She can't hear you." So she says, "Well you give me some water." It says "No, I cannot."

This dialogue goes on. It rises to climaxes and comes down: the girl sometimes remembering her peer group in their moments of shouting their slogans and being involved. Death, in response, would rise up and tell the girl, "Your tomorrow will never die." Eventually, she gets to a sort of climax, where she's encouraging her peer group to carry on and she begins to go down and down. When she gets to the point where she can't complete her words, then Death says, "Now you are ready for my embrace. Come little girl, it is finished."

A very, very touching point that was often quite difficult to read. Then I was in Holland for a conference. I had sent it to the *Capitol Times*. They had it printed and the day I was leaving for Holland, I bought a *Capitol Times* at the airport and there it was.

At the conference, there was a poetry reading night: I read it and there were lots of tears. It wasn't long after I got back from the conference, maybe two weeks or so, when I was sent a copy of a Dutch translation. I must have given a copy to my fellow South African, Vernon February, who was in exile in Holland. We were at the University of Leiden. He must have passed it on to somebody.

Now, here's this translation. I was reading it. I know some Afrikaans, so reading Dutch was not that difficult. But it was even more touching as I read it in a new language. For some reason, I started to translate it into my mother tongue, Sesotho, and every time I hear the words, it touches me differently.

About The SOWETO Poem

I went through London on my way back to here; and somebody had said to the BBC, "You must have that poem read there." They had been reluctant. I went to Busch House, but I didn't know how the communication was going between Holland and London on this. The person in Holland said, "If you're not going to have that poem read, then send it back here. We want that poem." Eventually, I read it on the BBC.

Here, I read it on Wisconsin Public Radio, and National Public Radio took it over and it was broadcast nationwide.

The SOWETO Poem-Prologue[1]

The child was twelve years old, if that. She was wearing her school uniform. In the eyes of the South African police, she was not a child. She was one of a mass of anonymous, faceless Blacks rioting and looting. A policeman's finger pulled the trigger and she lay in the street, dying.

And what was the occasion for this tragic event?

On Wednesday, June 16, 1976, the South African police turned a peaceful school children's march into one of the most violent clashes between police and civilians in the history of that country.

The children were protesting against the compulsory use of Afrikaans, the language of the white Boers, as a medium of instruction in their schools. They associated it with the oppressive laws they lived under, and with the police. They also saw it as a culturally impoverished language, leading to a dead-end.

Police violence led to thousands being maimed, hundreds killed, and thousands more jailed, including children, many of them no different in age and innocence from the girl mentioned above. In-

---

[1] The above prologue was written in July, 1976, when this poem was first composed. Peace has never returned to SOWETO since. The Commemoration of the SOWETO Massacre on June 16, 1976 reopened the still-fresh wounds of the year before and unleashed more violence and more deaths of children at the hands of the police. To this day there is no peace in SOWETO which really means South Africa, as the children demand a complete overhaul of their educational system which they recognize as a means of perpetuating their enslavement. If six or ten are shot dead during an afternoon's confrontation, often provoked by the police themselves, it is no longer news to a world press which has better things to do.

Meanwhile the children have made their choice and have joined their parents, and indeed taken the lead in demanding the removal of apartheid and the total liberation of black people of South Africa.

August 25, 1977

deed, the carnage continues to this day, having moved all the way south to Cape Town.

But among all those incidents, covering so many different areas and involving so many people, one report kept haunting me: A girl, a child no more than twelve years old, had been shot by the police. That little girl was, for me, the individual manifestation of the terror and senseless brutality.

And that was the occasion for the following dramatic poem which came to me many days after the event.

The SOWETO Poem

Where am I? Why am I lying here in the dust?
   O, child of a woman, how can I speak the unspeakable to a mere Twelve-year old? Isn't that the problem?
Who are you? Where are you? Speak to me. Hold me tight. My mother does not know I'm lying here in the dusty street.
   O, child of a woman, I am and I am not, for I come after the final Darkness has closed in.
Darkness? What are you saying?
   Ouiet. Just rest a while, child of a man and a woman, seed of the Sacred union. Do not worry, little girl.
Seed of the sacred union?
   You cannot understand.
Mother.
   She cannot hear you, O child. You do not know what is becoming of you.
She will come, my mother. She will hear me. She will come.
   I have no comfort for you, O unfortunate child, barely twelve years old. I am now your only companion.
Touch me, I'm hot.
   No.
My head is swirling. Hold me.
   No.
Please, you thing.
   Yes, I am thing and I am no-thing. I must stay away from you as long as possible.
Can you go to my mother and tell her . . . ?
   I cannot.
Oh, I'm tired. I'm drowsy.
   Sleep. That dust now is hallowed ground, where you lie.

It comes back now. I was walking. Yes. From school. My books, where are they? What happened to me? Why am I here? Oh, mother.
> *Do not linger long child. Be released. Let me embrace you.*

Please.
> *Not now.*

This dryness in my mouth. I'm thirsty. Mother, bring me some water.
> *(I am merciful.)*

Then bring me water.
> *O, you heard me. That was not for you, child. How merciful I am You will, mercifully, never know.*

There were many people, Policeman. Guns . . . They shot me! Oh, mother they shot me! Shot . . . me. Why?
> *Because they feared you.*

Feared me? Me, a child? Those big, big men with guns and clubs and bayonets? Feared me?
> *In you, a child, more strength. You to them a greater threat in the young tomorrows waiting to be born. They fear your tomorrow, that's why they try to kill your today. You understand?*

Blood! I'm bleeding! They shot me!
> *Out of fear, child. But your tomorrow will never die. For, when I embrace you, you will live in the endlessness of time, in all the yesterdays, the oday's and the tomorrows which will become one thing.*

My mother kissed me this morning. She left for the white people's house to go and cook for them and wash their clothes and care for their children. She said she'd see me in the evening. I ate. I left. I loved the arithmetic. Good subject. The teacher, he is good. English. Hygiene—wash every day, brush your teeth, comb your hair, cut your nails short. Civics—who is your Bantu Affairs Commissioner? Who is the superintendent of your Location? In what ways is the pass good for you? That piece of paper which the policemen are always demanding from you, without which they throw you in jail! Oh, how our people suffer!
> *Don't tire yourself, little one. So young. So beautiful! So tender! Just lie there and rest and wait. Your tomorrow will never die.*

Afrikaans! Why in hell? Why-y-y? Comrades, they shot me. Yes, the cowards! They shot me. But I hear your running feet, I hear your call to arms. I see victory! See how I pull myself up from the dust! See how I clench my fist! See how I make the final salute! I hear the shout "TO HELL," echoing in the four corners of the earth! Yes, to hell with them! To hell with them! ... Oh, mother, will you know when you see my happy face that my heart remains here with my comrades? With you? Tomorrow is so beautiful!

Tomorrow shall be born for today is indestructible. No sun sets forever. You, child, are like a seed that must seem to die in order to produce a young shoot seven days hence.

Tomorrow is ours!

Brave child! You're like a meteor that blazes and lights the earth ere it is extinguished. The straying traveler sees the way and is saved. Then, child, let the meteor trail off to silence, deep silence, well-earned silence, peace.

Tomorrow lives! Soweto! Soweto! So ... we ... to ... So ... we ...

Now you're ready for my embrace. Come little one. It is finished.

HOLLAND—THE PERFORMANCE

Then, in 1983, I got an invitation from Holland to go for a year to a place called *Netherlands Institute for Advanced Study in the Humanities and Social Sciences* (NIAS, for short). We were all "fellows" of the institute, from different parts of the world—the United States, England, France—but also a good contingent of Dutch scholars. We would take coffee breaks. One day, I was having coffee and there was a Dutch fellow who was a musicologist, and a German fellow, who had come with his wife (I was also with my wife for this year) and we were chatting away. It just occurred to me, "I have that poem here and it's just been translated into Dutch. Let me bring it to the Dutch fellow." I had no intention for anything to happen, just for him to read the poem. And I gave it to him in the Dutch translation.

We were all sitting down. He started reading…reading. I could see something happening in his face. He got up. He was still reading. He lit a cigarette. He was beginning to have tears in his eyes. The other two people were totally mystified. They didn't know what that could mean. I knew. Even though I did not expect that reaction from him. But when I saw it, I knew why. When he finished reading it, he said, "Daniel, this poem is made for music. And I know a composer and I will take it to him." He took it to Bernard van Beurden.

At first it seemed that the performance might happen before we were dispatched and went back to our homes. Van Beurden already had ideas about what musical instruments he wanted to use. It was going to be performed in Rotterdam. Something didn't go right, and it didn't happen then.

I got a letter from Holland, from Groningen, which I was told was one of the more than progressive, indeed *leftist* cities in Holland, and that every year, in May, they held what they called the "For May Project." They devoted several days to activists' speeches, peace groups, and in the last few years they'd added music as well. This letter that I got said, "We are a choral group. We work with 'For May Project.' We always look for a piece to perform. As we were looking, we saw your poem and we thought 'This is an appropriate poem for this occasion. So, let's look for a composer'." And they went to exactly that same man from a few years back, Van Beurden, and said, "We've found our composer. His name is van Beurden and he's very excited about composing music to this piece. In fact, he had done it already."

May of 1990, my wife and I were the guests at Groningen. We were treated very well. We were given two weeks of just being pampered before the performance. When it did happen, we were *guests of honor.* We're sitting there before the performance began—my wife and I, and a friend from Amsterdam and his wife—when somebody taps me from behind. I turn around. And he whispers, "I am Bernard van Beurden." We meet for the first time there, waiting for the performance of my poem with his music to happen. It was wonderful, incredible. It was a moment of whispered excitement at that time, "O.K., we'll talk at the intermission."

The program consisted of many pieces that were played before "SOWETO," which was the main attraction or performance for that evening. There was a performance. Then there was an intermission. Meanwhile, I hadn't heard the piece myself at all. This was going to be the very first time. Then came two short performances and then a second intermission. I thought, "Wow."

During the first intermission, van Beurden and I met outside in the corridor and as we got more acquainted he said, "You will notice that I cut in the middle of the piece at one. I keep your piece there and then we go back to it after the '*ungh dey*'. The reason I did this, I hope you approve"—although at that point it was a *fait accompli*—"I did it for a good reason. That poem, and of course the music is sympathetic to the poem, it builds up to such a high pitch of emotional intensity that I feel that I should break it at that point and just calm the feelings and go back to pick it up." He gave the example of a formal French meal. "After each course, they bring ice that people have to suck in order to cleanse the pallet: so that they are actually ready to relish the next course. This was my thinking in doing this."

Eventually, the piece comes on. I'm all-tense, and I'm holding my wife's hand. The way it came on was very dramatic. You know the usual way the curtains are opened and the conductor comes walking in and there's applause. They did it differently. It was all dark. The stage was covered. Then, when they opened the curtains, the performers were all there, and the conductor was standing facing them straight; it was just like a picture. It took everybody by surprise, I guess, because everybody expected the usual. And it took some time before people broke into applause.

Then there was stage lighting that was all around the stage with different colors of lighting, which when the lights came on were changed so that they would resemble something like either a sunset or a sunrise; it was most beautiful. At the end of the performance, we were called to the stage to receive bouquets of flowers. What a moment. Van Beurden told me. "I've composed this piece to just go with the story, just go with the story. I've not doubled up words or anything like that; I just made it go with the story."

So I was able, even though I didn't know the melody, I was aware, as it was getting close to the end, that it was getting close to the end. Holding my wife's right hand in mine, we were clasping hands. As it was getting closer, I don't know what happened, my hand, holding my wife's hand, started to shake vigorously. Just shook. My wife held it and calmed me. It was such a moment that I can't explain: Was it the break in the tension, the waiting, the anticipation? I don't know.

There was a café next to the auditorium where a reception took place, in a cafeteria, and more flowers were given to our wives, and we signed each other's books. Posters had been placed all over Groningen, it was all over that place; they really, really prepared for my piece to be performed, it was really the focal thing for that performance.

The Groningen performance being over, my wife and I were, from there, planning to go to Amsterdam and stay with this South

African couple. Also, at that time, van Beurden and his wife also lived in Amsterdam. We were going to leave on a Monday afternoon. That Sunday afternoon he invited us to his flat and came to fetch us for tea and some drinks, just the four of us: me and my wife and him and his wife.

It was then that he said to me, "You know, Daniel, I've got to tell you that when I read your poem I thought of my daughter, who was twelve years old and had died in hospital because of the doctors' negligence. As an artist, as a composer, I've always felt that one day there'll come the right moment for me to acknowledge my daughter's death with a piece that I will compose. And, when I read your poem, I thought, 'This is it. This is the poem I'm going to remember my daughter with.' If you look on the cover page of the music sheet, you will notice that the piece is *Dedicated to Roos*, which is the equivalent of Rose."

My wife and I embraced him and hugged him. That was his story, his personal connection to this poem. How it aroused in him this feeling that there is no better lyric, no better set of words, no better poem for me to add my own artistic skills to at last recognize the death of my daughter. That really clinches the story of how this whole thing just connected us.

It is significant and also ironic that this "world premier" of my poem was received in Holland, the ancestral homeland of the Afrikaners who so brutalized my South African homeland. The personal significance of this connection of Holland and South Africa, 1652 and all that, happened a long time before this. There was so much anti-apartheid activism in Holland that at times, as when I was a guest at Neaps for a year, we were called all over the place to go and read poetry by these activist groups against apartheid. To me, that was a very strange irony. That the place where the people now practicing apartheid came from, their ancestral home, they are saying "We have nothing to do with what those descendants of our parents are doing there. We do not approve."

I understand, vaguely, that the Afrikaners during the apartheid era tried to woo some Dutch people to come and strengthen their resolve, strengthen them in numbers, expecting that they would agree with their policy of apartheid. The Dutch simply said, "No. No.

No. Out of our sight! We are not going to be connected with what you're doing there. We do not approve it and we're not going to be seeming to approve it." That was a very important irony in this whole relationship.

When my piece was performed there, I was reading it already to people who were—as in the saying "You're preaching to the choir"—people who were already *progressives*. On the other hand, I didn't consciously see this as an ironic situation. I just saw it as these wonderful people who were so much on the side of humanitarianism, on the side of equality, on the side of freedom that they would disagree with those people who originated from there. Who said, "No, we're not going to shake your hands at this time."

I wrote a play in 1991, a year after Nelson Mandela was released from prison. Clearly, at that time, the movement toward the universal franchise, Blacks participating in the voting process, was on since Mandela's release in February of '90. In fact, it became clear later that the process had started even before that, while Mandela was still in prison. When the apartheid government had realized that it would be a political blunder on their part if Mandela were to, for example, die in prison—he was too much of a world figure already by then, even while he was in prison—it was the wisest thing they could do to release him.

President P.W. Botha had felt that pressure; had made a gesture to release Mandela. He was pressured from both sides. His party was not going to accept the action of Mandela being released. They wanted to push ahead with their apartheid; no matter what might happen they were going to pursue their very right-wing conservative policies. On the other hand, world pressure on South African white presidents, at that time under apartheid, was also very strong. In the late '80s, President Botha told the world that he was going to make a very important announcement. World media were just waiting to hear this and everybody was assuming he was going to announce that Nelson Mandela would be released from prison.

Then, he made an "offer" to Mandela that said: "I will release you if you renounce violence." To which Mandela responded with a note that was taken from jail to be read by his daughter. Mandela's note said to Botha: "You, President Botha, first renounce the violence of apartheid on our people and then I will consider your request for me to renounce violence."

By 1989 or so, it was clear that Mandela's release was overdue, when De Klerk became President, and in '90 announced he was going to release Mandela "without conditions."

In a play that I call *The Mandela Saga,* with some music that I wrote after a year of observing De Klerk and his activities, it became clear to me that Mandela was to be warned, or maybe he saw it himself, that De Klerk was playing a double game. He was wearing two faces: one face was for the public—he was this hero who was nicked-named the "Gorbachev of South Africa" and shared the Nobel Peace Prize with Mandela—but, at the same time, he was secretly undermining the process of moving toward elections and creating a new constitution.

The message of the play was for Mandela to beware of De Klerk. I used some words, phrases, proverbs, like the Xhosa proverb that says: "Don't test the bottom of the river with both feet." Probe first with your stick before you put your foot there. I used the Trojan Horse analogy

I am 82 years old now, 2006, and taking some piano lessons. At this point, there's no longer a matter of "I'll become a professional musician and play all over the world." It's for my personal pleasure. Little tunes do come to my head. There are two pieces in the play that are chanted or sung by the group as they move around the stage in performing the *Mandela Saga.*

Now and again in the writing of my poetry, sometimes music comes in. I sometime lead my audience into engaging in singing with me. Some audiences are taken by surprise. But generally, it goes on just fine. One of the poems that I would teach them is a poem called "Mango." It came from my late wife, when we were still much younger, walking on the beach in Cape Town. I had never eaten a mango before. There was a vendor there who was selling some fruit, including mangos. My wife bought one. Gave me a taste. And it was so lovely. It was incredible. I was converted. My love for mangos never abated. A ripe, sweet, delicious mango is something else.

So I composed this longish poem that has a part that I sing and I get the audience to sing, and I would get my students singing: "I Love my love with a love like the love I love a mango. I love my love with a love like the love I love a mango. Mango. Mango."

Then I would say, "Now, hold hands with somebody next to you. Then, start swaying back and forth…back and forth. Now say: 'I love my love with a love like the love I love a mango. Mango. Mango'." We would have fun.

One time I was at a conference of World University Service in Switzerland. We took an excursion by bus to very close to the Swiss Alps. After sightseeing, talking, and having a picnic lunch, as we were walking around before we went to the bus, a young couple, man and woman, white, started harmonizing a tune. I was not too far from them. So I started humming, accompanying them. And since I was humming and I didn't have my mouth open, I enjoyed the fact that they suddenly heard this sound that was making their music even more glorious, and they didn't know where it came from. It got to the point where they were looking back and forth and then I would just look very innocent and keep quiet. And they would start again. Then this mysterious bass voice would start up. Before they threw themselves down an embankment or something, thinking they were hearing the booming bass voice of God, eventually I made them aware that it was me.

THE STRUGGLE CONTINUES

Back to when this web that controls where we go, whether we like it or not, led me to become a Professor of African Literature and Poetry here in Madison. Having accepted that, I don't know where I would be if some paths that had opened and then shut, if they had opened and not shut: Where would I be? Would I like where I would be at that time? Would where I would be have some downsides compared to where I am right now? I say, "I don't know. But I should take what I became and make the best of it." And that's how I view having ended up being a professor here at the University of Wisconsin. Having met some very good people. Having met some very bad people. Having had all these experiences.

It seems almost mysterious, my coming here, having concluded this journey, where for some reason I seem to be following Dr. Jordan, my mentor—from Cape Town to London, where he was for a little bit, maybe a year; From London to Los Angeles, to UCLA; and then from UCLA to become a founding member of this department, which I was recruited to after his death.

When one goes back to the time that I received that "imperfectly addressed letter" when I was working at the Johannesburg Magistrates Court for those "liberal" lawyers, and Jordan got me out of there to go and study at the University of Cape Town, reconnecting from the time he was my teacher at high school—it seems that we were destined for me to just literally follow him.

So I went to London from Cape Town, stayed there for a few months; went to Los Angeles from England, to UCLA, and stayed there for six and half years; and then I came here after he passed away. It's a strange sort of thing to happen. Of course, going to Cape Town from Johannesburg was planned: he had written to me that he had gotten some scholarship money for me. But, from then on, nothing else was planned.

This is where I am, and I've enjoyed every bit of it. Maybe not *every* bit; there have been bad moments, but on the whole it was a very good experience to teach here. I've no regrets.

I did have some serious interactions with the Board of Regents relating to my life and my being from South Africa. The university certainly was very liberal in many respects; but money is always something that complicates life, that complicates governments. Even after the state, under our pressure—the pressure of the anti-apartheid groups that demonstrated—when the divestment had really won, the Wisconsin State Legislature passed a law that no state institution should continue or should ever do business with companies that in any way were connected with or dealing with South Africa.

Even though the University of Wisconsin is a state institution, they were sort of reluctant to stop dealing with companies that were indeed connected with South Africa, despite the pressure applied by my group, Madison Area Committee on South Africa, and by some progressive legislators like David Clarimba, who was a senator in the state legislature.

We were in this meeting and one of the items was for the Regents to come clean on the question of South Africa. Why was it that they still hadn't taken a step to obey the law? David Clarimba was at this meeting. He took the podium and he said: "In plain language, the university is breaking the law of the state. Put aside moral and ethical arguments, the fact is the university is breaking the law of the state if you continue to deal with companies connected to South Africa." The next day, the Regents voted for total disengagement with companies doing business with South Africa.

Leah Tutu, Bishop Desmond Tutu, Selina Kunene, and Daniel Kunene in Madison in 1989

It is appropriate to conclude with Chancellor Shalala, who became a very strong advocate for the liberation of South Africa and supported activists like Archbishop Desmond Tutu and the Reverend Chikane, whom the South African government had tried to assassinate. Chikane was then Secretary of the South African Council of Churches in Johannesburg He was suddenly taken ill just before he was to come here. He was in Namibia to address meetings when he became very seriously ill. He was taken back to Johannesburg, where he got better.

He got here and was accommodated at Chancellor Donna Shalala's home. Then, suddenly, he would get so ill that he had to go to hospital, near death. Got to hospital and it would take a day or less before he felt perfectly O.K. He went back to Shalala's. My wife and I walked there to visit. After a few minutes with him, we noticed that his limbs couldn't support him; he needed help sitting up and standing and walking. I went to Chancellor Shalala and said:

"This man needs to go back to hospital. He needs to go to the hospital urgently." Shalala ordered an ambulance to come and get him.

We were in the hospital til the early hours of the morning. Again, in a day or less, he was the healthiest man you could think of. A doctor about Chikane's age—they say when a doctor is about your age they want to get deep into what's going on—interestingly, dedicated himself to finding out what was happening. Suddenly, a bright idea: "There must be something in the clothing; some stuff that Chikane's clothing had been poisoned with. Because, whenever he got to the hospital, took off clothes, got into hospital garb, he was almost immediately well." So, they came to the conclusion that it was a question of poisoning. The South African government had been trying to assassinate him that way.

The clothes were taken to some lab—on the West Coast, I think Los Angeles—where they specialized in situations of assassination by biological agents and poisoning of clothing. Donna Shalala just got him taken to a store to buy new clothes that he needed. He bought new clothes and never got ill again.

It was determined that this was an attempt to assassinate him. The main message here is that the contrast—between the time the Regents had to be pressured to be on the right side of the South African issue, and the time that we had a chancellor who was actually on her own on the right side of that issue—was quite a step. And we ended the university's connection to South Africa.

There is an additional observation about the future of the Odin Cinema and related changes in South Africa that should be made a part of this history. It's important to me personally, but it's also important to the entire Black community of Sophiatown of Johannesburg, and people of conscience the world over. This was a time when the apartheid government decided to sort people out and "package" them into their different colors and languages and cultural groups, when they were passing laws like the Group Areas Act, under which I was called a "disqualified person" to continue living in a house that I had had built for me.

In doing that, they engaged in a lot of destruction. A place like Sophiatown had some really, very solid buildings, very well built. It's true that many owners of properties would have their main house in front, and then they would use the backyard and build small rooms, which they rented out to people; so, you'd have a kind of little community in the backyards of people who lived and paid rent to the owner.

In 1952, Sophiatown was destroyed, was absolutely leveled to the ground, at a time when my late wife and I had already moved to Cape Town. We visited friends of ours who were living in Western Native Township, which were Municipal Housing that was really tiny – that's another issue.

This one Sunday, we got in their car, they were going to show us what was once Sophiatown. The street where Dr. Xuma lived ,where I met the Bishop from the United States, Toby Street, was leveled down. There were no houses, maybe little mounds, maybe weeds growing. And to mock it all, a sign: "There was a sweeping destruction of this place by marauding beasts, wild animals, wild people – absolutely mad." There had been a major destruction, but there were still some symbols of what it used to be.

The symbol that struck me, and I wrote a short story about the destruction of Sophiatown, titling it with this symbol and that was, "The Stop Sign." You still had tarred roads, tarred streets and at the end of the street, at the intersection, the stop sign was still there. But you had jungle grass and weeds all around the street where you were driving.

We were really going through a great trauma as we were taking this tour. I had lived in Sophiatown and places like Victoria Road, where the AME church was, where I met Pache, all gone. Good Street, where the Odin Cinema had been, leveled down. A place, a community that used to be as good as a good suburb, had been razed.

They called the groups that came to bulldoze, to level down the houses, "The Wrecking Group." How much more totally abandoned to destruction can one be, even in the nomenclature, no mincing of words: "The Wrecking Group." There were stories like you can't imagine: of families who might one night, they've just got into bed, and they hear this noise outside and they come out, and "The Wrecking Group" is busy destroying their house even as they are sleeping in it. And they would have to beg them, "Please wait. Can't you wait 'til morning?" There were stories of men going to work in the morning and then coming back and finding their wives and children with their belongings on the sidewalk and the house gone. This is how cruel and merciless it was.

And as for those little rooms that people sometime built in the backyard, well, the apartheid government said: "These are slums. We are helping to cleanup, to remove slums, and there's a very nice area we've built for you called 'Meadowlands'." People were carted in trucks and buses to this totally characterless place. People had to try to build communities again that had been destroyed in Sophiatown.

Coming back to Odin Cinema, it was a very hard, emotional moment to think, "This is the place. This is what remains of that place where I used to sing; where we use to have the orchestra coming there to play, leveled down, a few bricks here and there." I could not believe it. I still intend to write an essay or a poem, "If These Bricks Could Talk."

I did a lot of singing in Johannesburg and Cape Town. In Johannesburg I sang mostly at the famous Odin Cinema in Sophiatown, which had a capacity of about two thousand. It was described as the most modern non-European cinema in the southern hemisphere. The Odin was leveled down as part of the vicious and vengeful destruction of Sophiatown by the apartheid government. I had also formed choirs to sing gratis on invitation and also to entertain ourselves at our respective homes, especially on Sundays.

The pianist George Peterson lived in Newlands and taught at one of the "Colored" schools. He accompanied me always, and our first "hit" was "Where'er You Walk" from Handel's oratorio (if my memory serves me right) at an NEUM concert at one of the town halls. I don't remember which—Mowbray, Salt River, Woodstock—maybe all of them at different times. Meanwhile, I was also composing my own music, both solo and choral, some in English and some in Sesotho, my mother-tongue. I formed and conducted a choir which I named the SOYA Choir, and which sang at most of the Movement's concerts.

RETURN TO THE ROOTS:
South Africa, Thirty Years Later
By Daniel P. Kunene

PART I

It's July 2, 1993. My wife, Selina, and I stand ready to board the Van Gaalder bus to O'Hare on the first lap of our journey back home to South Africa after thirty years in exile. We left South Africa on Friday, the 13th day of September, 1963, on a journey to the unknown at a time when any "unknown" out there was preferable to the hell that South Africa was, since the monster of segregation had matured into the more unabashed apartheid formally instituted in 1948. In fifteen years, the system that has been compared to Nazism had grown totally arrogant and defiant. It considered itself the model of race relations that the world eventually would emulate. "Those whom the gods wish to destroy, they first make mad." In our political organizations before we left, we believed Euripides's words implicitly and completely, for we saw the madness grow apace. We only wished the gods would hasten the process by shortening the madness and getting to the real business, for while the gods have an eternity, we each have but a meager lifetime.

Many people have died since we left, some of them very close to us. From reports, we know also that many people are wallowing even deeper in poverty than at that time, and many communities have been destroyed in the mass movements of people under the notorious and whimsical "resettlement scheme." My widowed sister,

Magdaline, whose first son, Jabulani, was imprisoned on Robben Island in the wake of the SOWETO students' revolt, had to fight a determined and sustained war against being moved from the tiny town of Edenville, where all of us were born, to the Bantu Homeland, Qwaqwa, of which she was told she was now a citizen. I salute her courage and sheer determination in facing the system and wrestling it to the ground. She did not do it as a political statement, but out of a determination to be left alone. She is one of the many unsung heroes and heroines of the struggle.

We are happy, Selina and I, that we are going to be reunited with our families. But we are also very apprehensive. What are we going to find? We have long clung to the image of the South Africa we left behind in 1963. In our talks to American audiences, we have proudly referred to some of the black values that have enabled our people to survive the vicious onslaughts of apartheid. Yet we also know that life's hard knocks must have left their marks, scarred bodies and souls.

My wife is not well. It saddens me so much. We have lived most of our years in exile in good health. We have been active in the anti-apartheid movement—calling for American companies to stop supporting apartheid, and for an economic boycott, as well as cultural and sports boycotts. It made us happy. It kept our hope alive. We carried anti-apartheid placards proudly. We annoyed the South African government, which we came to know had rather massive dossiers on our activities. Those were the happy days. But in the last three years or so, my wife's health has steadily declined. And now she is obviously not well.

As we stand by the bus outside the Memorial Union, I feel embarrassed by all that luggage! When I was a child, anyone who visited Johannesburg, the city of gold, even for a brief stay or work stint, was supposed to bring presents for everyone. Not some silly mementos; they needed trousers, shirts, blouses, dresses, jerseys, practical things like that. Now there we were returning from a huge "Johannesburg" after a huge absence, working in huge jobs and making huge money. And we imagined their need was huge back there. Hence our huge luggage.

We are lugging heavy winter coats on a hot, humid, muggy Madison summer day. I feel those who see us will either think us mad or envy us. They will guess we are going to the other side of the world. At O'Hare we reorganize our luggage, and it is a little more manageable.

Our flight to London on British Airways is very restful. The dinner is good. The night is very short, since we lose six hours. We arrive at Heathrow in the morning, and our connecting flight to Johannesburg only leaves that evening. So we get a room in the Heathrow Hilton and rest and shower and sleep. As we weave through the airport that night to go to our boarding area, we begin to hear some Afrikaans, and more of it as we get closer. The associations with apartheid are unavoidable—police raids at night, pass laws, jail, children shot in SOWETO and throughout the country by Afrikaans-speaking police to enforce the use of Afrikaans as a medium of instruction in their schools, Bantu Education. The whole damn system. Suddenly, it's as if all whites in this area are Afrikaans-speaking South Africans and hostile.

This is the longest lap of our journey, over eleven hours of airborne time. We arrive at Jan Smuts Airport tired and ready to recuperate. The strain of the journey has taken a toll on my wife in particular, because she is not well. On our long walk towards the immigration control gates, she keeps saying she is thirsty, but there are no water fountains around. As we stand in the line that now seems interminable even though we are now just a few feet away from the gate, she keeps saying she is thirsty. I break off from the line and go to a rather formidable looking white woman wearing a kind of uniform and ask her where we can get water. She looks curiously at me, shrugs her shoulders and, with a strong Afrikaans accent, says she does not know where we can get water; there aren't even any cups there. The nearest place, she says, will be the women's toilet after we go through the gate. She hesitates for a moment, and then says I should call my wife out of the line. She walks us to a gate not in operation, beckons an official who comes and examines and stamps our passports quickly, and she points where to go to reach the toilet. Selina comes out after some time, looking a little refreshed.

My visit to South Africa has a business side to it as well. I have been invited to be one of three international keynote speakers at the 1993 biennial conference of the African Language Association of Southern Africa ("ALASA93"), whose theme is, appropriately, "Building on the Past—Looking to the Future," scheduled for July 6–9 at the Witwatersrand University in Johannesburg.

Several other universities have invited me to visit them during my stay in South Africa following the conference. Selina and I are going to have a mini-tour of the country as we visit different academic institutions. As part of all this, we are met at Jan Smuts Airport by the president of ALASA, Prof. Rosalie Finlayson, who is accompanied by her husband, Ken.

We are accommodated in the Sunnyside Park Hotel on the north end of Hillbrow. The irony of all this is that, upwards of forty-five years before this, I was a page boy in a tight-fitting, brass-buttoned uniform with a cap to match at a residential hotel in the then lily-white Hillbrow. When not answering phones and going hunting for the residents to come and take their calls, I would be standing at the door, opening it for the white patrons as they came and went. Or carrying their luggage as they checked in or out, with a coin occasionally tossed my way. Now I am the guest, and the young white receptionist wishes me and my wife a happy stay. "And please call the office if you need anything," she says as she gives the keys to the porter carrying our luggage.

Of course, Mandela has been out of prison three years now and the country is, indeed, "looking to the future." One of the conference organizers, Molly Bill, came into the picture earlier today when she drove us to her house, where we rested, had lunch, and took baths before she finally drove us to the hotel.

We spend the morning and afternoon of Monday, July 5th, lounging around the hotel, getting used to being back. In the evening we are driven to the Holiday Inn, where the ALASA board has arranged a welcome dinner in our honor. I don't know anyone in this group of mostly white Afrikaner men, except for Molly and Rosalie. There's a great deal of chatting and joking, once everybody is relaxed. Following the dinner, Molly and Rosalie make brief welcome speeches. In my response, I thank ALASA for inviting me, but find it necessary to allude, if only briefly, to the policy of apartheid which strove so hard and so long to keep us apart. I remind my hosts this was not the first time I had been invited by my South African colleagues but that, for reasons we all know and deeply regret, "it has not been possible to accept till now." I see some heads nodding and I know my message is understood. This is the beginning of a long, slow healing process.

The Doke Centenary activities begin on Tuesday, July 6th, with a series of lectures. During lunch I am asked to chair the panels in the second half of the afternoon. In the evening, immediately following the panels, we go to the Senate Building, where the Doke Exhibit is to be officially opened by the vice-chancellor of Wits. Among the speeches is one by an African teacher from Lambaland, where Doke did his missionary and research work as a younger scholar in the early 1920s. He is accompanied by an African priest who is clearly his intellectual and spiritual mentor. He speaks without a script, from the heart, as he himself says. The saga of his and his priest's hard four-day journey on public buses and other not-so-comfortable means of transportation at their own personal expense, to be at the Doke celebrations, is clearly meant as a testimony of how important it was for them to come, and how determined they were. He states that they were sent by "the elders" with a message of gratitude and appreciation for Doke's missionary work in Lambaland. The speech brings many people close to tears.

I am also moved by the sheer honesty and sincerity and the deeply-felt sentiment. However, something in me rebels. This is like a throw-back to the old colonial and missionary era—the fawning gratitude and almost canine loyalty to the white missionary/master I find disturbing. It's all so anachronistic, just as if the past we hoped had gone forever suddenly comes alive before our very eyes.

Speaking out against apartheid.

The speeches over, there is suddenly a burst of singing by a mixed choir that moves to center stage in front of the podium. A good, solid, beautiful, non-professional but wonderfully harmonious group. They sing wedding songs and choral pieces in solid four-part harmony. This strikes a chord deep down in me. This is how we sang as pupils in our schools, an indescribable blend of team effort as a choir and individual virtuosity, self-expression, and sheer enjoyment of what you were doing. Individuals might strive for audience attention and get individual applause. My wife sang in such choirs at school too, and our reactions are similar. But when they sing old Caluza songs that I sang as a little boy in school and that I now sing silently with them, I feel this is a great part of our homecoming, and I feel a sting in my eyes and have to control this lump rising in my throat. (This is a reference to Reuben T. Caluza, a well-known Zulu composer, pianist, and choirmaster, whose songs we sang in our schools.)

Among the guests is Mrs. Vilakazi, M.A., D.Litt., who, to Wits's eternal shame, remained a lowly "language assistant" in the Department of Bantu Languages, under Prof. Doke, until his untimely death on October 26, 1947. She is introduced to us. She asks the inevitable question, "When are you coming back?" and without waiting for an answer: "You must come back and help to rebuild our country." She is not unaware of the risks, and she adds: "But you can't all come here and die."

Wednesday, July 7th, is the first day of the ALASA conference. The first keynote speech is by G.N. Clements, a linguist from the Sorbonne. I feel flattered that he has quoted from my 1961 Ph.D. thesis to reinforce some of the arguments in his brilliant paper, and that he advocates its publication.

We are expecting my brother, Peter, and his wife, Yvonne, from Kroonstad, who have been invited at my request. They aren't there by lunch time, but Molly Bill allays our fears, saying they are only expected in the afternoon. She was in charge of the arrangements for their coming. But we are still worried, and just as we are getting ready for a major manhunt, suddenly there's Peter at one of the registration tables! There's so much excitement, many embraces. Thenji, Peter's daughter, and her husband are waiting outside at the car with Yvonne. Peter and Yvonne are being provided complimentary room and board by ALASA, as my guests.

Tonight, I am to receive an Honorary Member Award from ALASA. So will Prof. C.T.D. Marivate, whom I met many years ago when he visited the University of Wisconsin. I am introduced rather elaborately by Prof. Johnny Lenake. The standing ovation that follows brings me close to tears. I feel so unworthy, and to see this whole auditorium on their feet and applauding and looking at me makes me feel like a tiny little dot. I look at my wife, close to the front row, and smile. She smiles back. To break the tension, as I get on the podium to make my acceptance speech, I joke about the award just handed to me by Prof. Finlayson. I hold it high and turn around and say that's what they do at the tennis championships.

After my speech, Prof. Marivate receives his award. He devotes a significant amount of his speech to praising me and my work, and how I have inspired him and numerous students of African languages and literature.

For my keynote speech on the morning of Thursday, July 8th, I am introduced by Prof. Chris Swanepoel. I feel he is speaking from the heart as he summarizes the main points of my career and his own personal appreciation of my work, and then he calls me to the podium.

Prof. Chris Swanepoel and the author.

Not long into my speech, I know I have captured my audience. I'm in control. I just have to maintain the pace, the tone, the mood changes in the paper. I conclude by applying my analysis to the woes of much of black independent African states in a hard-hitting criticism, with an implied warning for South Africa when its day comes. I propose the Black Consciousness Movement philosophy of the late 1960s and early 1970s as a good model to follow.

The audience's response is enthusiastic. I receive a standing ovation as I conclude. A White colleague later tells me I swayed them from one mood to another much like a conductor directing an orchestra. I am, understandably, jubilant. Chris Swanepoel concludes the session with an appreciation of my presentation that, he says, confirms the high esteem in which I am held.

Having gone to bed late last night because Peter, Yvonne, Selina, and I sat up discussing some family business, we missed the third keynote at 8:30 this morning, Friday, July 9th. Prof. Eyamba Bokamba, the keynote speaker, tells me later that in his speech he referred to his students as my "academic grandchildren," since he himself has been taught by me. Though I regret I was not there to hear the compliment, I still feel it was a wise decision to sleep late this morning. It is the last day of the conference, and things are obviously winding down.

We have a week's gap between the end of the conference at Wits and our visit to the University of Cape Town. We use that time to visit our families.

It is now Saturday, July 10th. Shortly after lunch, Rankele and Thenji Nthebe drive us to Kroonstad to visit my brother Peter's home. We are very happy about the opportunity to be driven, since public transportation is so dangerous, with politically motivated massacres in trains, buses, combi (mini-van) taxis. We drive past places where such killings occur daily. SOWETO. Sebokeng. Thembisa. We also pass by a hostel we are told has acquired a terrible notoriety for the killings there. At one point we ride parallel to a combi taxi crammed with passengers, as they always are. We notice several passengers turning to look at us. Selina and I feel uneasy since many people have remarked how much I look like Nelson Mandela.

During our stay with Peter and Yvonne, we plan to drive to my home, Edenville, where I have not been since I went to say goodbye to my father, weeks before we left for America. My mother had already passed by that time. Since our departure, my father has died, and so have other relatives, including a sister, an aunt, etc. The Edenville visit is therefore going to be a pilgrimage to the dust and stones of my beginnings. It is going to be hard visiting there, for life has also taken its toll on some of the other people. I am, therefore, more apprehensive than happy about the anticipated visit. At a stop in Vereeniging to fill up, I recall the Sharpeville massacre of March 1960 and its aftermath. Sharpeville Township is the black labor reservoir attached to white Vereeniging.

After Vereeniging, we soon cross the Vaal River into the Orange Free State Province, where Kroonstad and Edenville are situated. The two are very close to each other and, at one point, Edenville will be only eighteen miles to our left as we proceed to Kroonstad. I begin to see familiar names of railway stations, sidings, little towns that I passed so often years ago as I traveled between home and Johannesburg by train—Serfontein, Rooiwaal. Suddenly I see a road sign to EDENVILLE! The mere sight of it makes my heart pound, and my palms get clammy. When the car turns to go in that direction, I'm near panic. I can't just go *accidentally* to Edenville. I've got to psyche myself for it, brace myself for it. I ask, "Are we going to pass through Edenville?" "No," I'm told, and after a few kilometers we leave the Edenville road and once again pick up the one to Kroonstad. I feel as if fate has played a trick on me. My feeling of anxiety drops, and I breathe easier again.

I am now looking out for a little station called Heuningspruit. Should be coming soon, yes, there it is: HEUNINGSPRUIT is about eighteen miles or fifty-four kilometers from Edenville and was (perhaps still is) its railway link. This is where, as a little boy, accompanied by my older brother and sister, I had my first view of a train. When I saw it approach, it confirmed all the frightening stories I had heard about it: the earth shook, the black steam engine looked like a huge monster bearing down on us. But above all, Heuningspruit brings back to my mind my father. I always remember the day he hugged and kissed me, very happy and proud and laughing. I was again on my way back to Kroonstad Bantu High School, where, despite all obstacles, I was making excellent progress.

The approaches to Kroonstad are quite different from what I knew—new roads, some freeway-style overpasses, modern road signs. We pass through the white town into the inevitable sort of no-man's-land buffer between it and the black township complex we are heading for, which, we realize, to our consternation, is covered by a thick black cloud of smoke. We are told the smoke comes from the thousands of coal stoves used by the residents. We are to learn later that, though many residents have electricity and own electric stoves, they seldom use them because they get bills that are so outrageously high, often higher even than those paid by huge department stores with all the power they consume. Sometimes even people without electricity receive bills! The black cloud is frightening, and I feel a choking sensation just looking at it. We bore into it, and it is suddenly considerably darker as we negotiate the potholed streets that are in such stark contrast to the smooth ones in the white area.

Needless to say, Peter and Yvonne are excited to see us again. They quickly lead us into the house to get away from the irritating smoke that smells so strongly of charcoal. Peter is a junior high school principal. Yvonne worked in a clothing factory for years and held a supervisory position by the time she retired. They have a beautiful house where they live with their grandson, Pana.

Sunday, July 11th, is the day I have both looked forward to and dreaded. We drive to Edenville today. First we try to buy flowers to take with us. No success. Everything is closed. As we drive the twenty-eight-mile stretch, I try hard to identify old landmarks. They're all gone. The road runs at a different area altogether. I give up. It's as if a portion of my childhood is irretrievably gone. The old gravel road on which I often pedaled a bike to Kroonstad or back home, the farms, the tree lanes, twists and turns in the road, have been superseded by this modern two-lane tarred highway. As we get close, Peter points out Edenville Location to us. One man has built a double-story house, Peter says. In Edenville Location! Before I left, such a thing was not known, even in the white town.

As we enter the Location, now called Ngwathe, I am struck by several things: There's that beautiful double-storied house to our left, and a little way ahead, a night club. A NIGHT CLUB IN EDENVILLE LOCATION! Less than one hundred yards away there is a sprawling shantytown, shacks built with metal sheets of all types, mostly rusty, with some new shiny ones in between. To our right is the old Edenville Location, the one that nurtured me. It is a decaying dump of mud houses on dusty tracks for streets. The three images in this odd mixture constitute a powerful metaphor for South Africa that is both dying and reborn.

After a few bumps and shakes of the car, with people moving leisurely out of the way, Peter says, "There's our house." He stops the car opposite it. I see my brother Philip, my parents' last-born. He looks wasted. We all get out of the car, silent and solemn. We walk through the gate and see several people waiting inside the house, most of them standing, clearly because there aren't enough chairs, all of them with tears in their eyes. This is my first visit since my father died many years ago. My sister Sophia, my Aunt Boni, my brother-in-law David Malete, and others more distant, are also gone. The tombstones on my mother's and my father's graves were erected and unveiled in my absence. We have been told the unveiling was a big event, with lots of supporting relatives and friends, many of them from Kroonstad. I feel the tears in the eyes of this reception group are not only due to the fact that I am returning like some long-lost brother or uncle or grandpa or something, but plain and simple because life has not been so kind to them, and my coming is a reminder of that fact. In this mixture of emotions, I feel certain the fact that death has stolen away so many people in my absence is by far the most important.

As we enter the house, my eyes search for my sister, Magdeline. I look to my left and there she is, and, as she looks in my direction, she calls my name out loud and bursts out crying. I put my arms round her shoulders to comfort her, meanwhile controlling my own tears. She tries to stand up. It is difficult. She injured her ribs in a fall just yesterday. Magdeline, who fought the system for her right not to be moved. Selina and I last saw her in 1979 in Lesotho. She has changed considerably. She has gained a lot of weight and lost some teeth which she obviously has no money to replace. Her two sons, Jabulani and Suping, are also here. The children of my sister Sophia are here too. I embrace them. They cry. I comfort them, but my eyes are burning too, beyond the point of control. I wipe my eyes and continue embracing each one individually, many young enough to be my grand-something-or-others.

Reunion on Daniel Kunene's first day at Edenville, in front of his parents home. Selina Kunene is third from the left, Daniel stands in front of the door.

When feelings have calmed somewhat and we are able to talk, I'm introduced to everybody. Peter suggests that before we settle down, we should pass straight to the graveyard to pay homage to the dead. Yes, let's complete our journey, I say silently, and squeeze the pus completely from our wounds so they can begin to heal. Some people walk since there aren't enough cars. We park just inside the cemetery. We start to walk, Peter leading the way. I am on the lookout for the tombstones bearing the names of my father and my mother. A mixture of anxiety and fear almost paralyses me. I spot my mother's gravestone. We stop by it, and as I read her name, what I both dreaded and needed the most happens. I break down. I have one arm around Selina's shoulders, and she too begins to sob. I tell myself it is good. Thoughts crowd my mind. The uppermost is, it was my mother who allowed no obstacles—and they were legion— to stand in the way of our receiving an education.

We continue crying for some time. When our feelings subside, Peter makes a little speech in which he briefly mentions the care and sacrifice our mother bestowed on us. I am surprised and impressed by the strength in his voice and I think maybe that comes from being a preacher, albeit a lay one. We look around for some small stones which we all place on the grave and I say, "*O re roballe*" ("Sleep wee for our sake") and everyone says similar appropriate words. The Bible verse and hymn title on my mother's grave are in Sesotho. Next, we go to my father's grave, some distance away. As we stand solemnly there, my mind rushes back to a moment, many years ago, when the voice from Western Union in Los Angeles read the terrible message of my father's death over the phone and I felt the walls of our apartment pressing in on me. Again, Peter speaks appropriate words, brief and to the point. Once again, we place stones on the grave and repeat our small dialogue with the ancestors. The Bible words, the hymns, and the family message on the tombstone are in Zulu. We then go to the graves of my sister Sophia, my Aunt Boni, my brother-in-law David, and some Mokhanelis, which is the family my sister Sophia married into. As we get back into the cars, I wonder aloud if the African Methodist Episcopal Church still stands where it was before I left. Yes, but in answer to my implied request, we cannot go there now. Custom, which I should have remembered, enjoins us to go straight back home by the same route we came to the graveyard and wash our hands communally outside the gate before we go back inside. When we get home, we find that a small tub has already been placed outside for that purpose.

We settle down inside and soon young girls, all of them relatives, bring hot tea and home-made cakes and we drink and eat and begin to converse. Peter has suggested that we also visit the homes of the deceased who are closest to us, just to touch the soil with our feet. At Aunt Boni's, we have to explain to the present occupant the nature of our visit. We stand on the grounds, we look around and reminisce a little, and then we leave. We then go to Sophia's and end up at Magdeline's.

Those who are traveling today—to Kroonstad and to Johannesburg—must leave early, we are told, since the highways have become dangerous with random politically-motivated trapping and killing of people who are the wrong color and/or political persuasion. Whites hunt blacks and, in retaliation, blacks hunt whites. There are especially some highways which pass through stretches of white farms where AWB (*Afrikaner Weestandfeweging!* / Afrikaner Resistance Movement) vigilantes patrol regularly, especially at night, on the lookout for black travelers. Rankele had earlier told us of an experience where he and Thenji were the targets of such a pursuit early one evening in Kroonstad. It took some quick thinking and clever and daring maneuvers at the wheel to end up losing their pursuers, who had followed them right into Kroonstad Location where, part of the way, Rankele had to drive with his lights off.

The entire day, as we went to the graveyard and back and as we visited the homes I mentioned, the abject poverty of the residents was impressed on me by the dilapidated, neglected, virtually rotting state of the houses: rusted metal sheets secured by wire strands covering window spaces, or rags stuffed there in place of windowpanes; walls in sore need of repair, some with dangerous cracks. There seems to be a general state of despair, a kind of malaise. To my mind, these houses underscore the fact that their original owners and occupants have long since died. But what about their present owners? Is the art of plastering the walls with earth mixed with cow dung to preserve them and make them look and smell fresh not practical anymore? Maybe this is a reflection of the country's political turmoil and lack of direction in the apartheid era that has robbed the people of hope and of the joy of living. Uncertainty and a sense of insecurity are a kind of death sometimes more terrible than physical death. Our house is no different. There are two wide cracks that separate it from top to bottom into three sections which will no doubt soon drift apart enough for the entire structure to come tumbling down.

Be that as it may, tonight, my first night home, I'm going to sleep in my parents' house. It is much more comfortable at my sister Sophia's house, now occupied by her daughter Mmamosa, where a bedroom has been prepared for me and my wife. But tonight, I'm going to sleep in my parents' house. Magdeline suggests I shouldn't. It'll be too cold and drafty, and the bed is uncomfortable with slack springs and a lumpy mattress. Furthermore, it's mid-winter here, after all. She suggests the thought is as good as having done it. I'm almost persuaded. But something in me insists I must go. If I'm uncomfortable, even if I catch a cold, so be it. If I lie awake all night, so be it. I suggest to Selina she might want to sleep in the more comfortable place at Sister Sophia's. But she insists she is coming with me. They pile a lot of blankets on the bed and warm the room with a paraffin heater some time before we go to sleep. My brother Philip offers to spend the night there with us, in an adjoining room. We turn off the heater, blow out the candle. The bed is uncomfortable, but not too bad. The mountain of blankets on us keeps us warm enough. Next morning, we feel we have had more sleep than we expected.

Now, I feel, a major purpose of my visit to South Africa has been accomplished, even though there's a lot of ground to cover yet, including Potchefstroom, Selina's birth town, and Cape Town, where we established our own home after we got married, and where our firstborn, Zola, died at four weeks old, and where our next two, Liziwe Boitumelo and Sipho Thamsanqu were born, and where I taught at the University of Cape Town.

Monday, July 12th, we move back into my sister Sophia's house. It's a beautiful, clear, sunny winter day. After breakfast we take chairs and sit outside in the sun. People still bask in the winter sun as they did in our childhood, as Selina also remembers. When it gets too hot, especially when you are sitting next to a wall, you protect your head and face, and continue to move around the house following the sun like a sunflower. People pass in the street. They all greet: "*Dumelang!*" and we all respond: "*Ee, dumela mme*" or "*ntate*" or "*ausi*" and so on, depending on the age and sex of the greeter. Some stop at the fence to ask my sister Magdeline: "Is this your visitor from far away across the seas?" and my sister responds: "Yes, this is he, *mme*," etc., and since this is usually an adult, I get up and go to the fence to greet with a handshake. They appreciate it very much. I feel each handshake is a link across space and time. It is all so leisurely, so relaxing, so unhurried. You feel at last you have become reconciled with time, that it is no longer your enemy. I feel now I have arrived. This is home.

Later this afternoon we visit my sister Magdeline's for a cup of tea. During the conference at Wits, I had begun to hear rather disturbing things about the total breakdown of discipline in the black schools. Starting at Edenville, I make a point of talking with the teachers whenever possible. I am told that the students' behavior is totally irrational and that they are disruptive and defiant of authority.

It is mind-boggling. Students come drunk to school. One day, two of them came supporting another who was too drunk to walk and dumped him on a seat in the classroom, and when asked why they even bothered to bring him to school, they burst out laughing. They walk in and out of the classroom at will while the teacher is teaching, sometimes complaining it's too cold inside and going to sit in the sun outside. Sometimes they are all outside and the teacher stays alone in the classroom because that is his/her teaching time. Students break windows and glass doors. One time, one student took an iron bar and walked along an entire wall, smashing the windows purposefully and methodically. When asked why, he laughed.

As we hear more and more of these horror tales, my mind actively looks for an explanation. Could one link this up with a trauma which these young men and young women are acting out of their systems? I inquire what the average age of these students might be. From the answers I get, I am able to link them up with the SOWETO student uprising and its aftermath. I hazard the guess that the defiance of authority today is a direct legacy of the defiance of authority as part of the struggle for liberation. Then it was the evil authority of the agents of apartheid, especially the police. Then the children terrorized those who collaborated with the system, such as members of the government-established township community councils. They got results. We applauded it. Children decided strike action for their parents: "You don't go to work tomorrow, Father." "But…if you do, I won't be responsible for what happens to you." They got results. Elders were terrified of the children. This was the beginning to look ugly. They boycotted classes and ended up not going to school altogether. But they were growing older and missing school, such as it was. Their slogan was "Freedom First, Education Last ."

One could hardly blame the children. Education for blacks was in disarray, with the military and the police constantly present on the school grounds, creating an atmosphere of tension and confrontation. The children had grown up with a distorted sense of values, of which perhaps the worst was that authority was there to be defied. Of course, there are other factors that contribute to this behavior, including lack of hope, lives without a future to strive for. Secondly, the daily killings, either political or due to the sheer breakdown of law and order in a system that is itself the very antithesis of law and order, must lead to a great deal of frustration which unleashes the most negative elements of human behavior. There are no boundaries between defying authority that is part of an oppressive political system and defying all authority. This was all so easy to predict, yet there was nothing we could do about it.

It is Tuesday, July 13th. This the day we return to Kroonstad and Peter and Yvonne will be coming to drive us back. It's another beautiful, sunny winter day, so after breakfast we sit outside again, chatting and responding to greetings from passing neighbors.

Yesterday a rock standing in the right-hand corner of the front yard caught my attention. This rock is part of my childhood. It's been there ever since I can remember, in that very corner. It is surrounded by junk and all kinds of debris, including stones, chips of bricks, and concrete. It looks like a place where all kinds of rubbish is swept up. Yesterday I stated my intention to clean it up. Now I ask for a shovel and a rake to go and clean up the rock of my childhood. Jabulani disappears and soon returns wearing a pair of overalls, ready to do the cleaning up. Suping and my brother Philip help him, and I later join them myself, for the satisfaction of dirtying my hands doing it.

The backyard, which was a rich orchard of largely peaches when I was a child, with low crops like beans, pumpkins, peas, carrots, and so on grown among the trees every season, is now completely bare. It is now hard, solid ground. I am shocked, and I suggest that the soil could, maybe, be revitalized and new fruit trees planted. I hope someone will undertake to do it.

Peter and Yvonne arrive, and after tea at my sister Magdeline's house, we drive back to Kroonstad.

On Thursday, July 15th, our schedule takes us to my wife's birthplace, Potchefstroom, in the black township of Ikageng. As in Edenville, we are received by a whole group of relatives of different removes, extended family, young and old. The mood is lighter than at Edenville. There is even excitement and laughter. This is Selina's sister's house. Her name is Miriam. Miriam's house is pretty decent and presentable, built for her by her son Alpheus and her daughter Kganelo, who are twins. It is, in fact, an extension and improvement of what was Selina's and Miriam's parents' house. It is quite well furnished too. Both Alpheus and Kganelo are teachers, Alpheus the principal of his school. There are nieces and nephews and grand nephews and grand nieces. How close or distant is immaterial. Each one is claiming attention, which we give unstintingly.

Next morning, Friday, July 16th, we go to the O.K. Bazaar to buy flowers for the graves. As we enter, I recall many years ago when I was nearly assaulted by a tough white salesman called by secret phone to the department where I was trying to get service from the white young woman. My crime was that I objected to being called "John," the equivalent of "nameless nigger." He had come down some steps from an upper level, and I could see eye signals directing him to me. He came and stood right behind me, and the saleswoman, her nostrils flaring with excitement and anticipation, said, "Yes, John, what do you want?" Being aware of what was happening, I lay low. On my return to Cape Town I had written a long letter of complaint to the Johannesburg headquarters and an investigation ensued. They lied, which was no surprise to me. I was just happy that *some* action had been taken.

Today the interior of the store is very different. There's a lot of black staff in different positions—checkout and lower supervisory categories. They are friendly, they greet, they speak in Sesotho. Quite a transformation. We buy the flowers and leave in two cars for Stilfontein, a mining settlement, where Sarah, Selina's younger sister, is buried. The shanty town we drive through, with potholes as deep as ditches, is another example of a residential pattern we first saw in Edenville. We enter the cemetery, stop the cars, and get out. The emotional tension builds up as we walk towards Sarah's grave. We stand around it silently for a little while. My wife begins to sob, and I put my arm around her. I also cry, as we stand there holding each other tightly. We place the flower on the grave. Someone finds small stones which we place on the grave as we chant, "*O re roballe.*"

After we have slightly gained our composure, Selina says to me, "Would you like to say something?" I am full of words, but not the voice to carry them. I recall, for all those present, that the news of Sarah's death found us in Germany where I was a guest professor for one year at the Johannes Gutenberg University in Mainz. I had received the telegram at the door, opened it, and my grim expression prompted Selina to ask me, "Who is it? Is it Sarah?" She had been ill. I nodded my head. The funeral was going to be in six days' time. We mourned, with me nursing Selina and comforting her as best I could—doing the chores, cooking, and maintaining my schedule at the university. One afternoon, before the burial, I was in town when I was suddenly seized by an impulse to walk. I walked briskly, virtually marched down Grosse Bleicher, a wide street as its name implies, in the direction of the Rhine River—just walked and walked, as if possessed. I turned into numerous streets. I eventually retraced my steps to the tram stop at Schillerplatz, to return to Hechtsheim, where we lived.

When I finished talking, having managed only half of the above narrative, Ben, who has offered to come with us in his own car to carry more passengers, offers a prayer. He says very appropriate and comforting words. We place flowers on Sarah's baby son's grave as well, a little distance away. We repeat the same rituals as before. It is late afternoon. We intend to visit another graveyard in Potchefstroom before dark. On arriving there, we first stop by my wife's mother's grave. Her name was Selina – my wife is named after her. She died very young, in her mid-forties. After the rituals of flowers, stones, chants, a few speeches, we search for Selina's father's grave, which has no tombstone and is virtually impossible to locate. Furthermore, it's getting dark and we walk in grass that has nettles. Black cemeteries are not cared for by the municipality.

Next morning is Saturday, July 17th, and we go to yet a third cemetery to pay our respects to other departed relatives. Another of Selina' s sisters, Mary, popularly known as "Ou T"; Granny Mma-Monaisa, who died in her late eighties or early nineties; and Ouma Em (for Emily). We return home and once again wash our hands in a communal little basin.

By now, some trends have begun to emerge that I suspect are going to be confirmed over and over again as we travel to other towns and cities. The education crisis is one and perhaps the most important, since it affects the youth and is crucial to the country's future. Another one is housing, whose urgency can be judged by the shanty towns we have seen so far. Politically motivated violence that has become part of daily life in South Africa claims one's attention more immediately and intimately as one walks the streets and townships where it has occurred and is occurring. Also, there are unmistakable signs the people sometimes take drastic action to move toward achieving redress. And as a backdrop to all of this, there are the ongoing negotiations between the black organizations, led by Nelson Mandela, and white groups led by F.W. de Klerk. A feeling of drastic change is unmistakably in the air.

Did We Not Say?

Did we not say that
this battered SOWETO child
this baby weighed down by a killer gun
caged in prison cells like a murderer
lounging in foreign lands
without knowing the meaning of exile
whose years crept on him
as she shouted freedom first
and education last
whose youthful rising expectations
were sure to hit the rock
of the reality of power-hungry wolves
feasting on decay

would turn into an adult
devoid of dreams
ready to batter
the world that battered him?
To turn into an incestuous scavenger
feasting on the rotten system
that gave her birth?

Did we not say?
Did we not say"
       Daniel Kunene

Still to come: Cape Town, Port Elizabeth, King William's Town (site of the clinic established by Steven Biko), Umtata, Pretoria.

Suggested reading:

David Everatt and Elinor Sisulu, eds., *Black Youth in Crisis: Facing the Future.* Johannesburg: Raven Press, Pretoria.

William Raspberry, "Who Will Help South Africa's Illiterate Revolutionaries?" (Raspberry interviewing Dr. Ntatho Motlana), *Liberal Opinion*, May 23, 1994, p.7.

RETURN TO THE ROOTS:
South Africa, Thirty Years Later

By Daniel P. Kunene

During the summer of 1993, Daniel Kunene, accompanied by his wife, Selina, visited South Africa after thirty years in exile, most of it spent at the University of Wisconsin-Madison.

Part II

So, to Cape Town we go on Sunday, July 18th. As our flight approaches the city, we look for familiar landmarks, specifically Table Mountain and perhaps the University of Cape Town, which nestles at the foot of that mountain. Cape Town is home in a different sense from Edenville and Potchefstroom. This is where we created our own home after we married. This is where part of our blood, Zola, our first born, is buried. This the city from which we left South Africa on the *Pendennis Castle* on September 13, 1963, where the fragile link with the land and our friends and relatives was symbolized by delicate streamers held from the boat and from the land as the ship labored, tugged off from the pier by rugged little tugboats, the link that snapped and was to remain unmended for thirty years.

Prof. Sizwe Satyo, head of the Department of African Languages and Literature, meets us at the airport and drives us to the guest house, a restored old mansion, in Observatory, which, despite some modernization, has retained its elegance. We call our old friends Roddy and Hermine Wengrowe to tell them we have arrived. Hermine will pick Selina up tomorrow to spend the day with her. We are guests of the university till Friday next.

My first official assignment today, Monday, July 19th, is to give a talk to a first-year B.A. class on some aspect of literature. The class comprises only black students. I have been warned that the African literature classes have been divided into two groups, namely African mother-tongue speakers (Xhosa) and non-African mother-tongue speakers. The mother-tongue speakers, I am told, are able to read literature that the other group cannot. Another rationale for the separation is that, since English is the medium of instruction and discussion, the English-speaking students have an advantage over the non-English speaking ones in discussions and general class participation. The latter tend to feel intimidated. I feel extremely uncomfortable with this arrangement, but there is nothing I can do about it. I have not been given much direction as to the topic for this morning's presentation, nor any hint as to the level of comprehension and discussion to expect. In fact, it was left wide open: any topic I chose.

I have chosen a rather abstract topic, with the intention of illustrating from, *inter alia*, Thomas Mofolo's *Moeti oa Bochabela*. I have no sooner started than I realize I am not getting through to the class. The students' faces are blank. They are unresponsive. I ask if anyone has read Mofolo's book. "Raise your hands if you have." No hands raised. "Raise your hands if you haven't." No hands raised. I joke about "abstentions." No reaction. Conclusion: They have not read it. They don't' know it exists. Well, I think, Mofolo's is a Sesotho book and this is a Xhosa-speaking area. I ask if anyone has read A.C. Jordan's Xhosa novel, *Ingqumbo Yeminyanya*. There is neither yes nor no. I'm about to conclude they have not read it when a lecturer attending my presentation says: "But you *are* studying that book!" There's some embarrassed laughter. I don't know what to make of this. I fumble my way through the rest of that period. I feel this presentation has been a disaster. I should have been told what specific books they were studying and warned to make my lecture more concrete than abstract. The lecturers present feel differently; they say it was good and the students benefitted. I remain unconvinced. Tomorrow, I address the second-year group. I ask what books have been assigned to them. *Ingqumbo,* I am told. All right, *Ingqumbo* it shall be, with the standard pitched to their level. Today is Tuesday, July 20th. In addition to the second year B.A. class, I am also scheduled to address a faculty seminar today in the Department of English. The *Ingqumbo* discussion is very lively. We run short of time and express the wish to continue on another day if that could be arranged. I feel very happy and so does the class. I address the seminar on the journey motif in African literature. The discussion goes on reasonably well, and I'm satisfied. Selina again spends this day with Hermine, just relaxing at the Wengrowe home. In the evening, Roddy picks me up and we have a wonderful dinner together, reminiscing about old times.

Selina decides to spend the morning of Wednesday, July 21st, at the guesthouse. This is the day I give my main talk, which is the keynote speech I gave at the ALASA conference. Prior to the talk I am reunited with Dr. Vernie February, who holds a permanent research position at the University of Leiden's Afrika-Studie Centrum in Leiden, Holland. He is visiting the University of Western Cape, which has honored him with the position of "Professor Extraordinaire." It's an exciting reunion. He came for the presentation. I feel extremely happy about this talk. It comes off very well indeed, and the discussion is lively.

This afternoon, Prof. Satyo drives Selina and me to the Wolternade Cemetery, where Zola is buried. He first drives to the black township of Langa to pick up someone who knows the cemetery best to guide us in our search. The search turns out to be fruitless. Our information is too sketchy. First, we do not know which one of the thirteen or so gates to the mammoth burial place is the correct one. It soon becomes obvious that, even if we found the right gate, it would be absolutely impossible to identify the grave, though we have its number, since it has no tombstone or any other marker. When we left South Africa, we intended to return after my year's sabbatical, and we would have installed a tombstone at that time. Well, it turned out to be a thirty-year sabbatical!

This night Prof. and Mrs. Sathyo take us out for a special dinner treat. They have chosen the revolving restaurant atop the Ritz Plaza Hotel. It is a posh place and has live piano music this evening. As the restaurant revolves and reveals different parts of the city and landscape, our hosts explain what we see. One of the best sights is the ocean, and the white foam of the breakers on the rocks at the Seapoint shore create a ragged line along the coast. We also pass the pianist several times. At one point, we clap rather enthusiastically when he concludes a piece. The pianist notices us, and the next thing we know, he's playing "*Igqira lendlela*," the so-called "Click Song" popularized by Miriam Makeba. We laugh and conclude that this white pianist must have decided we were the sort of crowd that would simply love "*Igqira*." A white couple gets up and dances. We watch.

Before being picked up from the guesthouse on this Thursday, the 22nd, I call the Department of Births, Marriages and Deaths for assistance to locate Zola's grave. They give me the gate number and also verify the grave number. They give us the exact details of when our daughter was born, when she died, when she was buried. They also give the name of a caretaker to contact so he can help us find the grave. The caretaker, a "coloured" man, has an air of genuine sympathy. He gets in his car and asks us to follow him. He stops at the section where the grave is and begins to search, checking grave numbers, scratching at the bases of the low concrete rectangles built around some of them. He goes one direction, then another, then another, now and again checking the piece of paper we gave him. We begin to wonder, is the grave lost?

At last he stops by one grave and begins to measure with his feet. He does this in several directions. At last he stops, and with his foot he marks off a space on the ground and says. "Here it is." I ask, "Which side is the head?" and he points it out. We thank him. He tips his hat in a gesture of acknowledgement and sympathy and walks away to his car. Sizwe Satyo stands at a respectable distance trying to efface himself from the scene. We stand, tongue-tied. The silence, as we stand arm in arm by the grave of our first-born, is more eloquent than any words we might have spoken, if we could. I am the first to break down, Selina follows, and we stand sobbing there, trying to comfort each other with barely noticeable gestures of touching. Satyo remains passive at the distance he has created. At last we calm down. We look for ways to identify the grave for our next visit. Among other things, I carve a cross on the bark of a nearby tree.

Back at campus, I conduct a seminar for African Languages and Literature staff and senior students. After the seminar, Prof. Satyo drives me to the Wengrowes. Roddy and Hermine have arranged a sightseeing drive along the sea. They reveal some of their plans as we go along. We stop at different beaches to walk a little in the sand, maybe wet our feet a little, take pictures and so on. The houses here, in such suburbs as Llandudno, are huge mansions, some of them odd shapes, a veritable "conspicuous consumption" of wealth. It never ceases to amaze and annoy and frustrate me that some people can be so rich that they do unnecessary and sometimes downright nonsensical things with their money, while others, just a stone's throw away, live in rusty tin shacks with hardly any food to eat. This is a "conspicuous waste" of wealth. At our next stop, Roddy and Hermine point out peaks along the mountain range overlooking the ocean and tell us they are called "The Twelve Apostles." Of course, we knew about The Twelve Apostles before we left Cape Town, but had never been able to identify them. No better luck this time either. The apostles refuse to reveal their faces to us.

Abandoning the direction to Hout Bay, Roddy drives up to the top of Signal Hill. This is a great vantage point from which to see the city of Cape Town. The reason they have driven us here, they reveal as we wind our way up, is so that we can see the city lights come on at nightfall. Wonderful! As the darkness begins to gather, Roddy points out a blacker dot in the blackness of the ocean where a single light keeps flashing on and off. That, he says, is Robben Island. That brings a chill to my spine. The thought that people have been forced to spend up to thirty years of their lives on that island, in full view of the mainland, of "home," but despairing of getting away before the government had wreaked the last ounce of its terrible vengeance upon them, takes me through the most vexing, impotent anger. Many have died there, many psychologically damaged for life. But that also was the home, for twenty-seven years, of the likely next president of South Africa, Nelson Mandela, released in February of 1990. I ask myself, as I have done so many times, "Why do human beings do these things to each other?" I take a picture of the black spot in the middle of the ocean. Robben Island.

The city lights come on, one cluster after another. They come on on Robben Island too, a few flickering, individual light bulbs, it seems. I take a picture I feel certain will not come out. Roddy and I decide it's worth a gamble. One exposure. One can't go bankrupt on that!

From there, we drive to the city, all the way down to a place by the old docks called The Water Front. It was developed a few years ago, Hermine and Roddy tell us, as a kind of renewal and resurrection of the downtown area. It is close to the dock where, thirty years ago, we boarded the *Pendennis Castle*. The place contains shopping malls, ordinary shops, pubs, restaurants, curio and specialty shops. We first go around looking at a few shops. Then we stop for a beer. Following this, Roddy and Hermine deftly maneuver us towards a restaurant where they treat us to dinner. This has been an unforgettable, well-planned day, which unfolded as we went along, a wonderful outing with old friends going back to many years before we left the country.

On Friday, July 23rd, Prof. Satyo drives us to Stellenbosch University. I have never been to this university before, or in Stellenbosch town for that matter. It was a university that fully embraced apartheid, the brainchild of its intellectuals. But now, today, my wife and I are here at the university's invitation, with VIP status. Here we are hosted by Professors Jadezweni and Du Plessis, the latter being the head of the Department of African Languages. We are introduced to department staff as well as teachers from institutions which have an informal link with this department for furthering the training of their teachers. How ironic that the department is housed in the J.B. Vorster Building! One can't help thinking of the John Vorster Square in Johannesburg where black political prisoners were tortured under interrogation, and many died under strange, and sometimes not-so-strange, circumstances. But Vorster, former minister of justice and then president of South Africa, was at one time chancellor of this university even while he led the country deeper and deeper into barbarism. We are received very warmly.

I am asked to address the people gathered here on various matters, concerning the department's curricula, in particular the relationship of the language/linguistics area with the literature, a discussion that later inevitably includes oral and written as well as African-language and English-language literatures. There is a lot of excitement among the staff. The Africans among them are particularly excited, and I shake many hands at the end.

A special lunch has been arranged. We see more of the campus as we walk to and from the building where the restaurant is situated. This evening we are to leave for Port Elizabeth, so we cannot stay very long in Stellenbosch. We are given a gift of a half case of assorted Stellenbosch wines. After some photo-taking, we depart.

As we return to Cape Town, the approach is very impressive indeed, with Table Mountain dominating the scene. Despite the light rain and clouds, I take some pictures, focusing on Table Mountain, and hope for the best. Abner will take us to the airport from the guesthouse. As a farewell treat, we insist on having Cape Town fish-and-chips to throw our minds back to that little fish-and-chips shop we knew in Mowbray. On the way to the airport, Abner stops in Mowbray and buys us fish-and-chips, which we eat in the car as we drive. Rather greasy. We check in and I ask the rather amused staff at the check-in desk if we could take our unfinished fish-and-chips with us on the plane. Of course, they say, laughing. So, we do.

Selina and I have not been able to get seats together. It does not matter. It is not such a long trip. Maybe two to two-and-one-half hours at the most. I have a nice chat with a white businessman next to whom I sit from Cape Town to George, which is his destination. At George, my new traveling companion is another white man, an Afrikaner farmer. He is quite clearly furious about having to sit next to a black person. He is fuming as he squeezes past me to his wall-side seat. Maybe another forty minutes to Port Elizabeth. And this becomes the weirdest part of this trip, maybe of my entire South African tour. Or ever.

I turn to the man and say, "Hi." He mumbles a response. I ask, trying to draw him out: "Do you live in George or were you visiting here?" "Yes," he says. "You live in George?" "Yes, I have a farm here." As I am thinking what to say next, he asks me: "Where do you come from?" "From America," I say, consciously holding back the rest of the truth. Suddenly the man turns towards me and offers a firm handshake. "Well, I'm very glad to meet you," he says. Words to that effect. We fall into an uneasy, exploratory conversation. At least it was, on my part. I realize I'm committed to a lie, insofar as a half-truth is a lie. The man thinks I am an American negro, and he will talk to me on that assumption. I am willing.

In the process of the conversation, he tells me he does not like associating with certain people. Everybody has the right to decide whom he wishes to associate with. I mumble my agreement with the general principle. He goes on to state that he does not like being near black South Africans because they have a certain odor. It takes a lot to control my temper. Yet I must suppress even the slightest indication of the disgust I feel. The game must go on. I must hear more. I must not give him cause to be suspicious of my real national identity. He objects to blacks coming to his church for service. "They've got their own church," he declares. "Why'd they want to come to mine? They don't know the language." I interrupt: "You mean they come to the church but don't understand what's going on?" "Yes," he says, "so why do they come? They must go to their own church." I pretend that I'm as puzzled as he: Why would people come to a church where they don't understand the language the service is conducted in? In my heart I say, *You fool, that's a political statement, a sign of things to come.* But he believes that I'm puzzled like him.

Then there are the buses. Blacks, he says, leave their own buses and come and demand to ride in *his* buses. "So why do they leave their own buses and want to ride mine if they don't want to pay for it?" I corroborate. The fool. He is an anachronism, I tell myself. And an idiot to boot. All this ominous writing on the wall, the warning for the likes of him to mend their ways, he can't read it! "Are you going to P.E. [Port Elizabeth]?" I ask. "No, to Pretoria." I'm relieved. We're going to be met in Port Elizabeth, and the game might be up. I want him to go away believing he was talking to a different kind of black from the type he loathes.

"You know," he says, volunteering the information, "black people got no three-d." "Three-d?" I ask, amazed. "Yes, three-d," he says. "Do you mean three-dimension?" I ask, absolutely puzzled. 'Yes," he says, "three-d." "Well, why don't they have three-d?" I ask. With the faint smile of someone who knows these things, he says to me: "They never crawl on the ground when they are little, you know, like normal babies." "They don't?" I ask, truly amazed at this revelation. "No, they don't. You see, if you lived in this country you would see them. The mothers are always carrying them on their backs." "Really?" "Yes. Strapped with something to the mother's back." I say something like Ah or Oh. "Their feet are always hanging, they don't touch the ground until they are quite grown." "I see. So, that's why they've got no three-d?" I ask. "Yes," he says with great conviction in his voice. "You mean the mothers carry their babies even while they are working?" I ask, meaning to suggest to him some more sensible thing, such as, they get their sense of rhythm from feeling the mother's movements. He takes it differently. He thinks I mean when the mother goes to work for the white madam. I'm glad, because this makes him reveal more than I have asked. "No,' he says, a little confused, "when they go to work, they leave their children with their granny. You know, they always leave children with some relative." I refrain from asking if the granny or relative disallows the child to crawl. I'm satisfied the man is sure black people got no three-d. Must be one of the things that disgusts him about blacks. Such a perfectly normal thing as three-d! And they want to come to his church, ride his buses, and even vote. God forbid that the country should ever be cursed with a president who doesn't got three-d! Thus, my mind fills in the details he might have wished to.

We land at P.E. We spot our host for the weekend, Prof. Vuyiswa Maqagi. She's very excited to see us, and we spend a pleasant evening together. We extend our stay by one day, to spend Saturday, July 24th, there, mostly resting.

The day is spent in a rather leisurely manner. We are driven around P.E. for a brief sightseeing. We drive by "Khwetha Town." We are told that this "town" is, in fact, a modern version of a circumcision lodge. It constitutes part of the urban complex and consists of scattered shelters, each of which houses several "boys" in transition towards becoming "men." Past and present linking hands in a striking physical way, I think. The novitiates, we are told, are usually, and perhaps mostly, students from local secondary and high schools. When they are of the age to undergo the rites of passage to manhood, they choose a time for their seclusion, which will not interfere with their schooling, namely a school vacation long enough to allow them the free time to undergo their initiation, or traditional formal education, without interrupting their western-style education. This "lodge" is situated in a space between the black residential area where Vuyiswa lives with her family, and the white area, in a space that could have been a suburb of Port Elizabeth. She tells us that in the evening, fires are lit in these shelters for cooking, warming, and other purposes.

Our sightseeing also takes us past "Toilet town." This consists of privies made of corrugated iron sheets and stretching over several acres of ground. From a distance these look like giant tombstones, and our first impression is that we are looking at a graveyard. No, says Vuyiswa, who goes on to explain that since black shanty towns were springing up in all urban centers adjacent to black residential areas, including Port Elizabeth itself, the P.E. municipality had decided to provide some sites where future shanty towns would be built and provide toilets as a service. They are pit latrines, of course, not water-flushed. This would give the municipality some control over what has nationally become an urban phenomenon characterized by its spontaneity. Where, we ask as we have done so many times, do all these people come from? The answers vary, but sometimes overlap in certain areas. These answers are mostly conjecture: workers displaced from the white farms. Some farmers, we have heard, dismiss their black laborers and tell them to ask Mandela for a job. Some, most likely, come from the Bantu homelands, which many people rejected all along, anyway; maybe some from adjacent independent African states, refugees from the destabilized Mozambique, Angola, Lesotho, and so on. It's probably a combination of all these factors.

As we drive by a certain white suburb, our host tells us it's an AWB area. The AWB! The *Afrikaner Weestandfeweging!* (Afrikaner Resistance Movement.) This is a group of white right-wing extremists, the ones whose only response to the movement toward change is the rampant killing of any and all blacks anywhere and any time an opportunity presents itself. A South African counterpart to the KKK? One wonders. Gatsha Buthelezi is the only black who is welcomed most warmly in this area, our hostess tells us. Knowing that many right-wing conservative whites see Buthelezi as an instrument of divisiveness among blacks, that they see this as the only way they can cling to some of their outdated white-supremacist ideas, and that many of them have joined Buthelezi's Inkatha Freedom Party (IFP) as a result, we are not entirely surprised to hear this. Indeed, we have seen many times on South African television a white man appearing as a spokesman for the IFP.

What is surprising is that Buthelezi has apparently never stopped to ask what is in it for them. What do these white extremists stand to gain by supporting him? I remember that, in 1990, one of the aftermaths of Nelson Mandela's release from prison and the dawn of a new era in South Africa was that a significant number of right-wing whites were seen joining the Inkatha movement. The general sentiment, as voiced by some of them, was: "Our only salvation now is in joining Inkatha."

Visions of the so-called "black-on-black" violence, of the palpable presence of a "Third Force" manipulating things from behind the scenes, flash through my mind. An AWB suburb? Is this a sign of things to come? Of a separate white "homeland?" But it's not entirely surprising when one recalls how strongly President F.W. de Klerk advocated the retention of the Bantu homeland system in an interview by Ted Koppel in the wake of Mandela's release from prison.

On Sunday, July 25th, Vuyiswa drives us to the airport for our morning flight to East London, where we are to be met by car to be driven to Umtata. It's a long way, we are told, approximately four hours. Our driver is almost an hour late. He is a lecturer at the University of Transkei whom we met at the ALASA conference at Wits. He has been asked by Prof. Dorcas Jafta, who will be our host at the University of Transkei, to make a detour to drive us through the Ciskei, so the trip becomes a sightseeing and educational event. This is wonderful, since we have not been in this part of the country before.

This route will take us through King William's Town, our driver tells us. Excellent, I say. In that case we should make a further detour and go see the Zanempilo Clinic, established by Steve Biko, Mamphela Ramphele, and others. He has not been there himself, he says, but he will ask the way at King William's Town. Following the directions he is given in King, our driver soon leaves the tarred road and we travel on a gravel road for several miles to Zinyoka, the village where Zanempilo is situated. After a brief search, we arrive at this small, unassuming, rectangular building with whitewashed walls.

Daniel and Selina at Zanempilo Clinic established by Steve Biko and others in Zinyoka

The clinic is open. Only one person is around, a nurse. Our driver explains to her, in Xhosa, why we are there. We are visitors from America and we would appreciate being shown the place. The nurse obligingly shows us the various rooms, which include an examining room, a labor room, and a dispensary. The marvel of this place is what it symbolized when it was first built: The reawakening of a downtrodden people given a new sense of dignity and human worth through seemingly little acts of self-reliance and self-redefinition. That was what the Black Consciousness Movement did.

As we walk from one room to another, I feel a sense of awe. I stand where Biko stood, where his sense of purpose, his vision of the future of his people, blossomed into the reality of a clinic built by blacks and staffed by blacks, where the celebrated *ubuntu* of black people found concrete expression through the courtesy, kindness, understanding, and care with which the staff, comprising "educated" young blacks, treated the users of the facility, who were largely "uneducated," illiterate, and often older. It gave them hope and a new sense of identity. Realizing that was a freedom more fundamental and enduring than the breaking of the physical chains of bondage (since it rebuilt the shattered lives of the people), the government panicked, invaded the place, arrested Biko, and banned and banished Mamphela Ramphele. For this seemingly little act, Biko was brutally murdered by the police while in custody.

The nurse tells us also about the church at the back of the clinic. This too was built by black people with their own hands to replace the tiny structure that originally served as a church. When we are about to go outside to walk on the grounds, we ask the nurse to pose with us for a photograph. She declines, but says we are free to take the pictures. We do, with the clinic as background, and afterwards the church.

As we drive back over the bumpy gravel road towards the tarred highway, I cannot help conjuring up the picture of Biko in shackles, naked, locked in the back of a police van, driven to a prison 800 miles away, for the crime of awakening a people's sense of dignity. I pee on the side of this deserted road. It gives one a sense of freedom, of abandon. We reach the highway and resume our journey. It does not take long before we reach the Ciskeian border.

"*Wamkelekile eBisho* ("Welcome to Bisho") says a sign. Our driver stops and points out to us a soccer field not far from where we stand. That's the place where the massacre of ANC supporters took place shortly after they passed the "Welcome" sign and entered the Ciskei to demonstrate the unity of South Africa as a country and the need for the re-incorporation of the Bantu homelands into South Africa. The president of the Ciskei, Gqozo, ordered the massacre. All Bantu homelands do most of their dastardly deeds at South Africa's behest. This was no exception.

There is a little shopping center, with shops like Spar situated in multiple-story buildings. Bisho is the capital of the Ciskei. The brand-new town of Bisho, which consists of the shopping center, office buildings, and government administration buildings some distance away from where we are, was built in order for the Ciskei Bantu homeland to have a capital. The natural capital would have been King William's Town, but the whites in King would have had to move, and they refused. Simple. Then Bisho was conceived and born, to grace the head of the Ciskei Bantu homeland.

After this detour, we have to drive for what feels like an eternity before we rejoin the bigger highway linking East London and Umtata. The road seems interminable. Village clusters occasionally adorn the otherwise bare landscape. The surrounding hills do little to relieve the bareness and monotony of the stark winter countryside. As we cross the border to enter the Transkei, the driver slows down but is motioned to pass.

Here sheep, goats, and cows graze unmindfully along this modern two-lane highway. Mostly they keep away from the middle of the highway, to which they are so dangerously close. But occasionally you come across a casualty, and you wonder how the humans in the automobile fared. Or a cow slowly ambles its way across the highway, stops, apparently confused, looks around either because it does not know where to go or is in no hurry to go wherever it is it wants to go. All traffic stops in the middle of this modern highway in deference to this bovine disorientation. I am so tired of sitting in the car. Selina dozes on-and-off in the back seat in this seemingly interminable journey.

Another stop. The driver tells us that to our left (facing where we are going) is the village where Nelson Mandela was born. He cannot point out the exact house. I take a picture. On the opposite side of the highway he points out a red-tile-roofed modern mansion. That, he says, was built for Mandela to live in whenever he visits his birthplace. Mandela, who was in on the planning of the house even while he was still in jail, decided to have the house designed to the same plan as the Victor Verster Square, the last prison in which he was confined. We are totally amazed to hear this. Why? We keep asking. Why would he want to perpetuate the memory of that experience? Was Mandela referring to Victor Verster Square when he said, in one of his speeches after his release, that jail was really not that bad?

We cannot wait to reach Umtata. The journey has been long and often tedious, punctuated only by the places of interest we have seen. We pass Idutywa. We don't have much farther to go, our driver tells us. At last we arrive in Umtata. We are accommodated in the Protea Hotel. That evening we are entertained to dinner by our hostess, Prof. Dorcas Jafta. We are reunited with an old friend, Prof. Lucas Mbadi, who lived in our house in Cape Town when he was a graduate student there. We also meet Prof. and Mrs. Thipa, among others.

It is Monday, July 25th. We are picked up by Prof. Jafta for our first and only full day on the campus of the University of Transkei. I am to give two lectures, I am told: one in the morning to a large first-year class, and one in the late afternoon to a senior group, which includes "extension" people. Prof. Thipa leads us to the hall where the morning class is meeting. As we walk in from the back of the hall to proceed down the sloping aisle to the front, suddenly, apparently at a signal, the entire class stands up. This creates an atmosphere of reverence. We are honored, we are respected. There is more to it than just a professor from some foreign country who is going to speak to a class, walking with his wife. This demonstration of respect creates a new mood, and it casts us in a more elevated role than we had anticipated. We get to the front and take our seats, and this class of well over two hundred students sits down. Prof. Thipa introduces me and I get up to address the class.

No sooner have I started than I know this is going to be a big success. I have my audience and, I am certain, my audience has *me*. There is perfect silence, only writing. For the first time in my travels, I feel there's a hunger for education that is sometimes lost in the pandemonium of violence, disruptive behavior, lack of discipline, and defiance of authority that now characterizes the black youth in this country. There is a yearning for knowledge that I see in these young faces, and there is a readiness and a willingness to learn. Am I wrong? Is this behavior reserved for me alone because I am a distinguished visitor? I do not think so. It is unstudied. It is natural. It could inspire you with a sense of mission.

Following the lecture, there are some questions from the audience, after which my host conducts me back to my chair and asks me to sit, which rather surprises me because I am expecting us to leave the auditorium. No sooner am I seated than a man's voice breaks out near the back of the room. All heads are turned to where the voice is coming from. I look up, and I see a young *imbongi* draped in his ceremonial skins, holding a ceremonial stick, coming with measured steps down the aisle. My God! He is singing my praises! It all gushes out of his mouth with amazing ease and fluency. Spontaneous? My doubt is soon erased. Otherwise, how did he get all those points from my presentation which he incorporates into his poem? As he moves down toward the place where I am sitting, I ask myself, "How am I to behave? How does one receive this kind of compliment with grace and proper decorum?" At first there is some sniggering from the young audience. I interpret it to mean: *How can this fellow do such a primitive thing before such an important guest from America?* The sniggering quickly dies away. I believe it must be because they see how seriously I regard the tribute.

The poet comes and continues his praising in front of me, now turning to the audience, now to me, as he addresses some words to me. It is all in Xhosa. Now and again my name comes in either directly or in a genealogical reference, one of the highest forms of praise, introduced by a phrase the equivalent of "the Son-of-So-and-So." It is a struggle for me to keep the tears from rolling down my face. I remember Alex Haley hearing a *griot* singing his praises when he entered the Gambia as the descendant of Kunta Kinte and the celebrated author of *Roots*, when he said how he fought back his tears, because, he argued, one cannot be bawling all the time, or words to that effect. I succeed in driving the tears back into my chest. Yes, my chest, not my eyes. Tears come from the chest. The eyes are merely a passageway. When the *imbongi* finishes, with a request to God to bless and protect me, I get up spontaneously and embrace him. There is prolonged applause. He is a natural, a recognized poet. Afterwards, we are treated to tea and snacks, shown around the campus, and then driven back to the hotel for lunch and rest.

The afternoon lecture is preceded by a visit to the vice-chancellor's elaborate office. He is not happy about the political situation. In fact, he makes it plain that, much as some people might try to persuade one to return to South Africa, this is not the time. There is too much uncertainty, he says. "If you are settled in a job where you are, don't come back." He has advised his own daughters who are overseas not to return to South Africa at this time.

My evening lecture, which takes place in a large auditorium full to capacity, goes well, even though it does not connect quite as well as the morning one. This is followed by a few questions, after which the *imbongi* comes out again to sing my praises once more. There is quite a bit of ululating from some women in the audience, electrifying the atmosphere. When this is over, the audience is requested to remain seated, and my wife is called up to join me on stage. She is introduced briefly, and then two girl students come on the stage carrying gifts for us. Another unexpected event. We can hardly contain our excitement as we rip the wrappings apart to reveal an ornamental pipe with beautiful multicolored beadwork around the stem, a Unitra tie, Unitra pens, a little wooden cloth-draped doll decorated with colored beadwork and attached to a key ring, etc. We are overjoyed. We kiss on the stage, to the tremendous joy of the capacity audience and the host's admonition: "You younger folks, take note!"

The lecture is followed by another reception, more speeches, more hints for a speedy return. We are then driven back to the hotel where we have dinner. Before we finish, my old student and friend, Dr. Wandile Kuse, and a friend who studied at Northwestern University, Dr. Pule Phoofolo, accompanied by another ex–University of Wisconsin student, Dr. Jeff Perez, come in and walk towards us. We are all excited. They leave us alone and go to the bar, where we later join them. It is a wonderful evening, and we part rather late to go to bed.

Our flight to Jan Smuts Airport on Tuesday, July 27th, leaves after 3:00 p.m. We occupy the morning with a brief round of sightseeing, mainly the campus, where I take a few pictures. I have noticed, after my first few hours on the campus of the University of Transkei at Unitra, that the entire campus is under one roof. As we were conducted from one building to another, it soon became obvious that all of the buildings were interconnected. So even when you climb wide "outside" steps, you are still "inside." I wondered aloud about the wisdom of this, and feared that a structural weakness or defect in any one part could affect the rest and one day the entire campus might simply crumble down because a crack developed in one corner.

During the campus tour, Dorcas tells us that the dining hall had borne the name "A.C. Jordan Dining Hall," but some rather ignorant activist students had demanded that the name be removed because they did not want the names of "settlers" or "imperialists" on campus buildings! I ask, "Have they never heard of *Ingqumbo Yeminyanya*? Which is an idle question because, in fact, the book is constantly prescribed for African literature classes. We have also asked Dorcas to drive us to a place where we can buy some handicrafts. It is a windy, dusty day, so windy that I am rather concerned about the small aircraft which will carry us to Johannesburg. Fortunately, as the day wears on, the wind subsides considerably.

At Jan Smuts Airport, Prof. C.T. Msimang, who is to drive me to Pretoria to stay at the Unisa guesthouse as visiting professor at Unisa, and by my brother's daughter, Thenjiwe, and her husband, Rankele Nthebe, meet us. They are here to drive my wife to Potchefstroom to stay with her sister, Miriam, while I will be at Unisa for about twelve days.

It is a little after dark when we arrive at the Unisa guesthouse. Prof. Msimang leaves me there to settle in. About an hour later he returns and we drive to a restaurant, picking up Prof. Louw on the way. I remember Prof. Louw from many years back, from the early fifties, to be exact, when he was a student at Stellenbosch University writing a dissertation on the Zulu ideophone. I remember how he used to visit the University of Cape Town to discuss his research with me and Prof. Sam Guma when we ourselves were students at UCT. I wonder what he looks like now. Prof. Louw and I recognize each other immediately, though we realize, of course, that many years have gone by since we last saw each other.

At the dinner we are joined by Unisa's professor of Venda. As we are looking through the menu, I suddenly burst out laughing as my eyes pick out an item called "ladies' loins and rumps." While I don't want to be rude, I also can't miss the opportunity to poke fun at the waitress by pointing out the item to her and saying it out loud. She smiles. I wonder if I dare to order that item. It sounds so… so x-rated, fit for mature adults only. I tell myself I will not be corrupted by this place. Meat and potatoes! That's what I'll have.

I have been informed that I am being invited by Witwatersrand University to address them on the following day. This had originally been scheduled as a free day for me, so I am rather disappointed. On the other hand, I do look forward to speaking at Wits.

I am picked up mid-morning on Wednesday, July 28th, by one of the young black lecturers from Wits where I am received and hosted by Prof. Gule. I renew my acquaintance with Molly Bill and Bob Herbert and some other faces I first met at the ALASA conference about three weeks ago. Molly Bill takes me for a quick lunch at a nearby Italian restaurant. On the way back to campus, I make a quick stop at the Wits University Press to talk to its editor, Eve Horwitz.

Wits has picked the topic, "Time As a Narrative Organizing Element in Nyembezi's Novels." The talk goes well. As we wait for the elevator to leave the building, Nhlanhla Maake comes to me to apologize for missing my talk, explaining that he had to rush to Thokoza Township where a friend of his had been stabbed. Fortunately, it was not fatal, but he was admitted to the hospital. Who knows the motivation of this particular act of violence?

I am driven back to Pretoria.

On Thursday, July 29th, I give my first formal lecture—at 8:30 in the morning! The topic picked from my list for this lecture is "Criteria of Excellence: Who Owns Them?" I feel good about the lecture, which is followed by a lively discussion cut short by time as the next users of the room are waiting at the door. Following lunch, I spend a portion of the afternoon in my office and then go back to the guesthouse. The rest of the day is routine.

There is not much activity on Friday, July 30th. After lunch the campus is mostly deserted. One gets the usual campus TGIF atmosphere. In the early evening I am picked up by Ken and Rosalie Finlayson for dinner with Prof. Msimang and his family in Mamelodi. During the approximately thirty-to-forty-minutes' drive, I soon observe that Ken barely slows down as he approaches the stop signs at street intersections, and then accelerates and crosses without stopping. This happens largely as we drive through or near black residential areas. Ken explains that at the first stop sign, he looked through his rear-view mirror and noticed a combi taxi driving behind us and apparently not slowing down in approaching the intersection. He remarks, "If I had stopped, we might have been hit." Apparently, it is generally expected that stop signs are there to be ignored except to avoid a collision.

I meet Prof. Msimang's wonderful family. The Swanepoels soon join us, and I meet Anne-Marie, Prof. Swanepoel's wife, for the first time. Prof. Serudu and his wife also join us later. It's a wonderful evening. The conversation drifts from one topic to another. The one that sticks in my mind is the one I have heard so much in different parts of the country, namely the lawlessness, lack of discipline, and total lack of commitment to education in the black schools. What makes it worse is that teachers themselves are taking advantage of the situation to become lawless and intractable to the principal, thus exacerbating an already ugly situation.

The South African Democratic Teachers' Union (SADTU) is said to encourage teacher delinquency by sometimes calling unnecessary strikes, with the supposedly "striking" teachers having a lot of idle time on their hands, yet unable to say what the strike is about. Those few children who are trying to attend school seriously are thus left in the lurch. Some teachers, we are told, take advantage of this to concentrate on their own private studies. One Unisa professor says he sometimes spots some whom he recognizes, and he makes comments to their faces about the irresponsibility of their actions. Why aren't they reported to the authorities? They are reported, we are told, but the government does nothing about it, arguing that it is afraid to infringe on the teachers' individual rights. The teachers therefore engage in their delinquent acts knowing that they will receive all their pay in spite of work days missed.

It becomes obvious to me that this total chaos in education for the black child works as much in the government's favor as the political violence that is switched on and off at will. That is why teachers are rewarded for skipping teaching for no good reason. The more such chaos exists at all levels, the more time it buys the white government to remain in control. It makes one wonder about the origin of SADTU itself.

On our return to the guesthouse in Pretoria, we see traffic lights being sometimes ignored around the same area where the stop signs were also being ignored. It's the law of the people, I surmise: Where the law is too rigid to make sense, they ignore it.

This day, Saturday, July 31st, I am going to be a guest of the Swanepoels for dinner and spend the night with them. I throw together some leftovers for my lunch, and I do some bits and pieces of work. Mainly I am waiting until Chris Swanepoel comes to drive me to his house at about 5:00 p.m. On arrival there, I meet the Swanepoels' two teenage sons, Kobus and André, and their mother, Anne-Marie, whom I met last night. They are a wonderful family, who give me a very warm welcome. By the time Chris came to fetch me, he had already built a wood pile in a half steel drum (cut top to bottom), ready to be kindled for the *braaivleis* or barbecue. This is a wonderful idea, I tell Chris. I have never seen one like this before. The grill part consists of a thick wire mesh that covers the entire surface of the open part of the slit drum. The cooking surface is nice and wide. Furthermore, the fire is made of wood only. Contrary to my expectation, the wood embers hold the fire long enough and strong enough to barbecue meat for all of us.

Chris and I stand around the fire having cold beer while he barbecues the meat. I feel a bit chilly, and Chris lends me a sweater.

Other members of the family are busy inside preparing the rest of the meal. I notice the piano and, loving music as I do, I state my wish to have someone play the piano sometime during my visit. I learn that the two young men, André and Kobus, play musical instruments, Kobus the cello and André the violin. Anne-Marie plays the piano. Suzanne, the Swanepoels' daughter, currently in Cape Town, is also a musician, I am told.

"What about you?" I say to Chris half-jokingly, half-seriously, thinking how odd it would be if he were something like *only* a professor of African languages and literature at Unisa with all this musical talent and activity around him. "I'm supposed to be a baritone singer," Chris responds modestly. "My God!" I say, "the entire family!" I am excited, emotional, and perhaps even a bit sentimental about all this.

"Good Lord, my family was a singing family! All of us!" I blurt out. "We even staged concerts in our house!" I am emotional about it because it reminds me that, had I grown up in any other country but South Africa, I would have been a musician. I sang, trained, and conducted choirs and composed choral pieces that I taught to singing groups. I made attempts at learning to play the piano, which was my favorite instrument, but was always frustrated by lack of money to pay a piano teacher and had no piano on which to practice.

I remember how, as a child, I used to turn over a chair with steel rods bolted underneath to brace it, and twang them with my fingers, listening to the different pitches from the four rods and even trying to "play" them in harmony. I remember how, as a teenager in Johannesburg, I was offered free lessons by a white professional pianist at a hotel where I worked as a page boy; how I had to travel at least two hours on foot and by tram to reach a house in Western Native Township where I attempted to practice while family members were carrying on their normal activities and conversing all around me as I tried to concentrate. I remember how the lady pianist was summoned to the hotel office by the manageress and warned never again to allow me to practice on her piano in her room, something she had done as a desperate move as she realized my plight, and how I too was raked over the coals by the same manageress and reminded that my only relationship with the residents was as a servant. Did I want to keep my job? Of course, I did. And that ended that, and the lady pianist left the hotel not too long after this incident.

Oh, I remember many more things about my fruitless efforts to realize my life's calling, which would be too tedious to recount here, but which crowded into one brief moment as I heard about the Swanepoel musical family. Am I implying that if I had been white I would have become a musician?" YES. A great one. By which I mean if South Africa had not been so cruel to its black citizens and had I had the same opportunities as white kids, I would have been among the greatest. I remember that, as a young teenager, whenever I dozed off briefly, I would wake up with the most angelic choral music in my head receding away from me and strongly accented by the red/pink color of the inside of my eyelids, which could also be slowly clearing away at the same time as I returned to full wakefulness.

After breakfast on Sunday morning, August 1st, Anne-Marie, André, and Kobus form a trio to play some music for me. It's a mini-concert staged specially for me. While Kobus cuddles his cello and André holds his violin and bow in readiness, Anne-Marie sits at the piano. They start to play the first piece. Chris is sitting on the floor next to the chair I'm sitting in. As they begin to play, a picture of my family, especially my father and mother, with us children sitting on the floor and singing from a *tonic sol fa*–notation musical piece, flashes in my mind, and I have to struggle to push back my tears. I think I have succeeded, and that they have returned deep down into my chest. But, looking at the mother and two sons playing, I soon realize that I am fighting a losing battle.

In order not to spoil the concert and have to explain what brought it all on, I stand up quickly and rush to my room where I let it out quickly and briskly, and regain my composure before returning to my special concert. I wonder if they noticed, and if so, what they thought brought it on. They play about three pieces altogether. At the conclusion, I embrace each one to express the deep appreciation I feel.

Chris and Anne-Marie drive me back to the guesthouse, where I spend the rest of the day doing odds and ends.

It is Monday, August 2nd, and I am going to be shown around the campus today. I look forward to it very much, especially the stop at the publishing section of Unisa. My book, *Heroic Poetry of the Basotho*, first published by Oxford University Press in 1971, has been published from here "for exclusive use by Unisa students" ever since 1983, when it went out of print at Oxford. I had heard way back that the book was considered the "Bible" of students studying the heroic or praise poetry of Southern Africa. Professors Lenake and Swanepoel, I am told, were responsible for keeping it alive by requesting that Unisa publish it. They have told me that they see its continued use way into the foreseeable future.

My guide, who comes to pick me up from my office for this tour, is Yvonne Mashingo. I tell her I will not forget her name because she bears the first name of my sister-in-law and the last name of a tall, handsome man who worked as a waiter at the hotel in Johannesburg where I was employed as a "page boy" many years ago, the same one where my piano-learning attempts were brought to an abrupt end. The tour takes me from one building to the next, with Yvonne giving me a very articulate and interesting explanation of the function of each one. She knows the campus inside out and is an excellent "PR" person.

I see one of the largest and most modern auditoriums I have ever seen, where, *inter alia*, graduation ceremonies are held. I wonder if they ever fill it. Yvonne knows the histories of the different structures, the emblems, etc. The library is also very modern and well equipped. I ask to go to the stacks where works of African literature are shelved. We can only spend a limited amount of time here, of course, since there are other parts of the campus still to visit. We visit the archives, and I feel a sense of history around me as I see names and works of old linguists and collectors of oral traditions gathered here.

The publishing department is our last stop. I am introduced to Mrs. Van der Walt who is in charge of this area. I am simply amazed at the amount of publishing that is done here, the largest university publishing house… in the country? In the world? I don't remember which. Mrs. Van der Walt is very polite and efficient. She is excited to hear that I am the author of one of their publications, and one of their hottest items at that. She orders tea and meanwhile discusses with me some of the technicalities of Unisa's relationship with primary publishers whose out-of-print books the republish.

She brings out records of the sales of my book, and I realize that it isn't doing too badly. I try to order my book for my African poetry class back at the University of Wisconsin, only to be told that Unisa's contract with Oxford University Press specifically excludes sales outside of South Africa. How ironic! So many professors can use my book, but not me! This is obviously a situation to be corrected. Faxes begin to fly, and the anomaly is finally resolved. Yes, the book's author may order it for his classes, wherever in the world he may be.

Tonight at 7:00 p.m. I am going to be entertained to supper by Prof. Rosemary Moeketsi, at her house. She is planning to invite several colleagues and friends to meet me. I know someone is going to pick me up, but who and what time I'm not exactly sure. At about five-thirty my phone rings. It's Prof Lenake, calling me from Reitz in the Orange Free State. He tells me that he and Prof. Swanepoel are supposed to drive me to Prof. Moeketsi's house, but Reitz is almost three hours' drive away from the guesthouse where I am. I have no choice but to sit and wait.

The phone rings a few more times, and eventually the plans change. Prof. Moeketsi suggests she bring the dinner and some of her guests to the place where I'm staying, thereby cutting time and travel by half. Does the guesthouse have a stove and a refrigerator? I tell her yes. In fact the kitchen and the lounge/dining room are both quite spacious, very pleasantly furnished, and scrupulously clean. She estimates it will take them about forty to forty-five minutes.

They arrive in just over half-an-hour, she and four guests. The normally rather cold and sterile guesthouse is suddenly alive. They have brought the food in big containers, as well as some wine and beer, which go into the refrigerator together with the desert. Prof. Moeketsi has also brought a bouquet of flowers in a vase. Wonderful! We enjoy the conversation, the food and drinks. Pictures are taken. Johnny Lenake and Chris Swanepoel arrive and join the party. This turns out to be the best alternative to the original plans.

What a wonderful evening this has been. I take the flowers to my room and say goodbye to my hosts-cum-guests.

RETURN TO THE ROOTS:
South Africa, Thirty Years Later
By Daniel P. Kunene

Conclusion

It is Tuesday, August 3rd. This morning I address the Department of African Languages and Literature on the topic, "Time as a narrative organizing element in Nyembezi's novels." Not long after I start, and as I warm up to my topic, the door of the auditorium at the far end from the rostrum opens, and a rather heftily-built woman comes in accompanied by a man. They come straight down the aisle towards me, past where the rest of the audience is sitting. My first impression is that they are enthusiasts who are late for my lecture and who want to come and sit close to the podium. But what happens next startles me and brings my presentation to a screeching halt. The woman, who I now realize is on the warpath as she comes and stands right in front of me with the man who comes trotting down the aisle with her, looks up at me and shouts, "When are you going to finish? I am supposed to have this room right now. I have a guest speaker who is supposed to have started already. When are you going to stop?"

I am stunned. I look at my host, Prof. Themba Msimang, who is sitting close to the front, and I shrug my shoulders and say, "Prof. Msimang, I commend myself into your hands," or words to that effect. Prof. Msimang tells the woman he reserved this room for my lecture, and says there must be some mistake, would the woman go outside with him to try to settle the matter. The woman follows

Prof. Msimang with the gentleman I assume is her guest speaker following her like an obedient puppy. Before the door shuts behind them, I make a joke about the incident that brings the house down with laughter, which I'm sure the woman hears. I tell myself she deserves it. Prof. Msimang, always ready to see the funny side of things, later tells us what happened outside the auditorium. It was obvious that a mistake had been made in the office that allocated the room. So, he says to the woman, "I am sure we can settle this matter through negotiation with the space management office." Whereupon the woman, who is now rather distraught, shouts, "Negotiation! Negotiation! This country has got into a mess because of *negotiation*!!" And Themba is laughing his infectious laughter as he narrates the incident.

I look forward to an evening at the Finlaysons for supper and drinks. After this morning's experience, I feel I cannot wait to relax and share conversation, food, and drinks with friends and colleagues, and indeed *negotiate* a few things. Prof. Swanepoel drives me to the Finlaysons' house in the late afternoon, but he cannot stay. Prof. Rosalie Finlayson is dressed resplendently as he welcomes us from the end of this long, tunnel-like passage leading toward the living quarters of the house. This is a part of Pretoria with large estates and mansions, including some consulates and embassies. It is called Waterkloof. Ken Finlayson is his usual amiable self as host. I get reacquainted with Prof. Finlayson's mother, whom I first met when she accompanied her daughter to the guesthouse a few days ago. She is absolutely charming, and she and I enjoy quite a long conversation together. There's music and lively conversation among all the guests, who are colleagues and students. At the end of the evening, I am given a ride home by one of the guests. In a BMW!

Wednesday, August 4th, is a routine day: breakfast at the guesthouse, lunch with colleagues at Unisa, some time in my office. For supper, Prof. Lenake takes me to a very nice restaurant somewhere close to the Waterkloof area. It's quite a long drive but it's all worth it. The food is excellent and the service efficient, courteous, and even personally friendly. I keep having to remind myself that I *am* back in South Africa, being served by white waitresses and wine stewards, and that thirty years ago this would have been unheard of.

Return to the Roots: Conclusion

Thursday, August 5th is the eve of my departure from Unisa. I look forward so much to being reunited with my wife tomorrow at Potchefstroom. I have called her almost daily since we parted at Jan Smuts Airport on our arrival from Umtata almost two weeks ago. I give my second-to-last workshop. The topic is "Dialogue in C.L.S. Nyembezi's novels."

I was invited this morning, apparently on the spur of the moment, to have lunch with one of the lecturers, Ms. Hlumela Motlhabane, at her house in a Pretoria suburb. On the way there, she picks up a friend from her place of work. She lives in what appears to be a growing suburb of Pretoria. It is integrated and, as if to prove this, as we arrive there my hostess's daughter, about eleven, arrives from school with her white schoolmate.

Not long after we get to Hlumela's place, we are joined by Rose Moeketsi and perhaps two other people, all lecturers or assistants in the Department of African Languages and Literature at Unisa, whom I had already met on campus and at the Finlaysons' party.

It is a pleasant and relaxing afternoon, cut short by the need for me to get back and prepare for my departure the next day. Furthermore, this same evening, I'm to be entertained to dinner by Prof. Chaphole, whom I met at the conference at Wits, and who teaches at the Soweto campus of Vista University.

Evening comes. Prof. Chaphole picks me up from the guesthouse. He is accompanied by his wife and another woman. Chaphole has chosen a very exclusive restaurant in the city, in a building with a front that resembles a public office building, with many wide concrete steps leading to the front entrance. It specializes in Italian foods but serves other entrees as well. The place is empty. It feels unhomely. We are seated not far from the entrance, near the reception counter. We are not particularly happy about this spot, and our understandably suspicious minds tell us this is unofficial apartheid. Why isolate us to the spot where we will be disturbed and subjected to drafts as people come and go? And where we would be isolated from the rest of the diners? Furthermore, Prof. Chaphole had reserved our table so long in advance. We tell the man in charge, who seems to be doing everything by himself—receiving diners, taking them to their tables, seating them, etc.—that we want another table.

He is a tall, rather reddish-complexioned man whom I assume is Italian. He is very obliging, saying we could pick any table we chose. So we move to another table. More people start coming in, and it begins to feel homely. The man is also joined by two black waiters, one of whom is assigned to our table. He brings menus which are big and rather intimidating, the sort of menu that brings all conversation to a halt as you try to figure it out. We make our choices and settle back to our conversation.

I keep wondering what it's like to be a Vista professor. Thoughts of my conversation with the young lecturer from Wits who drove me there for my lecture on July 28th, and of my brother's experience of "apartheid" treatment by a white woman receptionist at another Vista campus (in Welkom, Orange Free State) keep coming into my mind. Would I accept even the most lucrative job, even as a visitor, to a place like that? I imagine myself subjected to racist white authority, which has become totally alien to me in my thirty years away from South Africa. I know, for example, that students at Vista in Soweto set buildings alight not long before my wife and I returned to South Africa. I know this was a political act, a rejection of this modern version of the "bush" college. It seems to me that this "ghetto" college is no different except for its urban setting, unlike the "bush" colleges, which mostly had rural settings.

Inevitably, questions about my plans for the immediate future have been directed at me from various members of this group, meaning, in short, "Come back!" This sentiment has been thrown at me so many times during our tour! People are aware of the "brain drain" that has been one of the tragic consequences of apartheid and would like to see the whole thing reversed. Again, the question flashes in my mind: Vista? It's been a pleasure and an honor to be a guest at Unisa, University of Cape Town, Wits, University of Transkei. But Vista?

The evening winds down. It's been wonderful. The food has been superb and the service excellent. I appreciate Chaphole's hospitality, and after dessert and coffee, they drive me back to the guesthouse.

Friday, August 6th, is my last day at Unisa. I give my final workshop. This afternoon, Themba Msimang is going to drive me to

Potchefstroom. As we walk toward the lecture room, I keep thinking my hosts want to milk me to the last drop, and I love it. It's been such a wonderful visit. This is a sweet and sad occasion. The family we have become in the past twelve days is about to split. During the workshop, my friend Chris Swanepoel takes several pictures. At the conclusion, I am presented with a copy of the department's brochure and a picture is taken while Prof. Msimang, as head of the department, hands it to me. As the audience leaves, there are emotional handshakes, embraces, and good words.

I rush back to the guesthouse to say goodbye to, and thank in different ways, a wonderful, dignified black woman called Sophie. Sophie, a Venda woman, is the housekeeper at the guesthouse. She is tall and dark brown in complexion. She has a ready smile and you know that, in spite of her politeness and the lowly tasks she performs, she is conscious of her dignity as a person. In fact, her attitude tells you she does not regard her job as lowly; she is proud to do it and derives satisfaction from doing it well. Sophie gratefully accepts the items of food remaining in the refrigerator that I give her. In thanks for her services throughout my stay, I pay her at least twice what I was told was reasonable, as indeed I did also each time she did my laundry.

Prof. Kunene at the University of South Africa at Pretoria guest house with the "jail keys."

I pack my suitcase, put together my papers and books. Chris Swanepoel has fortunately agreed to mail the bulk of my books and papers for me. I walk back to Unisa where I join Themba Msimang, Chris Swanepoel, Johnny Lenake, and other friends for our last lunch together. Themba takes care of a few small administrative details to conclude the financial arrangements of my visit.

Back at the guesthouse with Themba and Chris, I ask Chris to take a picture of me dangling the huge bunch of long steel keys that operated doors at the guesthouse. The bunch reminds me of jail keys!

We load the car. I give Chris a goodbye embrace, and Themba and I are off.

Political violence has never let up. It has gotten worse. When Selina and I first arrived, it happened mostly on weekends, but it has now become a daily occurrence. I keep wondering why so many people have to die for the handful of power-hungry dupes and incurable racists refusing to accept the extension of human rights *as civil rights* to other human beings who happen to be black. I am convinced that the demand for a separate, autonomous homeland for the uncompromising extreme right-wing white racists is a prelude to serious attempts to destabilize and otherwise undermine the new government envisaged for some time in 1993. So too with the demand for an independent, autonomous KwaZulu homeland. The question is not only why so many must die for the gratification of these bigots, but why so many are *willing* to kill and be killed in defense of such retrogressive goals.

Black residential areas like Sebokeng, Thembisa, Katlehong, and Boipatong have become the chronic victims of such politically directed and controlled violence and have in the process inevitably generated their own violence, which has taken a life of its own by creating hostilities, grudges, and desire for revenge where such did not exist before. The de Klerk government has responded by having troops stationed permanently in these so-called townships, but the troops are known to encourage rather than reduce violence, to help Inkatha troublemakers fighting against ANC supporters, and generally to make the situation worse. The people of these townships want the army out of their areas and have made this perfectly clear to the authorities. Instead, as Themba and I cruise along towards Potchefstroom, barely one-third of this one-and-one-half to two-hour journey, we meet the vanguard of an army convoy headed for Johannesburg. We have heard in the news that significant reinforcements of the troops already in the townships were contemplated. I wonder: To what end? Is there going to be war? It is a frightening aspect, this interminable line of army trucks with soldiers armed to the teeth, trundling their way towards Johannesburg.

Natal, an empty show of force by police and army, 1984 -Photograph by Ian Berry

Such scenes were becoming an all-too-common experience in the emerging South Africa. We have passed some apparent roadblocks as we wove our way past a black residential area adjoining the city, but have, fortunately, not been stopped. We now wonder aloud if the army might decide to stop us and ask us a few questions. I say to Themba, "I so wish I could take a picture of this convoy, but that might be a fatal mistake as they would have an excuse to shoot us and claim we were pointing a gun at them." Needless to say, Themba fully concurs. Some of the units have stopped by the wayside, maybe for the soldiers to relieve themselves and enjoy a smoke, each soldier balancing a gun in his hand. The convoy is endless, and we only come to the tail end of it as we reach the outskirts of Potchefstroom. I estimate we have passed nearly one hundred miles of army trucks, certainly no less than seventy miles.

After driving through the white part of Potchefstroom, with its beautiful buildings, shopping centers, and tarred roads, we enter Ikageng Township and negotiate the inevitable potholes, rubbish dumps, and clouds of dust to reach my sister-in-law's house, where she, my wife, and some relatives are waiting for us. Unscathed! What a relief. But I'm concerned for Themba, who has to drive all that distance back alone. He does not seem much concerned. He takes off his jacket and relaxes while my sister-in-law's daughter makes tea, which she serves with some of the home-made cakes we love so much. A conversation ensues. I keep reminding Themba not to leave too late, wondering, among other things, if he might find himself driving behind the military convoy we met on our way here, which would slow him down considerably in the two-lane highway. Themba eventually leaves. I ask him to telephone that evening so we know he arrived safely.

At last I am with my wife again. She looks slightly better. She has told me in our telephone conversations how well her sister, Miriam, was looking after her. Tomorrow we leave for Kroonstad and my brother Peter's house. Before that we plan to visit some of the graveyards of relatives again, particularly the grave of Selina's father, which we were unable to locate on our previous visit.

We also have to find someone to drive us to Kroonstad, since Peter and Yvonne are not able to fetch us this time.

Daniel and Selina Kunene leaving the guest house at the University of Cape Town

It is Saturday, August 7th. We have been warned not to go to the graveyards too late, since Saturday is the day for burials and we may find ourselves caught up in a funeral procession. But first we must ensure that there is a car to drive us to Kroonstad this afternoon. We can only think of Mr. Matlawe, a relative of my wife's family by marriage, a sort of "uncle-in-law" to my wife.

"Well, maybe. We'll see. O.K. I think so. I think so, definitely. Yah. It's O.K.," says Matlawe.

"How much?" we ask.

"Well, we'll see when we get there. I can't say before we get there because I don't know how far. When we get there, then I can tell you."

Well, we just have to take it, and be ready for whatever figure he might come up with when we reach Kroonstad.

Kgani, Miriam's daughter, drives us to the graveyards. She picks up Manotshi, a cousin of my wife's, who knows exactly where each relative's grave is, visits them regularly, and keeps them clear of weeds. We first buy artificial flowers in town, and then off we go to the cemeteries to say goodbye to the departed ones. I am determined to take pictures of areas where the new "loan" houses and the shanty towns stand side-by-side, separated only by a street. Someone drives me there in Kgani's car and I take some shots.

We have a rather late lunch. There is the sadness of parting, the reluctance to say the final goodbyes. Uncle Matlawe, who is apparently very strict on time, comes approximately ten minutes early. He has someone with him, a kind of co-pilot. This somewhat disorganizes us, especially when he goes outside and sits in the car. We feel under pressure. We aren't quite ready. But at last we leave, approximately fifteen minutes past the set time. Miriam comes with us since there is room in the car, and this will give all of us a few more hours together.

After filling up in town, Uncle Matlawe's "co-pilot," who is in fact the pilot, drives in a direction we are not used to. I keep my peace, believing they know a shorter route than Peter and Yvonne usually take. But for quite a while it looks as if we are heading for Cape Town. I eventually ask: "Is this the way to Kroonstad? I've never traveled this way before." "Yes," they answer, "we turn left at Orkney to proceed to the Free State." It turns out they have taken a much longer route, which Peter confirms when we meet that evening. Not out of malice. We get to know later that Uncle Matlawe is terrible with directions. He is sure he knows, but in fact he doesn't. Miriam confirms this when she calls us about their safe arrival back in Potchefstroom. On his return trip, Uncle Matlawe took a different direction, trying to correct his first mistake, but they ended up in Parys, a town at a far right-angle to where they wanted to go. But they eventually reached home.

Peter and Yvonne are not at home when we arrive. They have warned us this might happen, since they had a previous engagement away from home, hence their inability to fetch us from Potchefstroom. When they get back, amid all the excitement, they unlock the bedroom we have come to consider "ours" from our previous visit. Ah, what a wonderful surprise! Now we know why the room was locked when we arrived. It's been arranged like a bridal suite with fancy linen and frilly pillowslips. It's just gorgeous. We are so excited. We embrace them and tell them how much we appreciate it. We spend a pleasant evening together.

We wake up to a beautiful Sunday morning, August 8th. I am thinking about the "Three Million Gang," which terrorized the black townships of Maokeng, Seeisoville, Gelukswaarts, Phomolong, and other black ghettoes. Mention of the "Three Million Gang" sends chills down people's spines. My continued interest in the causes of violence leads me to probe into the specific manifestations of it.

It was at Edenville that I first heard stories about the "Three Million Gang." Now we are in Kroonstad, its headquarters and sole field of operations till its demise. Murders by the gang, we are told, took all kinds of sadistic forms. The story was told of a man who was thrown to the ground and repeatedly plunged through with a gardening fork. The victim was a black policeman regarded as being too soft in his treatment of his fellow blacks.

The police instigated the formation of the "Three Million Gang" to terrorize the people, especially those who protested and resisted police acts of brutality.

Is there any significance in the phrase "Three Million" in the gang's name? we ask. None. It means absolutely nothing. And there, it seems to me, lies the full horror of it. An ordinary object, this time a number, has been hijacked from its regular, normal signification and transformed into a symbol of violence and death. Like the number "thirteen" in Western European folklore—high-rise buildings were built with the thirteenth floor omitted. When you reach twelve, skip to fourteen. The terror of the name "Three Million Gang" lay precisely in the fact that it stood for nothing but pure terror.

The gang's leader was a black young man called George, also known as Diwitty. He and his gang had the full support and protection of the police and the courts. George's personal involvement in the reign of terror unleashed on the townships, including his own personal murders, were repeatedly reported to the police by eye-witnesses. George would be taken into "custody" and released the same day, without any charges brought against him. Instead of punishment, the police rewarded him by bestowing on him the honorary title of "King George."

Phomolong Township was the center of the gang's activities. They terrorized the residents of Phomolong so that they fled, and the gang moved in to occupy the vacated houses which by now carried the scars of violence in doors and windows where only the frames remained, around some of which was evidence of arsonists' fires. The gang abducted young girls as concubines, and no one, let along their parents, dared to intervene. They declared Phomolong a "No-Go-Zone." They nicknamed it "Beirut." When "Beirut" erupted, streets would be littered with rocks, and tires would be lit up to prevent traffic from going through. These pictures materialize into a numbing reality as we are driven, this Sunday afternoon, on a tour of some of the worst-hit areas. Since Peter has other business on this day, it has been necessary for us to hire a taxi. Our driver is both enthusiastic and nervous. "Beirut," he announces, as we negotiate a corner. "This is where it begins."

"Wow!" I say.

"Good Lord!" says Selina.

Signs of death and devastation are all around us! We are tempted to whip out our cameras and take some pictures, but we fear it might not be safe. Yes, confirms the driver. We shouldn't even stop the car to look, he adds. This might identify us as curious sightseers. "Beirut" is now an abandoned town, and through my mind flash such images as "bombed city," "ghost town," "Hiroshima," "terror-by-rule-of-law." These shattered window panes, missing windows and doors are like lifeless eyes and mouths and nostrils, giant skulls symbolizing the ravages of war. The fact that the houses in this segment of the ghetto are identical adds another dimension, the soul-destroying monotony of a military barracks. It gives one an eerie feeling to know that people have perished there or abandoned the place in flight.

Among the people George assassinated was a man whose son was himself a gangster of some notoriety in Johannesburg. This turned out to be "King George's" fatal error. Our informants tell us that the victim's son, on receiving the news, started preparations for a face-to-face confrontation with the "King" to avenge his father's murder. Then one day he drove to Kroonstad and traced George to the railway station. When he came on the scene, a parking lot in front of the station, George was happily chatting away with some acquaintances or friends. The stranger from Johannesburg came and stood right behind him and called his name: "George!" The "King" turned around, startled, and there was a split-second, eye-to-eye contact, followed by the stranger pulling a mask over his face and rapidly pumping bullets into "King George's" face and body. The people rejoiced; their murderer was dead. The police mourned; their "King" was dead. On hearing the news, the people poured out into the streets and celebrated, and the police came out to the townships in force and paraded up and down in an act of intimidation.

George's notoriety made him into a legend, and we were told there was another version of his assassination, namely that it was carried out under different circumstances by some white woman. Who knows what the implications of that story might be? Our informants assure us, however, that the stranger from Johannesburg was arrested and is still serving his sentence. The "Three Million Gang," now leaderless, began to disintegrate.

Our driver takes us through other areas. Among the things we would like to see are schools. Talking to teachers at Edenville, we had become aware that all was not well in the school system, so we are curious to see some school buildings, even though there is no activity there, this being a Sunday. One that captures our attention as we drive in its direction is a secondary school with a large mural of the map of Africa on a wall dominating the approaches to the school. The purpose of this map was primarily to inspire the students with a sense of a larger identity than that of blacks trapped like mice in the confines of apartheid. The purpose of the map was to join them with the rest of the African continent and generate in them a sense of being part of the sweeping changes that have taken place, down to the very borders of South Africa.

But now, the entire school shows ample signs of ruin—gardens, once beautiful, now trampled to bare ground; windowpanes broken; doors no longer locking properly because they have been forced; windowless and doorless lavatories with seats ripped off. These are not the ravages of the "Three Million Gang," but have been wrought by the students who are supposedly there to study and to move toward their future. But that may be precisely the problem: They have lost all sense of *future* that would make their *present* meaningful and worth nurturing. Africa stands sad and weeping at the wanton destruction, yet likewise proud, always looking beyond the storm clouds into that future that has eluded these students.

But destruction by your hand, when forced, is not destruction by your hand. If you suffer from dementia induced by intense persecution, and in your demented state you commit the most heinous crimes, you cannot be held morally responsible for those crimes. The ultimate moral responsibility belongs to those who induce your deranged mental state. It should have been obvious that the authority-defying children of Soweto in 1976 and onwards would mature into today's authority-defying young adults of the ghetto.

To be able to put all this into perspective, I talked to teachers old enough to have been practicing their profession in 1976. In the heat of the struggle against oppression symbolized most poignantly by apartheid, it was difficult for those involved in the struggle from a distance to avoid glamorizing the children's actions, including their subversion and perversion of the normal parent-child, adult-child, teacher-child relationships. Normally, parents had the authority, made decisions, and, if necessary, *made* the children obey their orders. In school, teachers had an *in loco parentis* relationship to the children with all the responsibilities that went with that relationship of surrogate parents. 1976 changed all that. During the children's revolt starting June 16, 1976, in Soweto, which soon spread to other parts of the country, these roles were reversed. The parents and the teachers were given orders by the children. Not a pretty sight.

At that early stage, the children considered the teachers to be part of the Bantu Education system they were rejecting. I asked if they demanded that the schools be closed and the teachers go home. No, said my informants, on the contrary they wanted the schools to remain open. Schools were convenient places for them to meet and organize. But the teachers were to do what the students told them. One reported instance was that of a group that called the teachers together and laid before them the new ground rules. They, the students, were thenceforth going to do whatever they wished for whatever reasons. Specifically, the girls told the teachers that they were going to wear make-up to school, stretch their hair, paint their nails and lips, wear broad figure belts, and do anything to make themselves look very attractive. And, to add a touch of tragic humor, they warned the male teacher not to come proposing love to them when they saw them looking so beautiful! Where would they get the money to do all that? Asked the helpless teachers. From their men, the girls answered.

It was not an easy time to be a teacher or a parent. That was the price paid for the political gains from the children defying apartheid laws and their agents, the police. Apartheid corrupted the children and they carried their corruption into their adulthood. And the younger children, growing up in this environment of recalcitrance and acts of extreme violence, themselves became defiers of authority and potential perpetrators of violent acts. At this secondary school where we are being shown around, the telltale multiple security locking, barring, and bolting system on the door to the principal's office tells a story of its own.

Continuing our tour after the school, we pass the remains of the "mayor's" garage, i.e., a filling station with auxiliary services like changing tires and minor repairs. It is a charred ruin that was burnt down because he was a "sell-out." He was participating in the municipality's fraud of pretending that blacks had a viable, self-sustaining city of their own. The truth is that, like all other black townships, the Kroonstad black townships were, and are, no more than cheap labor dormitories for blacks serving the white masters and madams in the white city where the real mayor and the real city council are. The "Mayor" of Maokeng was therefore benefitting from apartheid by helping to perpetuate it. (Shortly before the April 1994 elections, the "mayor," claiming to be a member of the ANC, attended an ANC rally that Mandela was addressing at a stadium in Maokeng. The crowd was incensed and demanded that he should leave. But, with his usual magnanimity and diplomacy, Mandela intervened on the "mayor's" behalf, arguing, rather disarmingly, that if he, Mandela, could work with de Klerk, his erstwhile jailer, for change in South Africa, why couldn't he—and everybody else—work with the likes of the "mayor?")

Tomorrow, we plan to go to Edenville. We intend to come back the same day. We call them to let them know. One of my nieces who works in a store in Edenville town will come home during lunch time to be with us. It is more than a mile which she covers on foot, morning and evening.

On Monday, August 9th, we are slow getting ready to leave. It's partly because Peter and I first go to a bank in town, where he does his banking business, to cash my check from Unisa. It turns out not to be as difficult as we had feared. He also takes rolls of film for developing and printing. We'll pick them up tomorrow. We fear we might miss my niece because she will have returned to work. We buy some Kentucky Fried Chicken to provide everybody's lunch at Edenville. Peter stops shortly after we leave Kroonstad and hands the wheel over to me to drive. I re-adapt quickly to driving on the left side of the road.

As we approach Edenville, I realize that I will never get used to the changes I see superimposed on the Edenville of my childhood, even my early adult years before I left for the United States. The "winds of change" have wrought new themes on the story of the tiny town I once knew. As we get closer, we see my niece, Mmamosa, walking briskly home. I am happy that we did not miss her. I stop the car and she rides with us the rest of the way. We first go to her home, the house of my late older sister Sophia. My sister Magdeline and my brother Philip come to join us there. My niece makes tea for all of us. We decide to have lunch before going to the cemetery, so that my niece can go back to work. Reluctant to part with us, she takes a little longer that her usual lunch break. Thereafter, Peter and I drive her back to town where we say our final goodbyes.

Back at the Location, we visit the graves of my parents and my sister Sophia, and some of my in-laws, the Maletes and the Mokhanelis. When we get back, we pass on to Magdeline's house, which will be our last stop before we return to Kroonstad. Once again we are entertained to tea and some biscuits. We settle down to a conversation, but it is clear that, as they say, we are sitting on one buttock. We keep reminding ourselves that highways are dangerous after dark, we must be sure to get back to Kroonstad while it is still light. As in Potchefstroom, I want to take pictures of the dwellings, especially of the old Location, the reminder of my childhood. I want to have a permanent record of the degeneration that I see. After I take a few shots, we bid farewell to my sister Magdeline and my brother Philip, and we are off back to Kroonstad.

We mostly spend Tuesday, August 10th, doing odds and ends. We go to pick up the pictures. We examine a few. They've come out very nicely. Peter wants me to meet a distant cousin who works somewhere in town. We meet her on the sidewalk and exchange greetings. She is very excited to see me. We have a brief conversation in which we try to establish family connections in the genealogical tree. As we stroll back to the car, Peter sees a classmate of mine from my high school days, Pearl West, who later trained as a nurse and was a senior in the Boksburg-Benoni Hospital, where my wife was a junior trainee nurse.

Years ago, my wife (then still my fiancé) talked very highly about Pearl West's patient, clear, and sympathetic approach in teaching her juniors. I was then in Cape Town studying for my Master's Degree. And then, some years later, when my wife and I were married and living in Cape Town and my mother was seriously ill, it was Pearl West, Peter told me, who very kindly and sympathetically tried to persuade my mother to go to the hospital in Kroonstad, where she now worked, and promised her the best care the hospital could give. My mother, who believed that was the time to have her family around her rather than be isolated in some hospital, thanked her but refused to go.

Pearl and I had shared several years of high school study together. I am therefore very excited as Peter and I follow her and catch up with her. She cannot believe her eyes. We have an animated conversation, as each obviously tries to recapture the faces we knew in our youth. She has now retired from her nursing. I tell her my wife will be very excited to hear that I saw her.

I have indicated to Peter that I would like to visit Mrs. Cingo, the widow of the man who was principal of Kroonstad Bantu High School during those years when Pearl West and I were classmates, Dr. Reginald Cingo. So Peter calls Mrs. Cingo to arrange it. I indicate I would also like to visit Dr. Cingo's grave, with her permission. It will be OK on both counts, she says. She will send her son, Sanana, who runs a small pharmacy next to her house, to pick up Selina and me early the next morning to go to the graveyard first and then come to her house for a visit. At the house, we reminisce about my student days at Kroonstad Bantu High School, when her husband was principal there. Selina and I have planned to leave Kroonstad for Johannesburg on Thursday, August 12th, stay with the Nthebes, that is Rankele and his wife Thenjiwe, Peter's daughter.

We spend Wednesday, August 11th, largely preparing for our departure the next day. This is the day I have a brief glimpse at the old Location which, in my student days, was simply known as "Kroonstad Location" and was divided into an unrecognizable dump of raw earth and corrugated sheet-iron walls that lean precariously. The dirt streets are eroded into a succession of potholes. Again, the sense of death is prevalent, death not of the flesh, but of the soul, of the joy of living, of the will to go on. It seems people living here (for, incredible as it may seem, these dumps are still occupied) have lost all sense of the purpose of living. They are simply vegetating from one day to the next.

Our driver from Potchefstroom had strayed into this heap of rubble now called "Old Location" when we missed a turn going to Peter and Yvonne's house the previous Saturday, and I did not recognize it as a place I once knew. But this is where Teacher Makae, Teacher Matsepe, Teacher Tlhapone, Rev. Tlhole, Rev. Lipholo, and we youngsters and workers of all descriptions lived. Some landmarks have simply succumbed to the ravages of time, despair, and neglect. The Anglican Church is one of them, that once-magnificent building (for a black Location, that is). There's no trace of it. Teacher Matsepe's house as long been reduced to a mound of dust.

We also take advantage of this uncommitted day to simply sit and relax and chat, though, with the hour of parting getting close, we seem to have become paralyzed: So much to say, but all of it somehow blacked out of the mind. Though my wife is holding out bravely, I am now impatient for us to be on our way back to the United States, so she can resume her treatment of natural remedies and vegetarian diets so badly disrupted by our intense tour and well-intentioned but incompatible diets that have inhibited her progress.

On Thursday, August 12th, Peter and Yvonne drive us to Johannesburg. Halfway there, Peter hands the car over to me to drive the rest of the way. We first go to the elementary school where my niece, Thenjiwe, is principal. We are shown around the school, which is isolated from any of the townships and by that fact alone gives the impression of being less prone to disruptive attitudes. We drive to the Nthebes' house with Thenji. Peter and Yvonne are going back to Kroonstad the same day. We have a quick cup of tea and biscuits, and they are soon on their way. That evening, at my niece's house, we watch a video of Chris Hani's funeral. Hani was secretary general of the South African Communist Party, and former chief of staff for the ANC military wing, *Umkhonto Wesizwe* (The Spear of the Nation) or MK. He was ideologically much more radical than Mandela and, at the relatively young age of perhaps middle fifties, was a favorite of the youth. He was gunned down outside his home in a white working-class suburb of Boksburg which he was trying to integrate. How much of a rival to Mandela he would have been for the position of first black president of South Africa was to remain unknown.

Selina and I spend much of Friday, August 13th, going from one bank to another trying to convert our rands to American dollars. I get snubbed by the white assistants at several of them. I feel it's not only a matter of carrying out government restrictions on exporting rands, but deliberate acts of meanness. We have virtually given up and are returning to the car where our driver is waiting for us, when we decide to try one last bank. The United Bank receives us most courteously and the woman helping us does our conversion with no fuss at all.

Next, we visit Raven Press, where I have a long conversation with Glenn Moss, its director. I have three books published by Raven, *A Seed Must Seem to Die* (poetry), *From the Pit of Hell to the Spring of Life* (short stories), and *Thomas Mofolo and the Emergence of Written Sesotho Prose* (literary analysis). We have a lot to talk about and we are there for about an hour and a half. We rejoin the driver and return home.

Saturday, August 14th, is a day for packing and getting ready for our departure the next day. But we also go souvenir hunting. We are driven to the city center (downtown area), where a weekly open market of all kinds of crafts is held. Of course, it is meant to cater to the tourist market and there are all the indications of mass production. We are nonetheless able to come up with some reasonably good purchases.

First thing on the morning of Sunday, August 15th, Rankele loads up our luggage, which is rather big because of gifts we have been given by relatives and friends during our stay, as well as our own purchases. Even though our flight leaves at eight in the evening, we decide to get to the airport around three, and certainly not later than four to take care of formalities prior to our flight.

As we cruise along the network of highways, there are long spells of silence in which my mind wanders and occasionally recaptures in haphazard order some of the high points during our visit: Stellenbosch, Wits conference, Edenville, square miles of shacks mushrooming all over the country, Cape Town and our friends Roddy and Hermine, blacks and their "three-d" deficiency, Unisa, Themba Msimang, Chris Swanepoel and his family, my brother George in Odendaalsrus who has gone completely blind. Now and again the mind dwells on one picture. Graffiti, anonymous voices, irreverent, often prophetic, sometimes humorous, such as the one that said "I was a member of the Anglican Church until I put *tu* and *tu* together!" A work of genius, I thought, when I was told about it. Besides, who knows what color or political persuasion the person is? Frustrated white Anglican, expressing his/her dilemma? An artist simply succumbing to the creative urge?

Min(e)d Words

Graffiti sprayed on Soweto walls
Anonymous
Pervasive
Powerful
Alive

Graffiti infiltrates all the layers of
The mind of the driver cruising by
The mind of the combi-taxi with its sardined cargo
The mind of the cyclist squeak-squeaking on the dust-ridden street
The mind of the foot-slogger rousing to rebellion the sleeping sand
The mind of the tourist chewing a Cuban cigar and wiping the sweat

from his double chin with a white handkerchief
The mind of the white South Africa answering tomorrow's questions
with yesterday's stale clichés

Graffiti is life writ large
with all its infinite questions
is the mind's window to blurred futures
like misty mountains on distant horizons
never stagnant
never stale

No graffiti on suburban walls
Like the late Berlin Wall
So alive with the people's provocative art this side
So sterile-ly blank and pale as death on the other

Graffiti
Your irreverence is infectious
You are life's exuberance
You are life's hope

Graffiti on the wall
Graffiti on the wall

Oh, there's the sign to the airport. Chris and Anne-Marie Swanepoel join us at the airport to say goodbye as previously arranged. Chris accompanies me to the exchange bank, which turns out to be a blessing since, once again, I am faced with problems that are only solved when he makes a personal check in the same amount as mine and I sign mine over to him.

We are back on the main floor. It's early evening and, as we stand around, there is suddenly a burst of singing from some part of the airport. It grows louder and louder. What could it be? I cannot banish a nagging fear that this might be a prelude to some violence about to erupt at the airport. But such lovely singing! Does not sound anything like a war song. It's a mixed choir, which comes to the concourse where we are, arranges themselves, and begin another song. I think, by the way, there was a time not so long ago when the police would have come out in force and arrested these singers for "disturbing the peace." But today the choir has simply taken over the airport and people begin to gather around them. A young conductor directs some of the songs. I soon gather that he is on his way overseas for further studies, and that his choir came to bid him farewell the best way they knew how. But this turns out to be a generous farewell to all who care to accept the gift.

Choir at the airport, bidding farewell

My wife and I are thrilled. We were received with song at the ALASA conference celebrations of the Doke Centenary when we first arrived, and now we are flying out on the wings of song! Goodbye, South Africa! Goodbye, our fatherland! Not a goodbye but an *au revoir*. Having seen each other again after thirty long years and renewed our bond, we shall see each other again and again and again. For, as they say in Zulu: *Abakhe babonana bayobonana futhi*! (Those who have once met will meet again!)

Daniel and Selina Kunene returned to Madison, Wisconsin on Monday, August 16, 1993. Selina Kunene died on Friday, October 22, 1993.

Epilogue—
for Selina

Were it not for this thing
this closing of the eyes
this stopping of the breath
this stiffening of the limbs
this cessation of speech
this departure of the body heat

We would have been playing our favorite game
chasing the butterflies of our dreams
lolling in the enveloping warmth
of the world we moulded with our own hands
which is the real world
which is always around us
which is invulnerable and strong in its farailty

But this thing
this closing of the eyes
this stopping of the breath
this stiffening of the limbs
this cessation of speech
this departure of the body heat
it came upon us
it came between us
it came to spite us

Yet we shall dream on
beyond speech and breath and eyes that don't see
eyes that for their blindness see more
take in new landscapes beyond the limiting horizons

as we leap with nimbler limbs
unfettered by tendons and ligaments and veins and vessels
that defy our orders
and our heat shall rise
and we shall talk and we shall laugh

beyond the prison of mortality

Daniel Kunene

EDENVILLE (1996)

In preparation for our departure, in particular to prepare my children's minds as to what they might expect during our forthcoming three-week sojourn in South Africa, I had put together an itinerary in which I gave them as accurate a description as I could of the South Africa I knew before I departed with my wife and two oldest children in 1963: I told them about Edenville, my birth town; Kroonstad, where I went to high school; Odendaalsrus, where my older brother had lived and taught school while his wife pursued her nursing career. I told them about Cape Town, where I obtained my master's and doctoral degrees from the University of Cape Town and was a lecturer till our departure; where my wife practiced her nursing and midwifery; where our first child was born and died in infancy.

I told them about distances, climates, weather eccentricities; where we should go at certain points of time in our visit—for example, Cape Town at New Year's was a must, what with the minstrel show of colorful costumes, umbrellas that bob up and down to music with a beat so fast that the minstrels often trot rather than walk its rhythms. And, of course, the southeast wind that cascades down the rugged cliffs of Table Mountain toward the sea and drapes the white cloud, the "table cloth," in massive folds over the top and the slopes of the mountain. There was also the cable car that we could ride to the top of Table Mountain for a commanding view of the city, the suburbs, the sea, and beyond to the faraway mountain ranges on their long journey north.

I hoped and prayed that Edenville and Odendaalsrus and Kroonstad and Beaufort West and Cape Town still existed as they had been when I last saw them; that the wineries of Stellenbosch, Paarl, and Constantia still spread their bounty over the landscape. It would, of course, be no major tragedy if some of these things were not as I recalled them. Or maybe not even there anymore! Just a slight embarrassment that daddy's or grandpa's memory hadn't been so reliable after all.

By the time this trip was planned, my daughter and first-born, Liziwe, lived in Novato, north of San Francisco, with her husband Fritz and their two teenage sons, Somori and Thiyane; one son, Sipho, was in New York; and my two other sons, Luyanda and his wife, Linda, and Wandile, my last-born, lived in Los Angeles. We were all going to meet in London and then fly together to Johannesburg.

One looks back. There's always that looking back. There's always the inevitable evaluation of the choices one has made. Of those other choices one could have made. Or, more accurately, the chances that tantalizingly presented themselves, then withdrew the promise without an explanation; indeed, the dreams, the opportunities one hoped for, but which always turned out to be castles in the air stubbornly defying the power of gravity. There is the speculation as to how one's future might have unfolded if that choice or that other one over there had been made, rather than this one. I sometimes tease my children, saying: "You know, none of you would be here, would exist, if I had made that choice or that other one, and not this one."

For example, what if the African American Bishop of the African Methodist Episcopal (AME) Church, visiting Dr. and Mrs. A.B. Xuma from Louisiana in the middle of the 1940s, had followed up on his promise to obtain a music scholarship for me on his return to the United States? The Xumas, who lived in Sophiatown, Johannesburg, had invited me to their house to entertain the bishop and his wife with my double quartet choir. I had written a piece specifically for the visitors, and they were highly impressed. But, alas, the bishop never got back to me, even when, in desperation, I wrote to remind him of our conversation, in which he and Dr. Xuma had actually discussed how best to obtain traveling papers for me in light of apartheid's restriction on freedom of movement by Blacks. Had

I gotten the scholarship, I would, without any doubt, have married someone other than my children's mother. We laugh and shiver at the thought and declare that we would not have wished that particular future—or any other—over the one that has brought us all together.

Or I could have gone to England in the early 1940s, urged and encouraged as I was by an Anglican priest, one Brother Giles, to further my education there. I was then working in Johannesburg after my high school education was brought to an abrupt halt by lack of money for school fees and books. When Brother Giles made his proposal, I was engaged in private study, which I squeezed into my spare time to complete my matriculation, a university entrance requirement. The very thought of studying in England excited me—best education, no color prejudice. But this Utopia was, so to speak, torpedoed by the fact that World War II was at the height of its fury and the high seas were not a very safe place to be.

But again, we say the future we are now living is the best future, for it has brought us all together. And now here we were, all of us, in 1996, about to embark on a family pilgrimage to my origins, the place that molded me, and my future, that had brought us all together.

My past was not an easy one. It never was for a black person in South Africa, economically and socially, with all that that entails, such as terrible schools with their terrible facilities. In fact, in Edenville *Location*, there were no schools, no facilities; things taken for granted in Edenville *Town*, the white half, just a stone's throw away. Churches served as school buildings during the week. And that pulpit was always towering over you, looking at you. God was always hovering around and frightening the wits out of you, what with hell so easy to attain and heaven so difficult. What could you do to escape the everlasting fire waiting to engulf you, the wailings and the gnashing of teeth? I know I personally cringed at the very thought of gnashing my teeth. Come to think of it, I did not know what gnashing meant. It just sounded too terrible for any reasonable person to wish to experience, like grinding your teeth with your mouth full of sand.

Schools?! Without free books?! With compulsory school fees?! Uniforms too?! Without any of which you were barred from attending?! Schools? With no libraries? I did not know the *word* "library." Not even in high school. You read your schoolbooks, passed your exams (or failed them or dropped out of school), and that was the extent of your reading. Except, of course, the Bible, which you read for school and listened to being quoted and elaborated upon in loud clichés by the preacher on Sunday.

We, my children and I, were going back to these roots. The future was going to meet its past. Face to face.

I do not believe in futures that never come, that are always tomorrow, next month, next year: Futures that outlive their owners. For me, there is no question who is boss between me and my future. I own my future. It wouldn't be there except for me. That is why I want it to come and let's sit down and have a friendly chat. For instance, I would like to ask it why it took one direction when I was desperately trying to coax it in another. I want to tell it whether or not I'm satisfied with the way it has turned out, the way it has served me. So, when I say "Today is my future," that statement makes perfect sense to me. It also makes sense that futures realized beget new futures, yet to be striven for.

In other words, the future that has arrived is not static, but is no sooner here than it generates new vistas, new fields to explore. It is like reaching the summit of a hill you have been clambering up with hope and great expectations. You no sooner reach the top than new horizons beckon you from far away, challenging you to climb new hills, head for new summits. And it is in one's striving toward the new challenge, the new future, that one is actually living it. We are living the next millennium right now in our anxieties, our doubts, our fears, and our nail-biting anticipation.

So fiercely are we engrossed in our fantasies of this "coming," that we might be so tired we'll oversleep on January 1, 2000! Yet it is precisely in this moment of embracing that which is yet to be, that we acknowledge that the ever-flitting futures whizzing past us are constantly opening new vistas for us. Otherwise, the realized future is no more than a *cul de sac*, a trap from which there is no escape. It defines death as nothing else can.

Edenville (1996)

So, here, before a tottering red-brick house, the house that breathes the countless stories of my childhood, we stand, here in Edenville Location, living one of my endless futures, my desire to bring my children home, for them to see the sun rise and set where I used to see it rise and set when I was a child.

Earlier today, shortly after we arrived at Edenville, Fritz had "sneaked out" with his video camera to record spots and sweeping panoramas of where we are, comment on what he sees, capture moods. I only become aware of this later. For my part, at this time, I was being celebrated simply yet completely by my sister, my nieces, my nephews, and all the little ones who were intoxicated with the pleasure and the pride of the arrival of their relatives from America.

There was music playing in an almost exhibitionist fashion on the stereo. It is the type of music, it seems to me, that has grown out of the years of struggle, of violence, of confrontation of youth and children with police, of torture and mutilation, of death; of a strange mixture of hope and despair. Its breathless rhythms are often combined with words and phrases normally associated with the slow, lilting, melancholy tunes of sad hymns that long for heaven; but now loud, lively, almost violent, taunting you to get up and dance.

All these elements are blended together into new idioms, new statements, all the more powerful and intriguing because of the contradictory elements straining against each other. As if heaven and hell were dancing a lively tango.

It is euphoric, this music. And it is a challenge to the powers that have been, that are, and that shall be, to recognize the patient, hopeful waiting for a new future to arise. The future begotten by the demise of apartheid, the future now striven for in South Africa is that of a liberation translated into visibly improved living conditions, a movement in the direction of a new life; of a more fair distribution of the good things of life—some sense that a victory has been won; some sense as to who won it, and to what end. Feelings of this sort find a suitable vehicle in this type of music. For, let it be acknowledged, there is a sense of transience in the new South Africa, that things are yet to be defined, true and meaningful destinations yet to be reached. The present is but a picnic at a roadside stop, with a long journey yet ahead.

I am seated at a table with one or two of my nephews. The music seems to energize the young women and children moving back and forth preparing refreshments and food. The sounds of conversation, laughter, calling someone, clanking of pots and pans and dishes, water running or splashing, these all mingle with the music, and the effect is more than uplifting, it is slightly intoxicating. I am awakened from this state of semi-hypnosis by Fritz's voice as he walks in and repeats several times: "Humble beginnings, Dad, humble beginnings!" He had located the red-brick house, photographed it and its surroundings with his inimitable commentaries. The rascal couldn't even wait to be properly introduced, I say to myself.

Humble beginnings! An eloquent phrase, those two words, whose effect was to join a piece of my past, and the realized future being currently celebrated, into a larger meaning. WE HAVE ARRIVED, EDENVILLE IS THE TRUE ARRIVAL, AND TIME IS STANDING STILL....

I continue to give talks on South Africa and African Liberation, too numerous to list individually. They include the period from the fifties to the two-thousands, i.e., from the critical years of the heyday of apartheid to the turbulent nineties as the country painfully inched towards democratic elections on a universal suffrage. Current talks include a critique of post-1994 elections, including the Truth and Reconciliation Commission. I continue to give talks, read poetry, and perform other services concerning South Africa and other topics, to different groups and organizations.

"Nkosi Sikelel' iAfrika"

(Dr. Phyllis Jordan–1998)

In a letter dated April 1998, Dr. Phyllis Ntantala Jordan, wife of A.C. Jordan, sent the following missive.

Dan,

This hymn, *Nkosi Sikelel' iAfrika,* now the National Anthem of South Africa, was composed by Enoch Sontonga, a teacher in the Transvaal, in 1894. It was made popular by his school choir singing it at school concerts—a feature of African education in the past.

Pixley ka Seme, founder of the ANC, then barrister in Johannesburg, asked Sontonga for permission to have it sung on the day of the inauguration of the Native National Congress—later the African National Congress—at its first conference in Bloemfontein in December 1912. From that day on, *Nkosi Sikelel' iAfrika* became the anthem of the African people, sung at the close of every gathering—meeting, conference, school choir competition, etc.

Sontonga, a Xhosa, wrote the lyrics in Xhosa and not in the mixture of Xhosa and Zulu as the people tend to sing it today. That being the case, choirs should sing it in the original lyrics of Sontonga. This is the proper thing to do, if not for anything, just out of respect for Sontonga, the composer.

The reason why it is sung in this mixture, is because the music is singable—if I may coin such a word—in all the southern African languages. It can be sung in Zulu, Shona, Lozi, Nyanja, Swahili, Sotho, and this is what the people have done. As members of an audience, individuals may perhaps, be excused for using the lyrics they are comfortable with. But, as a National Anthem, sung by choirs, that is not acceptable. Let us do the right thing (as we do with other national anthems) and sing it in the language in which it was written. That way we will not only be elevating it to the level of a real National Anthem, but also showing our sure respect to Sontonga, the Composer.

Copies of this composition should be at the Cory Library for Historical Research in Grahamstown, South Africa, which took most of the Lovedale Archives when Bantu Education was introduced. The music of most of the African composers—Xhosa, Zulu—was published at Lovedale, the only African Press in those days. Then came the Morija Press for Sotho.

Phyl
Taylor, Michigan
April 1998

Nkosi Sikelel' iAfrika   *God Bless Africa*
Nkosi Sikelel' iAfrika   God Bless Africa
Maluphakam, uPhondo Iwayo   May her Banner stand up high
Yiva Nemithandazo yethu   Hear also our prayers
Uyisikelele; Uyisikelele   And bless them; & bless them
Yiza Moya!   Come, Holy Spirit
Sikelele, Nkosi Sikelele   Bless, Oh Lord! Bless.
Yiza Moya!   Come, Holy Spirit
Sikelela, Nkosi Sikelele   Bless, Oh Lord! Bless
Yiza Moya, Oyingewele!   Come Spirt, Holy Spirit
Usiskelele,   And Bless us,
Thina lusapho Iwayo.   Us, her Offspring

Enoch Sontonga,
1896

Honor at University of South Africa (1999)

This is the Acceptance Speech when awarded the Honorary degree of D. Litt et Phil., University of South Africa (UNISA), October 7, 1999.

Mr. Chancellor, Mr. Vice Chancellor, all the honorable members of this august institution, my friends who are here and everybody here whom I'd like to share this with and have come to share this with me. I am both extremely happy and very humbled by this singular honor: namely, the conferment on me of the degree of D. Litt et Phil by my alma mater the University of South Africa.

I have many people to thank: first and foremost, my parents and especially my mother who worked tirelessly to give as many of her children as possible the opportunity to obtain education under the most arduous and discouraging conditions anyone can imagine; and which perhaps some in this assembly today can empathize with. My parents, two beautiful people, whose beauty shone through their poverty and through which they did great things.

I thank my teachers. I remember their painstaking labors to bring out the best in us. Their authority over us as our surrogate parents, the *in loco parentis* status over us. I remember their love but also their canings. On my part not so much for not getting my work right, because I was told that I was very clever, not that I believed one word of it. But for the most part, the memorable caning was when I ran away from school and my mother chased me and gave up, because I was a very fast runner, and then these two big bullies sent by the teacher to come looking for me who chased me all the way to a neighboring farm and then escorted me like a common bandit back to school. The teacher gave me a good one that day, almost too good: in fact, I think it was too good. I'll leave the gory details to your imagination.

What I never understood was when they said, "it hurts me more than it hurts you." I never believed a word of it. But be that as it may, I reckon that is why I am standing here today; for I never wanted my father or my teacher to hurt themselves more than they hurt me.

I recognize the presence of my daughter, Liziwe Pointer, who came all the way from Novato in Marin County near San Francisco to be my sort of cheerleader in lieu of my late wife, her mother, to whom I owe so much. I thank all my children, in absentia, for their constant support and encouragement of Daddy or Papa. I recognize all my relatives and my extended family: brothers, sisters, brothers-in-law, sisters-in-law, nephews, nieces, and all the little ones whom I have given permission to call me grandpa, or even great grandpa, but who insist on calling be Uncle Dan. I guess I should be grateful for that.

I recognize my friends and my colleagues who are honoring me with their presence today. I say to them "Mr. Chancellor UNISA is the quintessential analogue of the diversity of South Africa. Under its imposing architectural design, virtually a university under one roof perched on a hill like a giant eagle about to soar into space, and through the many languages, literatures and cultures it promotes, it helps to move us forward towards the fulfillment of the words of visionaries like the prophet Nsikana in his praise poem for God, in the early 19th century when he said to God, "You are the great cloak that covers us all: You are He who unites herds that reject each other."

UNISA poses a challenge to the balkanization introduced into this continent by the Berlin Conference, which created numerous Berlin walls that crisscrossed and carved up the entire African continent: denied people their natural curiosity to come together; even though at first they might laugh at you for [what] might seem to them your queer behavior, your strange ways. The Berlin walls that were later to be used in a gigantic experiment with human beings to deliberately and in a calculated manner separate people who had been living harmoniously and peacefully together through the creation of artificial "nations "called Bantu Homelands.

The dislocation of the lives of millions of Africans through experimental resettlement schemes. The Berlin walls that kept us apart. In our efforts to reverse this trend, to break down these walls, to create a true *Rainbow Nation*, a government of national unity, tolerance, nay an acceptance of the differences that nature had deliberately, infallibly designed for us to have—UNISA, under its enormous wings, leads the way in meeting this challenge on the eve of the new millennium. Mr. Chancellor I thank you.

"Nkosi Sikelel' iAfrika"
(Dr. Daniel Kunenen—2002)

Professor Daniel Kunene, *The Madison Times* (June 2002), "Thoughts on the African National Anthem." Professor Kunene introduced the African national anthem at Madison's 13th Juneteenth Celebration, on June 15th in Penn Park. He spoke in the Heritage Tent.

"*Nkosi Sikelel' iAfrika*" was composed in 1896 by a Black South African school-teacher, Enoch Sontonga. It is a prayer. It beseeches God to come to Africa's help in its fight to regain the freedom taken from it by the White colonizers and settlers. The CD rendition I have brought is a vocal harmonized one, with soprano, alto, tenor, and bass. It is complete in itself. I will not sing with it.

There is one change in this rendition which I consider unfortunate. The original uses the word *uphondo*, i.e., a horn, referring specifically to the horns of a cow. In this rendition, *uphondo* has been replaced by *udumo*, which may be translated roughly as "glory" or "fame." I have experienced other performances in which this change has been made.

This change is unfortunate, because the image that Sontonga evokes with the use of "horn" is one that arises from the fact that the Black people of South Africa were a cattle-culture people. Cattle featured in all the important aspects of their lives, as they celebrated birth, death, puberty rites, marriage, and so on. Therefore, a cow entered into many metaphors and symbols in their languages.

In the context of this song, I see a depiction of a cow during a drought. As the water slowly dries up, it recedes from the pool's edge and the cow must wade into the mud to reach the water. The water is a metaphor for the Africans' lost or highly compromised freedom, and the mud, in which the cow can easily get stuck and die, represents the struggle to regain the lost freedom. As the drought gets more and more intense, the little remaining water becomes more and more difficult to reach, and the risk of getting stuck and dying is much greater.

Remember how Nelson Mandela was stuck in Robben Island prison as he tried to reach that water and regain the lost freedom. Remember how the leaders of the struggles throughout the continent had to risk being stuck in that mud to reach the water. The drought is intense. The water recedes farther and farther; it is reduced to a small ring surrounded by treacherous mud.

But the cow does not give up. It continues to go deeper and deeper into the mud to reach the water. As long as its horn is raised above the mud, there is hope. But, alas, the burden of the struggle, the mud, might lead to its neck getting tired and drooping and its horn getting stuck in the mud. However, the lure of the water is irresistible and makes the risk worthwhile. I think this image must not be thrown out from this anthem without much thought.

When Enoch Sontonga composed this song—because to him that's what it was, just another one of the many songs he composed—he did not think that one day it would be sung throughout the continent of Africa, and indeed in the African Diaspora, right here in Madison, Wisconsin, in the United States of America. It was an ordinary human act, which was good in its nature.

I want to address these remarks especially to the young people here today. The good human deeds you perform today might one day be celebrated as great deeds that have made a change in the world. Remember Rosa Parks when she refused to give up her seat in a bus, simply because she was tired and saw no reason why she should give it up for someone who got on the bus after her. She was applying the simple law of first come, first served. She did not think that one day that simple, good, human act was going to be celebrated in history.

"Nkosi Sikelel' iAfrika"

You do not plan to do acts that history will celebrate. Simply be satisfied that the deed you do today is a good, human deed. That's all. History will take care of the rest.

We will now hear the African national anthem. Please rise to receive and honor it.

A SECOND MARRIAGE (2003)

In 2003, ten years after the death of his first love and first wife, Daniel married Marci Starks. He was 80. It is a challenging example of stamina, will, and intellectual muscle and the love and care of Marci. It was a grand affair of tuxedoes and eloquent speeches. "The Clan" was there: Liz, Sipho, Lu, Linda, Wandi, Somori and Thiyane, Michele, Greg and Sage, and me celebrating this gift of a human being and his new bride.

Together they were beautiful—her dress a gorgeous mix of shades of gold, him in black tux and beautiful head of white hair. During his part of the vows, he asked, "Who's going to be first when the baby cries?"—and we all just cracked-up and, of course, so did Marci. It was a joyous moment. It was a joyous occasion.

She had heard him on WORT Radio and, as she tells it, "fell in love with that voice, with that sincerity and well eloquence." No wonder that would be so, for he was a participant and reliable host from the late 1980s to 2007, with guest appearances after that. An 1989 interview included his first wife, Selina, as they broached the topic of Miriam Makeba, her music, politics, and personal life, with special focus on her autobiography, *Makeba: My Story*. Other distinguished guests over the years include Ngugi Wa Thiong'o (novelist, playwright, essayist), Sonya Sanchez (poet extraordinaire), Fabu Mogaka (poet laureate of Madison), and Maulana Karenga (creator of Kwanza); and in 2003, WORT's Radio Literature Collective presented "A Story" with Marci Kunene.

Marci was a devoted partner and helpmate: she made sure he and his environment were clean and that he ate regularly and healthily. She provided the support and security that allowed for more international travel, the writing and publishing of numerous articles for local and national press, and five major books over the next ten years: *The Zulu Novels of C.L.S. Nyembezi* (2007); translation into English of Nhlanhla Maake's novel *Kweetsa ya Pelo ya Motho* (2009); translation into English of C.L.S. Nyembezi's Zulu novel, *Mntanami! Mntanami!* (English title, *My Child! My Child!*) (2010), for which he was awarded the Sol T. Plaatje Award by the English Academy of Southern Africa and the Karel Capek Award by the International Federation of Translators (FIT); and translation from Sesotho into English of Thomas Mofolo's novel, *Pitseng* (2011); then, amazingly, a 453-page novel, *Dawn to Twilight* (2013)!

She accompanied him November 17–20, 2004 to Frankfurt, Germany, where he read poetry and a paper on Maake's novels; and participated in storytelling at The 8th International Janheinz Jahn Symposium at Johannes Gutenberg University in Mainz, Germany. They traveled to South Africa, December 5–12, 2005, where he was a participant in The Wisconsin Idea Abroad: Week Away in Cape Town. He presented a paper on "The UW-UCT Connection Through A.C. Jordan and Daniel Kunene." The timing was in conjunction with the inauguration of the Southern African Large Telescope.

In February 2010, they traveled to Grenada, Nicaragua, where Dan presented his poem, "Peace," at La Otra, *Revista de Poesia*, which can be seen and heard on YouTube. And in 2011 to San Francisco, where he gave his acceptance speech for the Karel Capek (FIT) Award, also to be found on YouTube.

Honor at Cape Town University (2013)

21 December 2012

Dear Professor Kunene:

It is with great pleasure that I write to you on behalf of the Council of the University of Cape Town to invite you to accept the award of the degree of Doctor of Literature *honoris causa*. This invitation is in recognition of the impact of your scholarship that locates orality and oral poetry within modern linguistic and literary paradigms, and your significant contribution to preserving and opening the African tradition to a wider audience.

Honorary degrees are conferred at our graduation ceremonies. If you accept, which I sincerely hope you will, we will be pleased if you would be able to receive the degree in person...at one of our year-end ceremonies in the period 11 to 17 December 2013.

I would be grateful if you would keep this invitation confidential to your close circle until the University makes a formal announcement, which, of course, we will not do until we have your acceptance.

I look forward to hearing from you.

Yours sincerely,
Professor Thandabantu Nhlapo
Acting Vice-Chancellor

Being part of that "close circle," Liziwe, Sipho, Lu, Wandi, Linda, Marci, Michele Goodwin, and I knew it was time to start making plans. Nelson Mandela passed away on December 5, 2013. He was 95 years old. We had started making plans after the letter of December 12, 2012. Ironically or fortuitously, we all left for South Africa December 6, 2013: from San Francisco or Los Angeles or New York, meeting in London and meandering around mammoth Heathrow Airport until we found each other, joyfully, and a place to have lunch; then, flying together to Cape Town.

Dad, Papa, Dr. Daniel Pule Kunene, now 90 years of age, and still getting around independently, but assisted when needed by his wife, Marci, is receiving an honorary doctorate from the University of Cape Town. His literary accomplishments and contributions to African Languages and Literature include translations of major South African authors such as: *seSotho* novelist Thomas Mofolo's (1931) *Chaka* (2015) and Zulu novelist C.L.S. Nyembezi's (1950) *My Child! My Child!* (2010), for which he won the FIT Award in August of 2011. In all the Library of Congress lists 16 books authored by Daniel Kunene – five in the last ten years of his life, including a 453-page novel, *Dawn to Twilight* in 2013.

Lizzie had arranged for a driver to meet us at the bright and sparkling Jan Smuts Airport in Cape Town. And, sure enough, after customs and picking-up our bags, we saw the sign: POINTER & KUNENE PARTY. Sipho had arranged for us to stay at the New Kings Hotel in Sea Point, a very nice, clean, four-star, five-story hotel, with friendly staff and within walking distance to the beach. Papa, Marci, and Michele are staying closer to the university at the five-star Vineyard Hotel in Newlands, a really quite beautiful venue—a single-story white structure spread out over several acres, valets to greet our car, doormen to open doors for us, and a gorgeous lobby with bottles of South African wines displayed in framed cases.

We had dinner there that evening, Papa, Marci, Michele, Liz, Sipho, Lu, Linda, Wandi, and I. Papa was very, very emotional, even before we made a toast: "When we left South Africa…almost 50 years ago" he said, "I could not set foot in this hotel, except as a servant." Then he wept…seriously wept!! Then came the toasts, as we lifted our glasses: Lizzie spoke first: "To Papa, for this wonderful honor he is receiving." Then Sipho: "To the best Dad a child could have." Next Lu: "For the courage and foresight to sacrifice for a better future for all of us." Linda, raising her glass, insisted: "Thank you for these wonderful men." Again and again we raised our glasses. Finally, Wandi: "Thank you, Papa, for being a rock and a shield in our lives." Then, to our surprise, delight and gratitude, Michele insisted that she and husband Greg Shaffer (who wasn't even there) pay for everything—appetizers, wine, dinner and desert—for the nine of us, at a five-star hotel.

Liziwe, Daniel & Michele Goodwin, 2013

The love for "Madiba"—for Nelson Rolihlahla Mandela—is palpable, envelopes us! His portrait is everywhere... and, of course, in the hotel lobby, where Lizzie insisted on posing Papa with a photo of Mandela in the background. Their resemblance is uncanny, unnerving, unsettling, but there you have it. It's been 50 years! Fifty years ago, when Papa and Mama, Lizzie and Sipho set sail from Cape Town, South Africa for the United States. Fifty years ago, before the idiotic system of apartheid tightened its primitive grip on the people of South Africa.

On December 10, 2013, we visited the District Six Museum. I took a copy of my book from Africa World Press on Alex La Guma, *A Passion to Liberate: La Guma's South Africa: Images of District Six*; and got in exchange a copy of a book by Noor Ebrahim (curator of the District Six Museum). He told me about a new book by Blanche La Guma, Alex's wife: *In the Dark My Dress is on Fire*.

District Six was the Harlem, the South-Side Chicago, the West Oakland, the South Philadelphia of Cape Town. In 1966, in keeping with the illogic of the myth of white supremacy in general and the Group Areas Act in particular, District Six was declared a "White" area. What followed, in the late 1970s, was the destruction of homes and businesses in which generations of families had lived and worked. The intent was to erase District Six from the map and memory of Cape Town, if not the world. The District Six Museum is dedicated to the memory of this.

We left there and, rather than using "our driver" or a taxi, we decided to walk to the Cape Town Stadium, where a massive celebration, with thousands of people, was being held in honor of "Madiba" / Nelson Mandela. We passed the *Fugard Theater*, named for Athol Fugard, one of South Africa's most well-known playwrights (*Master Harold and the Boys, Bozman and Lena*). The theater, in the District Six area of Cape Town, opened with performances by the Isango Portobello theater company in February of 2010 and a new play written and directed by Athol Fugard, *The Train Driver*, played at the theater in March of 2010.

The Cape Town Stadium is a soccer and rugby stadium that was built for the 2010 FIFA World Cup. The stadium, a marvelous, beautiful structure, is located in Green Point, between Signal Hill and the Atlantic Ocean, close to the Cape Town city center and Waterfront. The stadium has a seating capacity of 60,000 and cost US$600 million to build. And this day, in honor of "Madiba" / Nelson Mandela, every seat is filled and we—Liz, Sipho, Lu, Linda, Wandi, Michele, and I—were there!!! Among that capacity crowd, that "Rainbow Nation," we were there! Honoring, as it turned out, the life of two great men: Daniel Pule Kunene and Nelson Rolihlahla Mandela. The ironies of life are many!!!

Honor at Cape Town University (2013)

Daniel & Liziwe - 2013

Luyanda, Daniel, Liziwe, Sipho & Wandile - 2013

SIXTEEN DAYS

Even as his 93-year-old body began to succumb to inevitable decline, he kept an intellectual vigor that was, to say the least, phenomenal. Remember, he published his first and only novel, *Dawn to Twilight* at 90. I was using it in my Humanities class. So, when, at 92, he came to California to visit family, he also generously gave a lecture to this class, with Liz, Somori, Sipho, Lu (filming), Linda, Wandi, and Marci (Dad's wife) present, on the use of the *leitmotif* in this work—in this case, the recurring theme of *water,* its necessity, its power, its use as a political tool.

Dad summarized this way: when two teenagers, Duma and Meisie, accidentally meet at a street water tap, and it is dry, they are both frustrated and their rather unlike temperaments emerge in different ways. She flares into a temper. He holds his feelings under control. A brief word jousting follows. The fact that they live in a white-controlled black township in South Africa immediately brings up the political meaning of the dry tap. They part abruptly, the young man afraid he'll be late for school, while the young woman holds school in contempt. But it seems a seed has been sown. How will it grow? What directions will their lives take?

Writing for the award-winning, Contra Costa College student newspaper, *The Advocate*, Robert Clinton provides enjoyable insights into this experience in his article, "Renowned Author Stirs 'Curiosity': Historical Injustices Displayed Through Published Works." Clinton explains that students, faculty, and family were treated to a presentation by Dr. Daniel Kunene, an internationally known author and a translator of African texts into English, who happens to be Professor Pointer's father-in-law. Dr. Kunene came to explain the metaphoric connections between socio-economic politics and everyday life in his new novel, *Dawn to Twilight*.

After explaining *leitmotif* as a unifying, dominant, recurring theme, he pointed out that the struggle for water is a recurring theme throughout the story and finds common connections—Location, class, and status. To begin, he requested two volunteers from the packed classroom to assist in acting out a passage from the book to set the mood of the story. His 92-year-old frame and calm but powerful voice led the students through the reading. He then asked the students to explain their interpretations of scenes and character motivations.

An author of sixteen books, he said to the class that he did not only come to lecture, but also to inspire conversation about the message behind the written words—namely, the criticism of apartheid and the restoration of African literature. At one point, about 30 minutes into his talk, he gave a thunderous clap with his hands, in a way only a grandfather could, to stop three young men in the back from speaking over students attempting to ask questions. Students asked him to return to the next class for more.

On Wednesday, May 11, 2016, sixteen days before he passed away, Dad received an email from Aubrey Yoffe:

Dear Professor Kunene, greetings from an ex-citizen of Edenville. I trust you will remember me. I now live in Sydney, Australia. A kind lady helped me get in touch with you through google and extend my fondest greetings and good memories. I left Edenville in 1953 and still maintained contact with David Malete for many years thereafter. I hope this stimulates your memory of that little village where we occasionally had discussions. I learned from google that you have attained many prestigious awards and heights which I knew you would attain having had those conversations with you in Edenville. You may recall I spoke to you when I visited the USA approximately 25 years ago. I look forward again to hearing from you after all these years. Warmest regards, Aubrey.

On May 14, 2016, thirteen days before he passed away, Dad wrote back:

Aubrey! Aubrey!! Aubrey!!!

What an auspicious time for you to get in touch with me when I'm trying to remember as many details of my past as possible! When every bit of memory, true or doubtful, or even unintentionally fictitious, is a brick in that wall? I started this project as an autobiography, but stopped not far from the beginning to ask myself is that truly what happened? Or, is that how it happened? Then I remember the term "poetic license" and decided I would copy a phrase some literary specialist call "faction," namely fact and fiction meshed together.

The Edenville I knew has almost entirely disappeared in the recent impact of the social, political events and their effect on the social, physical and over-all changes of the demography of the place. The current Edenville has usurped the place of that one, the one that I used as a background to my stories, to my characters' understanding of the meaning of life. I noticed that on my visit from the US to attend my sister Magdeline's funeral. I still cherish the Edenville in my stories, such as the collection From the Pit of Hell to the Spring of Life. *How could I forget features like the two streams, one that ran closest to the white town where we, children from the black side, pilfered pears from Baas Wessel's trees overhanging the shallow side of the black side of the stream? How, since we were mostly hungry? We filled the fronts of our shirts. We got home and our parents shared what we brought, no questions asked!!*

There was another stream which flowed closest to the black residential area, the "Location," featured by two large willow trees, one on each side, and flowing in the same direction. The two flowed closer and closer and more and more furious as they rushed to their point of impact to pour their increasingly furious waters into the Ngwathe River, towards their point of impact where they clashed their Armageddon. They have run dry! Sorry, I got carried away.

My children came from different parts of the United States last month to join me in celebrating my 93rd Birthday on April 13th. At that time they also decided to ask me if they could name my next great-grandson after me, namely Daniel, to which I agreed heartily. My namesake is expected sometime in August or September if I remember correctly. They also arranged to celebrate my Birthday on Skype, so many of us could actually see and talk with each other. It was a wonderful occasion. I call them collectively my "Clan."

It was wonderful hearing from you, Aubrey!! Do you have any of my books? If not, I will gladly select one or two and send them to you. By the way about over ten years ago, before I retired from the University of Wisconsin, I attended a "Black Literature" Conference in Brisbane. I flew into Sydney and stayed a few days there with friends I had met at a research center in Holland before continuing on my way to and from Brisbane to attend a "Black Literature" Conference. So, I saw a bit of Sydney. My friends were surprised a conference like that could be held in a place like that! They told me about the racism there, that it was nicknamed "The Deep North," mimicking America's "Deep South!" Is it still like that?

Much love, Aubrey, and once again, thanks for getting in touch.

Daniel

AFTERWORD

By Raj Shukla

Daniel Pule Kunene lived enough life for two, complete with two great loves. His first wife, Selina, departed in 1993, having shared with him four children, two grandchildren, and two great grandchildren. Ten years later, he was graced with the affection and care of Marci, whom he devoted himself to for 13 years until he came to rest. Over a glass of wine last week, Daniel's daughter, Liziwe (Liz) Kunene Pointer and her husband Fritz Pointer; his sons Sipho Kunene, Luyanda (Lu) Kunene and his wife Linda Fowells, Wandile (Wandi) Kunene, and Marci painted a vivid picture of a man who built bridges across continents and between people with his keen intellect, endless creativity, and deep compassion for all.

He was my neighbor and introduced himself with a kind of grace and good humor that was uniquely his. My wife and I came by to gaze at what would be our new home in the early summer of 2012. As we held hands on the sidewalk and imagined the life ahead of us, we heard a soft tapping from a nearby window. We looked up to see Daniel and his lovely wife, Marci, beaming their glorious smiles and raising a glass of wine to an odd pair of strangers who were dangerously close to trespassing. Like so many others in Madison and beyond, we fell in love with him and his family.

An emeritus professor of African Languages and Literature at the University of Wisconsin-Madison, Daniel used his skill with language to transcribe South African oral works, translate South African writers, create poetry and short stories, and dazzle friends with poignant and often hilarious oratory.

He lived in exile from his home country for 30 years and found the injustices of racism followed him from South Africa to the United States when the Kunenes arrived in early 1964. A year earlier, Vivian Malone had taken the first steps past George Wallace to register alongside white students at the University of Alabama. A young President Kennedy committed the nation to de-segregation that very evening. Just one day later in Mississippi, Medgar Evers was murdered in front of his wife and children for the crime of working toward a country free from discrimination. Dr. King brought his dream of a just America before hundreds of thousands at the March on Washington two months later—only weeks before four girls were killed during the 16th Street Baptist Church bombing in Birmingham. Two months later, President Kennedy was dead.

"This is a violent country," Daniel remarked to a young Liz Kunene about America, uncertain of the decision to move to a nation boiling over with emotion amid great social change. However, the opportunities a move offered could not be denied. During a period teaching in Los Angeles, the very emotions that gave Daniel pause led him to consider a position at the University of Wisconsin-Madison. The community's activism was exciting to Daniel and contributed to the family's choosing to make a life in Wisconsin… but not without sacrifice.

"They made the decision to stay in America and to leave everyone behind," recalled Sipho of his parents. "That must have been incredibly difficult." Perhaps their choice was made easier because they believed a stay in the United States was temporary. Liz noted that, much like so many immigrants, "They left South Africa believing they would return." To their surprise, the Kunenes would not return to South Africa for three decades. They adjusted to life at an urban university far removed from the South African countryside and Daniel shielded his children from harsh realities that existed even in "liberal" Madison.

"He sheltered us; he protected us" from the racial tension of the day. In fact, his children only recently learned of a petition to segregate their near west-side neighborhood during their youth. It was directed squarely at the only black family on the block (Kendall Avenue) at the time.

Daniel's passions to combat injustice in the world—even on his own street—fueled his constant activism. He was a prominent figure in the Madison Area Committee on Southern Africa (MACSA) which led the fight to ensure the city, county, state, university, and corporations would divest from the interests propping up the apartheid regime.

His activism was as personal as it was political. Lu remembers an image of his parents reading poetry to children in a local elementary school. "Part of their activism was to educate the community about Africa and South Africa and apartheid. Some of my dad's poetry—he came in to a parent show-and-tell and read some of his poetry and asked the kids about it. And the kids got it. They understood. That's how he used art to undermine an unjust system."

Daniel truly believed in education as a force of liberation. And his commitment as an educator never faded. Last year (at age 92), Daniel made the long trip to California to teach during Fritz's course at Contra Costa College. His family witnessed as Daniel cast a spell on the enraptured students. "When he got up before the class, the years melted away," recalled Lu. He found the same solace and inspiration in the poetry he composed to enlighten others. Said Wandi of Daniel's motivation, "He got so much out of the creative process and what he did. He would acknowledge and appreciate how it affected others. But like a lot of artists who are doing what they love, he was so focused in that moment of creation—that was important."

Sipho described what so many experienced in Daniel's poetry: "My dad always had a way of seeing things through a different set of eyes." And that rare gift extended to his relationships. Linda remains amazed that "a lot of our friends felt like they could call him for advice. He was generous of spirit and interested in their lives and interests. Everybody who met him walked away feeling they were special."

He was a scholar, an artist, a dissident, and an activist to his last days, but his greatest joys came during time spent with family and friends. During recent months, he reconnected with former students and old neighbors. He was given one final precious gift from his daughter and granddaughter: "We have a third grandchild coming—his great grandchild—who will be named Daniel," Liz said while describing the videoconference during which she shared this news with her father. They captured the moment and look forward to showing Daniel's namesake in the years to come.

The world will surely miss Daniel's unmatched talents. Our city will miss his unmistakable voice. I will miss his laughter. My daughters will miss his eager hugs. What he left behind will remain precious to all who knew him.

A card recently arrived at the family home with the famous Mahatma Gandhi quote, "My life is my message." Daniel's message was to truly participate in life with joy and curiosity. It will echo in the minds and hearts of his family and the many friends who honor him.

BIBLIOGRAPHY OF SELECTED WORKS OF DANIEL PULE KUNENE

The Beginning of South African Vernacular Literature: A Historical Study. Los Angeles: University of California Press, 1967.

The Works of Thomas Mofolo. UCLA: African Studies Occasional Papers Series.

Heroic Poetry of the Basotho. London. Oxford University Press, 1971.

The Ideophone in Southern Sotho. Berlin: Verlag Von Dietrich Reimer, 1978.

Pirates Have Become Our Kings. Nairobi: East African Publishing House, 1978.

A Seed Must Seem to Die. Johannesburg: Ravan Press, 1981.

From the Pit of Hell to the Spring of Life. Johannesburg: Ravan Press, 1986.

Thomas Mofolo and the Emergence of Written Sesotho Prose. Johannesburg: Ravan Press, 1989.

Tongue and Mother Tongue Trenton, NJ: Africa World Press, 2002.

The Zulu Novels of C.L.S. Nyembezi. Lewiston, NY: The Edwin Mellen Press, 2007.

Dithoko, Dithothokiso le Dithoheletso tsa Sesotho. Cape Town: Oxford University Press, 1996.

The Rock at the Corner of My Heart. Makanda, IL: Brown Turtle Press, 2009.

My Child! My Child! by C.L.S. Nyembezi. Translated by Professor Daniel Kunene. Cape Town: Longman, 2010.

Pitseng: The Search for True Love. A Translation of Thomas Mofolo's classic novel by Daniel P. Kunene. Lesotho: Morija Museum & Archives, 2013.

Chaka: Thomas Mofolo: New English Translation by Daniel Kunene. Cape Town: 2015.

Kero Court Chronicles. Madison: Daniel P. Kunene, 2015.

Dawn to Twilight. Madison: Daniel P. Kunene, 2015.

Scholarly Articles and Chapters in Books

"Song for Sekoto: 1913-2013." The Gerard Sekoto Foundation, 2013.

"Speaking the Act: The Ideophone as a Linguistic Rebel," in *Ideophones: Typological Studies in Languages #44.* F. K. Erhard Voeltz and Christa Killian-Hatz (eds.), Amsterdam: John Benjamins Publishing Company 2001.

"Oral Residuals in African Literatures." *Voices: A Journal of Oral Studies,* Vol. 2 (1999).

"Edenville." *Wisconsin Academy Review*, Vol. 46, No. 1 (1999).

"Thomas Mofolo," a ca. 9000-word article for the volume *African Writers* (ed. Prof. C. Brian Cox, University of Manchester) for Scribner's Writers' Series. London: Simon & Shuster, Prentice Hall International, pp. 479–493 incl. (1997).

"Return to the Roots: South Africa Thirty Years Later." *Wisconsin Academy Review*, carried a 3-part series of the narrative of my and my wife's return to South Africa in July–August 1993 (1994-1995).

"Acceptance Speech." *South African Journal of African Languages*, Vol. 4, No. 1 (1994).

"Characterization, Realism and Social Inequality in the Novels of C.L.S. Nyembezi." *South African Journal of African Languages*, Vol. 14, No. 4 (1994), pp. 155–162.

"Personal Testimony." *ALA Bulletin,* Vol. 20, No. 4 (1994).

"Southern African Literature, Oral and Written." *UNESCO: General History of Africa*, Chapter 19 (partial) of Volume VIII. Paris: UNESCO and Oxford: Heinemann, 1993.

"African-Language Literature: Tragedy and Hope." *Research in African Literatures,* Vol. 23, No. 1 (1992), pp. 7–15.

"Language, Literature and the Struggle for Liberation in South Africa." In *Perspectives on South African English Literature*, Michael Chapman, Colin Gardner, and Es'kia Mphahlele (eds.). Johannesburg: Ad Donker, 1992, pp. 497–513.

"Journey in the African Epic." *Research in African Literatures,* Vol. 22, No. 2 (1991), pp. 205–223.

"Language, Literature and the Struggle for Liberation in South Africa." In *The Question of Language in African Literature Today*, Eldred Durosimi Jones, Eustace Palmer, and Marjorie Jones (eds.). London: James Curry / Trenton, NJ: Africa World Press, pp. 37–49. Reprinted from original publication in *Staffrider*(1991).

"'Mandela Saga' Celebrates Personal, Political Conviction." *L&S Magazine*, Summer 1991, pp. 20–21.

"The Variety of Narrative Voices in African Literature." *Presence Africaine* (A), 1990. [Requested by editor for the special issue to Commemorate the Thirtieth Anniversary of the First Congress of Negro Writers and Artists]

"The Conjunction as Catalyst in the Novels of C.L.S. Nyembezi." In Festschrift for Professor Emeritus David Rycroft, in *South African Journal of African Languages*, Vol. 10, No. 4 (1990), pp. 338–344.

"Dialogue in the Novels of C.L.S. Nyembezi." In *Die Vielfalt der Kultur*: *Ethnologische Aspekte von Verwanttschaft, Kunst und Weltauffasung,* Karl-Heinz Kohl, Heinzarnold Muszinski, und

Ivo Strecker (eds.). Berlin: Dietrich Reimer Verlag, 1990, pp. 380–405 (Festschrift in honor of Professor Emeritus Dr. Ernst Wilhelm Muller on his 65th birthday).

"Malcolm X: An Invocation." A poem partly spoken partly sung, performed at Edgewood College on February 8, 1990.

"Fiction and Society in South Africa." In *Writers From South Africa*. Evanston: TriQuarterly Books, 1989, pp. 15–25.

"Introduction" [and commentaries] in *Exit Genesis* by Anna Yardeni. Trenton, NJ: Red Sea Press, 1989. [Review]

"Ingqumbo/The Wrath: An Analysis of a Translation." In *Connection Essays on Black Literatures*, Emmanuel S. Nelson (ed.). Canberra: Aboriginal Studies Press, 1988, pp. 75–87.

"Reuben T. Caluza: Ein Zulu-Komkponist und Sozialkritiker." In *Sudafrika: Nur Fur Weisse? Lesebuch Zur Apartheid*, Dr. Ute Luig und Dr. Volkhard Hundsdorfer (eds.). Berlin: Dietrich Reimer Verlag, 1987, pp. 226–241.

"Thomas Mokopu Mofolo 1876–1948." In *Twentieth Century Literary Criticism*, Dennis Poupard (ed.). Detroit: Gale Research Company, 1987, pp. 256–265.

"Position Statement on the IUPPS-sponsored World Archaeological Congress to be held in Mainz in September, 1987." In *Von Southampton Nach Mainz, Die Geschichte eines Verschweigens Dokumentation zu Den Auseinandersetzungen um den 11, Weltweiten Archaologenkongress Betreffs der Teilnahme Sodafrikas/Namibias, Herausgegeben Vom Asta Der Johannes-Gutenberg-Universitat Mainz, Zusammengestelit Von Bettina Schmidt und Andreas Meister, Asta Uni Mainz, Saarstrabe 21, 6500 Mainz. Erweiterte Auflage* (August 1987).

"Written Art and Oral Tradition in Southern Africa." In *European-Language Writing in Sub-Saharan Africa* (Chapter XII), Albert Gerard (ed.). Budapest: Akademiai Kiado [in Series *A Comparative History of Literature in European Languages*], 1986, pp. 1021–1044.

"Ntsoanatsatsi/Eden: Superimposed Images in Thomas Mofolo's *Moeti oa Bochabela.*" *English in Africa*, Vol. 13, No. 1, May 1986, pp. 13–39. [Leading article solicited for this special issue devoted to Thomas Mofolo and his works]

"Language, Literature and the Struggle for Liberation in South Africa." *Staffrider*, Vol. 6, No. 3 (1986).

"Journey as Metaphor in African Literature." In *African Literature Studies: The Present State/L 'Etat Present*, Stephen Arnold (ed.). Washington, D.C.: Three Continents Press, 1985, pp. 189-215.

"The Chaka Controversy: New Light on the Role of the Missionaries." In *Interdisciplinary Dimensions of African Literature*, Kofi Anyidoho, Abioseh M. Porter, Daniel Racine, and Janice Spleth (eds.). Washington, D.C.: Three Continents Press, 1985, pp. 113–127.

"The Peopling of a Story: A New View of Characterization in African Literature." In *The Next Decade: Theoretical and Research Issues in African Studies*, James E. Turner (ed.). Ithaca, NY: Africana Studies and Research Center, Cornell University, 1984, pp. 173–191.

"N. M. Khaketla, Poet and Humanist." *Concerning Poetry* (Special International Issue), Vol. 17, No. 2 (1984), pp. 2–23. [Solicited article]

"Ideas Under Arrest: Censorship in South Africa." *Research in African Literatures*, Vol. 12, No. 4 (Winter 1981), pp. 421–439. [Republished in *Ufahamu*, Vol. XI, No. 3 (Spring, 1982), pp. 204–221; request to republish in French translation was also made.]

"Levels of Communication in the Heroic Poetry of Southern Africa." In *Artist and Audience: African Literature as a Shared Experience*, Richard O. Priebe and Thomas Hale (eds.). Washington, D.C.: Three Continents Press and African Literature Association, 1979, pp. 60–76.

"Writer, Reader and Character in African-Language Literature: Towards a New Definition." In *Neo-African Literature and Culture: Essays in Memory of Janheinz Jahn* (1978). Extensive quotations from this article incorporated into *Twentieth Century Literary Criticism* (Gale Research Company).

"Neglected Literatures: The Case of African Literatures in the African Languages." *Council on National Literatures Report*, No. 7/8, 1977, pp. 11–15.

"Leselinyana la Lesotho and Sotho Historiography." *History in Africa,* Vol. 4 (1977), pp. 149–161.

"Shaka in African Literature." In Donald Burness, *Shaka, King of the Zulus in African Literature*. Washington, DC: Three Continents Press, 1977, pp. 165-192. [Special solicited essay]

"Writer, Reader and Character in African Language Literature—Towards a New Definition." In *Neo-African Literature and Culture—Essays in Memory of Janheinz Jahn*, Bernth Lindfors and Ulla Schild (eds.). Mainzer Afrika-Studien 1, B. Heyman, 1976, pp. 243–257.

"An Analysis of Stephen A Mpashi's *Uwauma Nafyala.*" In *Neo-African Literature and Culture—Essays in Memory of Janheinz Jahn*, Bernth Linfors and Ulla Schild (eds.). Mainzer Afrika-Studien 1, B. Heyman, 1976, pp. 258–266.

"Towards an Aesthetic of Sesotho Prose." In *Exile and Tradition*, Rowland Smith (ed.). Longman & Dalhousie University Press, 1976, pp. 98–115.

"The Imagery of Darkness and Light in Thomas Mofolo's *Moeti oa Bochabela.*" In *The Commonwealth Writer Overseas*, Alastaire Niven (ed.). Didier, 1976, pp. 255–264.

"The Crusading Writer, His Modes, Themes and Styles." In *Text and Context*: *Methodological Explorations in the Field of African Literature,* Mineke Schipper and Abiola Irele (eds.). Leiden: Afrika-Studiecentrum, (ser. *African Perspectives*), 1976, pp. 99–112.

Paper/panel on South African Oral Traditions in *Issue*, Vol. VI, No. 1 (Spring, (1976)., Bernth Linfors, Guest Editor.

"Une Soiree au Concert ou la Theatralite d 'une veillee'." *Revue d'Histoire du Theatre*, No. 1 (1975), pp. 87–96.

"Bantu Literature." *Encyclopedia Britannica* (US Edition). Chicago, 1974.

"L.M. Mwiinga's *Nyoko Ngumw*— A Critical Analysis." *BaShiru*, Vol. 4, No. 2 (Spring, 1973), pp. 65–80.

"Towards An Aesthetic of Sesotho Prose." *Dalhousie Review*, Vol. 53, No. 4 (Winter, 1974), pp. 701–719. [Later published in book form with other essays in *Exile and Tradition*, Rowland Smith (ed.), 1976.

"A Preliminary Study of Downstepping in Southern Sotho." *African Studies*, Vol. 31, No. 7 (1972), pp. 1–24. (Solicited for inclusion in *Festschrift Doke*, but received too late for that publication.)

"Metaphor and Symbolism in the Heroic Poetry of Southern Africa." In *African Folklore*, Richard M. Dorson (ed.). Doubleday, 1972.

"Problems in Creating Creative Writing: The Example of Southern Africa." *Review of National Literatures*, Vol. 1, No. 2 (Fall, 1971), pp. 81–103.

"Special Deverbative Eulogues in Sotho." In *Studies in African Languages and Linguistics*, Chin-wu Kim and Herbert Stahlke (eds.). Linguistic Research, Inc., 1970, pp. 123–133.

"African Vernacular Writing—An Essay on Self-Devaluation." *African Social Research*, No. 9 (1970), pp.639–659.

"Deculturation—The African Writer's Response." *Africa Today* (August-September, 1968), pp. 19–24.

"A War Son of the Basotho," *Journal of African Literature and the Arts,* (Spring, 1967), pp. 10–20.

"The Ideophone in Southern Sotho." *Journal of African Languages*, Vol. 4, Part 1 (1965), pp. 19–39.

"Southern Sotho Words of English and Afrikaans Origin." *Word* (December, 1963), pp. 347–375.

"Where Language Mirrors." *The New African*, Vol. 1, No. 8 (August, 1962), pp. 2–3. [follow-up on "Who is Your White Man?"]

"Who is Your White Man?" *The New African,* Vol. 1, No. 6 (June, 1962), pp. 8–9.

"Notes on Hlonepha Among the Southern Sotho." *African Studies,* Vol. 17, No. 3 (1958), pp. 159–182.

Selected Review Articles

Review of J.C.W. Van Rooyen, *Censorship in South Africa* (Kenwyn, South Africa: Juta & Co. Ltd., 1987). Reviewed in *Research in African Literatures,* Vol. 22, No. 1 (1991).

Review of David Rycroft and A.B. Ngcobo, *The Praises of Dingana,* (Durban: Killie Campbell Library and Natal University Press, 1989). Reviewed in *Research in African Literatures,* Vol. 22, No. 1 (Spring, 1991).

Review of Albert Gerard, *African-Language Literature*: *An Introduction to the Literary History of Sub-Saharan Africa* (Longman, 1981). Reviewed in the *Canadian Review of Comparative Literature* (August, 1983).

Review of Christopher Heywood (ed.), *Aspects of South African Literature* (London: Heinemann, 1976). Reviewed in *World Literature Written In English,* Vol. 19, No. 2 (1980), pp. 175–178.

Review of Rev. M. Ferragne, O.M.I. (comp), *A Catalogue of 1000 Sesotho Books* (Rome / Lesotho: The Social Centre, 1974). Reviewed in *Research in African Literatures,* Vol. 19, No. 3 (1979).

Review of Patricia E. Scott, *Mqhayi in Translation,* Communication no. 6, Grahamstown: Rhodes University, Department of African Languages, 1976. Reviewed in *Research in African Literatures,* Vol. 10, No. 3 (1979).

Review of Minnie Postma, *Tales from the Basotho* (translated from Afrikaans By Susie McDermid), American Folklore Society Memoir Series, Vol. 59 (Austin: University of Texas Press, 1974). Reviewed in *Research in African Literatures,* Vol. 7, No. 1 (1976), pp. 69–74.

Review of Mosebi Damane and Peter Sanders, *Lithoko: Sotho Praise Poems* (Oxford: The Clarendon Press, 1974). Reviewed in *Journal of Southern African Studies* (1975), pp. 249–251.

Review of Patricia E. Scott, *James James Ranisi Jolobe—An Annotated Bibliography*. Communication No. 1 (Grahamstown: Department Of African Languages, Rhodes University, 1973). Reviewed in *Research in African Literatures*, Vol. 6, No. 1 (1975).

Review of B.E.N. Mahlasela, *A General Survey of Xhosa Literature from its Early Beginning in the 1800's to the Present*. Working Paper No. 2 (Grahamstown: Department of African Languages, Rhodes University, 1973). Reviewed in *Research in African Literatures*, Vol. 6, No. 1 (1975).

Review of Christopher Heywood (ed.), *Perspectives on African Literature, Selections from the Proceedings of the Conference on African Literature held at the University of Ife* (New York: African Publishing Corporation, 1971).

Review of Jack Cope and Uys Krige (eds.) *The Penguin Book of South African Verse* (Baltimore: Penguin Books, 1968). Reviewed in *Africa Report*, Vol. 16, No. 4 (1971).

Review of S.M. Guma, *The Form, Content and Technique of Traditional Literature in Southern Sotho* (Pretoria: Van Schaick, 1967). Reviewed in *Research in African Literatures*, Vol. 1, No. 2 (1970), pp. 205–210.

Review of Jack Goody (ed.), *Literacy in Traditional Societies* (Cambridge University Press, 1968). Reviewed in *African Social Research*, No. 9 (1970), pp. 708–709.

Review of Trevor Cope (ed.), *Izibongo—Zulu Praise Poems* (Oxford: The Clarendon Press, 1968). Reviewed in *Journal of African Languages*, Vol. 8, Part 1 (1969), pp. 50–53.

Review of Ernest Cole, *House of Bondag*,(New York: Random House, 1967). Reviewed in the *Los Angeles Times*, December, 1968.

Review of Alan Drury, *A Very Strange Society* (New York: Trident Press, 1967). Reviewed in the *Los Angeles Times*, 1967.

Review of the film *Africa Addio*, for the *Los Angeles Times*, June, 1967.

Review of Derek Fivaz, *Some Aspects of the Ideophone in Zulu* (Hartford Seminary Foundation, 1963). Reviewed in *Linguistics*, No. 25 (September, 1966), pp. 120–128.

Review of M. Mohapi, *Temo ya boholoholo Lesotho* . Reviewed in *African Studies*, Vol. 16, No. 4 (1957), pp. 247–248.

Short Stories

"Maketoni," translated into Czech by Dr. O. Hulec, and published in the magazine *Novy Orient*, Vol. 1 (2002), pp. 25–30.

"My Future was Yesterday," *Matatu* Heft, 3/4 2, January (1988).

Russian translation of my short story "The Spring of Life." Biographical entry as follows: Daniel P. Kunene (UAR), "Istochnik zhizni," translation from English by S.R. Dubrovkin, compiler, Yu. Volpe, ed. (Raduga: Moscow), pp. 305–333 (1987).

"Blood Relatives" in *TriQuarterly* special issue from South Africa: New Writing, Photographs and Art (Spring/Summer, 1987).

"The Spring of Life" (unabridged), in Russian translation in the Soviet publication *Afrika* [an almanakh] (1983).

"Maketoni" in *Presence Africaine* (1983; special volume in memory of David Diop [1927 – 1960].)

"The Spring of Life" (abridged), published in Russian translation in the Soviet magazine *Asia and Africa* (1982).

"The Spring of Life," *Staffrider*, Vol. 4, No. 4 (1982).

"Me," *Okike*, No. 18 (1981).

"The Pit of Hell," *Wisconsin Academy Review* (June 1978), pp. 21–24.

"The Spring of Life," *Okike*, No. 11 (1973).

Memoirs; interviewed by Robert Lange with The Oral History Project of the University of Wisconsin–Madison (2006).

INDEX

A

African American(s) 3, 138, 154, 157
African Diaspora 304
African Language Association of Southern Africa (ALASA) 216–217, 220, 239, 247, 255, 285
African Literature Association 187, 327
African Literature in Translation 160–161
African Methodist Episcopal (AME) Church 20, 22, 25, 30–31, 49, 53, 59–61, 76, 113, 211, 290
African National Congress (ANC) 96, 110, 181, 187, 250, 269, 278, 282, 297
African Studies Program 155, 157
Afrikaners 77, 169, 202
Afrikaans 18, 22, 42, 79, 98, 169, 179, 181, 184–185, 190, 193, 196, 215, 329–330
Afro-American Studies Department 154, 156–157, 173
America vii, 2, 6, 33, 40–41, 47, 77, 130–131, 136–137, 139, 145–146, 152–153, 157, 161, 167, 185, 222, 244, 249, 252, 293, 304, 318, 320
Anglican (church) 110, 180, 281, 283
Apartheid vii, 1, 3–6, 8, 13, 19, 77–78, 91, 95–96, 98–99, 101, 103, 106, 116, 122, 125, 128–130, 133–134, 137, 145, 152, 167–169, 177, 181, 186–189, 193, 202–204, 208, 210, 212–215, 217, 219, 228, 230, 242, 265–266, 276–278, 290, 294, 311, 316, 321, 326

B

Bantu 7, 44–46, 48–49, 78, 80–81, 85–86, 92, 97–100, 104, 106, 153, 177, 179–182, 186–187,

196, 214–215, 220, 223, 246–247, 250, 277, 280–281, 298, 300, 329
Bantu Authorities Act 99
Bantu Education Act 97, 180
Bantu Education System 177, 180, 277
Basotho 4, 37, 67–68, 70, 83, 95, 158–161, 260, 323, 329–330
Biko, Steve 235, 248–249
Black American(s) 19, 76, 138, 154
Black Consciousness Movement 222, 249
Bloemfontein 39, 58, 297
Boers 50–51, 77, 169, 178, 193
Boksburg (So. Africa) 118, 120, 280, 282
Botha, P.W. 203
Boycott 4, 167, 169–170, 214
Brain Drain 266
Brutus, Dennis 2
Buthelezi, Gatsha 247

C

Cape Town viii, 4, 88, 90–93, 95–96, 98, 101–102, 104–105, 109–110, 113–116, 118, 120, 123, 127–129, 134–135, 140, 147–148, 188, 194, 204, 207–208, 211–212, 222, 229, 232, 235, 237, 241, 243, 251, 255, 258, 266, 272–273, 280, 283, 289, 308–312, 323–324
Capitol Times 190
Chaka 4, 8, 69–71, 310, 324, 327
Colored (People) 116, 188
Cronkite, Walter 98, 179

D

De Klerk, F.W. 204, 234, 247, 269, 278
Department of African Languages and Literature 4–6, 137, 155, 157, 237, 263, 265
Department of Bantu Affairs 106
District Six Museum 312
Doke, Clemens M 85, 89, 91, 218, 220, 285, 329
Durban 91, 330
Dutch 20, 22, 26, 40, 42, 50, 100, 116, 190, 199, 202
Dutch Reform 20, 40, 100

E

Ebrahim, Noor 312
Edenville vii–viii, 1, 13–14, 16, 19, 23, 29, 31, 34–35, 37, 39, 41–42, 44–46, 49, 53, 55, 58–59, 73, 214, 222–226, 229, 231–232, 237, 274, 276, 278–279, 283, 289, 291, 293–294, 316–317, 324
European(s) 27

Index

Evers, Medgar 2, 320

F

February, Vernon ix, 118, 190, 203, 239, 241, 308, 312, 326
Finlayson, Ken 216, 220, 256, 264
Fugard, Athol 312

G

Germany 4, 6, 8, 47, 147, 169, 232, 308
Goodwin, Michele ix, 310–311
Great Depression 33
Group Areas Act 95, 121–123, 139, 188, 210, 312
Gwangwa, Jonas 2, 5

H

Haley, Alex 27, 252
Hani, Chris 282
Holland vii, 147, 190–191, 199–200, 202, 239, 318

I

Immorality Act 99–101
Inkatha Freedom Party (IFP)

J

Johannes Gutenberg University 4, 6, 233, 308
Jordan, A.C. viii–ix, 2–3, 48, 62, 79–81, 85–90, 99, 101–106, 113, 115, 121, 124, 137, 140–141, 147, 151, 207, 238, 254, 297, 308
Jordan, Phylis viii–ix, 2–3, 48, 62, 79–81, 85–90, 99, 101–106, 113, 115, 121, 124, 137, 140–141, 147, 151, 207, 238, 254, 297, 308

K

Karenga, Maulana 307
Kennedy, John F. 2, 129–131, 320
Kenyatta, Jomo 103, 154
Kgositsile 2
Kroonstad 7, 41–46, 48, 78, 80–81, 85–86, 92, 220, 222–225, 227–228, 231, 271–275, 278–282, 289
Kunene, Daniel i, iii, viii, x, 1, 4, 7–9, 11, 26, 38, 74, 93, 102, 120, 135, 144, 149, 171, 199, 202, 209, 213, 226, 235, 237, 248, 263, 272, 285, 288, 303, 307–308, 310–313, 315, 317–324, 327, 332
Kunene, Ephraim 31, 35, 38,

56
Kunene, Liziwe   iii, v, ix, 1, 5–6, 71, 122, 125–128, 130, 184, 229, 290, 300, 310–311, 313, 319
Kunene, Luyanda   ix, 2–3, 138, 290, 313, 319
Kunene, Magdeline   ix, 225, 227–229, 231, 279–280, 317
Kunene, Marci   ix, 307, 310, 315, 319
Kunene, Philip   225, 229, 231, 279–280
Kunene, Selina   vii, ix–x, 1, 3–4, 9, 31, 110–112, 114, 118–120, 126, 146–149, 168, 185, 209, 213–216, 222, 225–226, 228–229, 231–233, 237–240, 243, 248, 250, 269, 271–272, 275, 280–282, 285, 287, 307, 319
Kunene, Sipho   ix, 1–2, 11, 71, 116, 125–128, 130, 229, 290, 307, 310–313, 315, 319–321
Kunene, Wandile   ix, 2, 11, 138, 253, 290, 313, 319
Kuper, Leo   91
Kutoane, Martha Mahloli   30

L

La Guma, Alex   312
Lesotho   vii, 34, 37, 67, 159, 187, 225, 246, 324, 328, 330, 332
Lord, A.B.   62, 160, 258, 275, 298
Los Angeles   2, 4–5, 133, 137–138, 140, 144–145, 151–152, 207, 210, 227, 290, 310, 320, 323, 331–332
Lutheran   31, 49

M

Maake, Nhlanhla   255, 308
Madison, WI.   vii, 3–4, 6, 116, 137, 139–140, 144, 147–148, 151–152, 156, 185–186, 207–209, 215, 237, 285, 303–304, 307, 319–321, 324, 332
Madison Area Committee on Southern Africa (MAC-SA)   3–4, 9, 321
Magubane, Bernard Magubane   ix, 2
Makeba, Miriam   240, 307
Malone, Vivian   2, 320
Mandela, Nelson   1, 203, 222, 234, 241, 247, 251, 304, 310–312, 326
Mandela, Winnie   110
Masekela, Hugh   ix, 2, 5
Mbulu, Letta   ix, 2, 5
McKay, Nelly   156–157, 163
Melville J. Herskovits Library of African Studies Archive at Northwestern University   11

Index

Mofolo, Thomas 8, 69–71, 238, 282, 308, 310, 323–324, 326–328
Moyo, Dambisa 6
Moyo, Steven 6

N

Natal 22, 27, 31, 49–50, 89, 91, 95, 101, 270, 330
Native Law 128
Ndawo, Ralph 82
Netherlands 8, 147, 199
New Era Fellowship 117
New York 131–133, 137, 148, 290, 310, 331
Nkosi, Lewis viii, 9, 168, 297–298, 303, 305
Nkosi Sikelel' iAfrica (the National Anthem of South Africa) viii, 9, 297–298, 303, 305
Nkrumah, Kwame 154
Non-European Unity Movement (NEUM) 115, 212
Nyembezi, C.L.S. 8, 255, 263, 265, 308, 310, 323–325

O

Orange Free State African Students Association (SASA) 78
Oxford University 159, 175, 260–261, 323

P

Pan African Congress 104
Pass Laws and System 106, 215
Peterson, Hector 182–183, 212
Plaatje, Sol T. 308
Pointer, Fritz iii, vii, x, 1, 290, 293–294, 319, 321
Pointer, Sarah ix, 6
Pointer, Somori ix–x, 71, 290, 307, 315
Pointer, Thiyane ix, 71, 290, 307
Population Registration Act 107
Potchefstroom 109, 118, 229, 231, 233, 237, 254, 265, 267, 269, 271, 273, 279, 281
Pretoria 120, 235–236, 244, 254–255, 257, 264–265, 268, 331

R

Race Classification Board 107
Racism iii, 2, 22, 90, 155, 163–164, 318, 320
Rainbow Nation 301, 312
Ralston, Richard 156–157
Raven Press 236
Rivonia Trial 1

S

Sanchez, Sonya 307

Sekhuthe, Miriam ix
Sekoto, Gerard ix, 2, 6–9, 324
Semenya ix, 2, 5
Sesotho 18, 23, 49–50, 57, 59, 62, 69, 71, 152–153, 158, 190, 212, 227, 232, 238, 282, 308, 310, 323, 328–330
Shukla, Raj viii–ix, 319
Skinner, Meg ix, 9
Society of Young Africa (SOYA) 116–117, 212
Soga, A 68
Sontonga, Enoch 297–298, 303–304
Sophiatown 8, 63–64, 110, 113, 145, 210–212, 290
South Africa(ns) 4, 215, 244
South African Communist Party 282
South African Democratic Teachers' Union (SADTU) 256–257
SOWETO vii, 82–83, 145, 165, 177, 182–184, 186, 188, 193, 195, 197, 200, 214–215, 222, 230, 235, 265–266, 277, 283
Starks, Marci ix, 307
Stellenbosch 90–92, 96–97, 242–243, 255, 283, 290
Student Nonviolent Coordinating Committee (SNCC) 3
Swahili 153, 298
Swanepoel, Chris ix, 221–222, 256–257, 259–261, 264, 267–268, 283–284

T

Tesfagiorgis, Freida High W ix, 6, 157
Township 16, 60, 63–64, 81, 109–111, 145, 178, 189, 211, 223–224, 230–231, 239, 255, 258, 271, 274, 315
Truth and Reconciliation Commission 295
Tutu, Desmond Archbishop 107, 209

U

Umkhonto Wesizwe (The Spear of the Nation) 282
University of California Los Angeles (UCLA) vii, 5–6, 91, 131, 133–141, 144, 147, 151–152, 158–160, 170, 174–175, 207, 323
University of Cape Town (UCT) 88, 90, 101, 127, 134, 255, 308
University of Fort Hare 88
University of Leiden 190, 239
University of Natal 91, 95, 101
University of South Africa (UNISA) 87, 159, 254–255, 257–258, 260–261, 264–266, 268, 279, 283, 299–301

University of Stellenbosch 90, 96
University of Transkei 247, 251, 254, 266
University of Wisconsin – Madison – 3, 48, 137, 147, 207–208, 220, 237, 254, 261, 318–320, 332
University of Witwatersrand 89–90, 168
Urban Areas Act 122

V

Van Beurden, Bernard ix, 199–202
Veerwood, Dr. 97–98
Vilakazi, V. W. 89, 220
Vorster, John B. 242

W

Wa Thiong'o, Ngugi 307
Watts, CA 140, 145
Wengrowe, Roddy and Hermine ix, 237, 239
Wesleyan Methodist Church 20, 25, 30, 53
White(s) 13–14, 16–19, 27, 30, 34–35, 41, 44, 48, 81, 86, 90, 98–100, 107, 122, 135, 137, 139, 141, 145, 152, 165, 178, 215, 227, 247, 250

X

Xhosa 68, 86, 88–90, 95, 98, 104, 106, 115, 117, 138, 141, 152–153, 161, 204, 238, 249, 252, 297–298, 331

Y

Yoffe, Aubrey 316

Z

Zambia 147, 157
Zulu 8, 14, 23, 31, 48–50, 70–71, 78, 85–86, 88–89, 95, 98–99, 152, 161, 220, 227, 255, 285, 297–298, 308, 310, 323, 326, 331–332
Zululand 49–50, 99

Index